STANDARD GRADE MODERN STUDIES

Britain

SERIES EDITOR: FRANK HEALY

JIM BRYDEN

KENNY ELDER

BRIAN McGOVERN

DUNCAN MURRAY

Hodder & Stoughton

A MEMBER OF THE HODDER HEADLINE GROUP

Acknowledgements

The authors and publisher thank the following for permission to reproduce material in this book:

Financial Times: Figure 3B; Glasgow Evening Times: Figure 4.64; Glaswegian: Figures lXX, 2J; Guardian Newspapers: Figure 1.8; Help the Aged: Figure 6.18; Herald: Figures 1W, lX, 1Z, 1AA, 1QQ, 1AAA, 1EEE, 1.10, 1.14, 1.15, 1.16, 1.19, 1.40, 1.42a, 1.43, 1.46, 1.47, 1.48, 1.49, 1.50, 1.55, 1.56, 1.57, 2.5, 2.6, 2.7, 3F, 3G, 3P, 3R, 3.10, 3.11, 3.12, 4M, 4O, 4Q, 4R, 4.10, 4.11, 4.14, 4.29, 4.31, 4.35, 4.36, 4.38, 4.39, 4.40, 4.45, 4.46, 4.47, 4.57, 4.59, 4.63, 4.65, 4.66, 5E, 5F, 5G, 5.7, 5.8, 5.10, 5.12, 6G, 6.13, 6.14, 6.20; Labour Research: Figure 4.27; Observer: Figures 1CCC, 1.52, 4.62; Scottish Enterprise: Figure 4MM; Stanley Thornes Publishers: Figure 2D; The Times: Figures 1LL, 4.32, 4.34; Times Literary Supplement: Figure 1.35b.

The publisher would like to thank the following for giving permission to reproduce copyright photographs in this book:

John Birdsall: Figures 4J, 4.33, 4.58, 6.9, 6.25, 6.28; Camera Press London: Richard Open, Figure 1Q; Ken Keane, Figure 2I; Help the Aged: Figures 4.24, 6E, 6K, 6.8, 6.27; The Herald and Evening Times Picture Library: Figures lM, 1R, 1T, 1IIb, Patrina Malone 1WW, 1.9, 1.12, 1.38, 4.51, 4.53; Life File: Dave Thompson, Figure 4.16; Mike Evans, Figures 4.8, 4.25; Andrew Ward, Figures 4.12, 6C; Jan Suttle, Figure 6.13; Angela Maynard, Figure 6.14; Tim Fisher, Figure 4N; Magnum Photos: Stuart Frankin, Figure 3M; Harry Gruyaert, Figure 4H; P A News: Sean Dempsey, Figure 1K; Stefan Rousseau, Figure 2.3; Figure 4.50; Popperfoto/Reuters: John Stillwell, Figure 1C; Ian Waldie, Figure 2.4; Renfrewshire Council: Figure 1TT; Rex Features London: Figure 1F; Tim Rooke, Figure lKK; Figure 1.1; Sky TV, Figure 1.5; Nils Jorgensen, Figure l.IIa; Today, Figure 3K; Ken McKay, Figure 3O; Douglas Robertson: Figures 1HHH, 1.45, 1JJJ, 1.44, 2C, 6.24, 6.26; Topham Picturepoint: David Giles, Figure 1.32; David Gaywood, Figure 3A; Tropix Photographic Library: M & V Birley, Figures 4T, 4.26, 6D, 6H, 6J, 6.23; Christian Smith, Figure 4T; Universal Pictorial Press: Figure 4.50

Philip Ford for the charts and graphs.

Every effort has been made to contact the holders of copyright material but if any have been inadvertently overlooked, the publishers will be pleased to make the necessary alterations at the first opportunity.

British Library Cataloguing in Publication Data
A catalogue record for this title is available from The British Library

ISBN 0 340 65557 7

First published 1997
Impression number   10 9 8 7 6 5 4 3 2 1
Year   2002 2001 2000 1999 1998 1997

Copyright © 1997 Frank Healy, Jim Bryden, Brian McGovern, Duncan Murray, Kenny Elder

Typeset by Fakenham Photosetting Limited, Fakenham, Norfolk.
Printed in Great Britain for Hodder & Stoughton Educational, a division of Hodder Headline Plc, 338 Euston Road, London NW1 3BH by Redwood Books, Trowbridge, Wiltshire.

The General Election 1997

Although this book was published under the new Labour government, the writing and production processes were well under way before the General Election of 1 May 1997. As a result of this there are occasions in the book where government policy, MPs positions and statistical data may relate back to the pre-election situation. Users of the book should be aware that it was not possible to fully rewrite the book to reflect the result of the election, but where possible updated information has been supplied.

Contents Foundation

Contents General/Credit

one

Representation at National and Local Level

The UK is a **democracy** which means that the people who live here have a say in how the country is run. The British people do this by voting for a representative at **local**, **national** and **European elections**. They vote for a **councillor** or a **Member of Parliament** who represents their views at Council Meetings or at Parliament in London.

- **Labour Party**
- **Conservative Party**
- **Liberal Democratic Party**
- **Scottish Nationalist Party**

Each political party tries to attract as many voters as possible so that they can win an election. They must try to put forward ideas that appeal to most of the voters. The political parties compete with each other in trying to gain support of the majority of the British people to win the election. Since 1945 no political party has won over 50% of the votes.

Elections occur quite often in Britain and Figure 1B gives a good idea of the main types of election.

Figure 1A   Renfrew District Councillors plant trees at Paisley Arts Centre, 1995

Source: Renfrewshire District News, *March 1996*

Type of election	Represents population	Representative
European Elections	European Union	Member of European Parliament (MEP)
National/ General Elections	Britain	Member of Parliament (MP). (Represents a constituency)
Council Elections	Local area	Councillor. (Represents a ward)

Figure 1B   The main types of election

The political party which wins the General Election becomes the government and it runs Britain for a maximum of five years. The Conservatives won a general election in May 1992, therefore the next election could be no later than May 1997. The Labour Party won on 1 May 1997.

Representatives normally, but not always, belong to a **political party**. The major parties in Scotland are:

Constitutional Monarchy

Figure 1C   The Queen in Parliament

Britain is also a **constitutional monarchy** but this does not have an effect on our representative democracy. All that this means is that Britain has a **Head of State**, the Queen, but she does not have anything to do with running the country. The government does that. The Queen's major role is to sign all of the new laws that have been passed, giving the **Royal Assent**, i.e. approval.

QUESTIONS

1 What does democracy mean?
2 What types of elections can people vote in?
3 What is the maximum amount of time between general elections?
4 Who is the British Head of State?

Separation of the powers of Government

The government is divided into three separate parts. Each has a different role to play in running the country.

Executive	Legislature	Judiciary
⬇	⬇	⬇
Cabinet & Civil Service	Parliament (House of Commons & House of Lords)	Courts
⬇	⬇	⬇
Put ideas for law to Parliament	Make/pass laws	Put laws into practice

Figure 1D   The government

The Legislature: (House of Commons & House of Lords)

The legislature is that part of government which looks at ideas and suggestions for a new law and decides whether or not it should become a law. The ideas for a new law are called **Bills**.

Bills usually come from the **manifesto** (the promises the Party makes to the voters) of the political party but can also come from other groups who want to change the law for one reason or another, e.g. interest groups like Help the Aged, or from professional groups like the Law Society.

There are three types of Bill:
- **Government Bills** – ideas for a new law which the government puts forward. Most Bills come from the government.
- **Private Member's Bills (PMBs)** – ideas for a new law which are put forward by individual MPs. Not all MPs can put forward this type of Bill. Each year all MPs' names are put into a hat and a number are drawn out. Those MPs whose names are drawn out of the hat can put forward their own Bill. They are responsible for writing it out and getting support for it from other MPs. PMBs which don't have the government's backing usually fail to become a law. Government and Private Member's Bills are usually ones which affect

2

people in the country, for example the BSE scare in Britain at present, i.e. Mad Cow Disease.

- **Public Bills** – this type of Bill usually deals with issues that affect a group of people or a person. For example, the control of guns in Britain will affect that group of people who own guns.

How a Government Bill is made

The original idea for a new law is put forward in a **Green Paper** and all the people involved with or affected by the idea are asked to give their opinion on it, e.g. MPs, interested groups and others.

After all of the opinions on the idea of a new law have been received, the government produces a **White Paper** which is the final version of the idea which will go to Parliament.

At Parliament the following process starts, usually in the House of Commons (Figure 1E).

At the House of Lords the whole process, stages 1 to 4, takes place again.

Stage 1   **First Reading** The Bill is introduced to MPs. There is no debate on it.

Stage 2   **Second Reading** The Bill is debated. A vote is then taken. The Bill can end here or go to the next stage; it depends on the votes for or against.

Stage 3   **Committee Stage** The Bill is looked at very closely by a group of MPs and any changes (called **Amendments**) are made to it and reported to the House of Commons.

Stage 4   **Third Reading** The Bill, after all of the Amendments have been made, is debated on. A vote is taken. If the Bill gains majority of votes it goes on to the House of Lords.

Figure 1E   The four stages of a new law

Any Amendments made to the Bill in the House of Lords are looked at when the Bill goes back to the House of Commons, and these are discussed. If there are no Amendments, the Bill will go from the House of Lords to the Queen for Royal Assent. Once a Bill has the Royal Assent it becomes a law and goes on to the **Statute Book**, where all laws are written.

QUESTIONS

1 What makes up the legislature?
2 Describe the three types of Bill in your own words.
3 Describe how a Bill becomes law in your own words.

Organisation of Government

The Legislature is made up of the **House of Commons**, which now has 659 elected MPs (each MP represents a **Constituency**), and the **House of Lords** with about 1200 **peers** who are not elected by anyone. Of the 1200 peers there are a number who are appointed by the government for life (life peers). The remainder are **hereditary peers** and their title will pass to their children when they die.

Figure 1F   The Houses of Parliament at Westminster

3

The 1992 and 1997 General Elections brought the following results (see Figure 1G):

Political party	Number of seats	
	1992	1997
Conservative	336	165
Labour	271	419
Liberal Democrat	20	46
SNP	3	6
Others	21	23

Figure 1G   Results of the 1992 and 1997 general elections

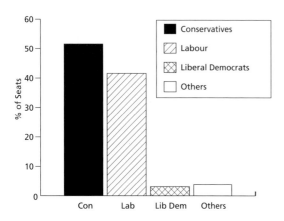

Figure 1H   Percentage of seats won by each party at the 1992 and 1997 general elections

Labour won the 1997 general election with an **overall majority**. This means that they gained more seats than all of the other parties added together, as Figure 1I shows.

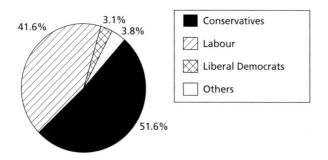

Figure 1I   Results of the 1997 general election

QUESTIONS

1 In what way can it be said that the House of Lords is not democratic?
2 Which political party usually becomes the government after a general election?
3 How many MPs are there in the House of Commons?
4 What is meant by an overall majority?

The House of Commons

In the House of Commons the government sits on one side and the **Opposition parties** sit across from them (see Figure 1J). After a debate, a vote is taken of those for and those against the issue being discussed. The MPs vote by going through one of two lobbies. One lobby is for those agreeing – the Aye Lobby. The other lobby is for those against – the No Lobby.

This type of voting is called a Division and the Aye and No Lobby are called the **Division lobbies**. The votes are counted by **tellers** who inform the **Speaker**, who announces the result.

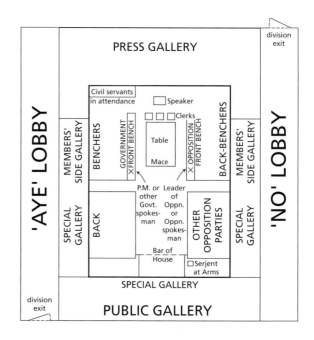

Figure 1J   The House of Commons

4

Front benches and back benches

Figure 1K   The front benches of Labour (1996)

The MPs who sit on the front benches have been promoted to form the **Cabinet** (they are the **front-benchers**). They are usually in control of a government department and they speak on matters connected to that department. For example, the Minister of Agriculture will speak on the BSE crisis.

The Opposition also has promoted MPs on their front benches and they are called the **Shadow Cabinet.** Continuing with the above example, the Shadow Minister for Agriculture will question or give their views on British farming.

Back-benchers are unpromoted MPs and they sit on the same side of the House as their political party, behind those on the front benches.

The majority of MPs sit on the back benches in the House of Commons, behind the leaders of their party. This explains why they are called back-benchers.

The Whip System

The ordinary MP can normally be expected to follow the **party line**, i.e. vote in the way that the leader of their party wants. But just to make sure that MPs vote as expected, each party has **Whips** and a **Chief Whip** who make sure this happens.

Along with the Chief Whip, who is a member of the Cabinet or Shadow Cabinet, there are a number of Whips to help keep the MPs in line. One job is to keep the back bench MPs informed of important debates in the House of Commons. To do this, each MP receives a written notice of the debates that will soon occur in the House of Commons. These notices are also called whips. (See Figure 1L.)

One-line whip

Lets MPs know that a vote will take place

Two-line whip

Lets MPs know that they should attend unless they have made an arrangement with an 'opposite' MP not to attend. This is called a **pair**. The Whip's office must approve this.

Three-line whip

MPs must attend.

Figure 1L   Whips notices

Sometimes even the Chief Whips cannot force MPs to vote with their party, as happened recently when some Conservative MPs refused to vote according to the party line when there was a debate about the European Union. In this case some of the **Eurosceptics** led by Bill Cash, MP, were asked to **abstain** rather than vote against their own party. However, some Conservative MPs did vote against their own party.

5

QUESTIONS

1 How do MPs vote in the House of Commons?
2 What name is given to promoted MPs?
3 Who sits on the front benches?
4 What is the job of the Whips?
5 What can MPs do if they disagree with the views of the party leader in a vote in the House of Commons?

Just a Job?

Figure 1M shows the different influences that an MP has to cope with. However, an MP might disagree with their party on abortion and vote according to their conscience. In 1992, a Conservative MP, Elizabeth Peacock, had to decide whether to vote for or against her party when the Conservative Government wanted to close a coal mine in her constituency.

MPs have been in the news recently over two different issues:

- **Nolan Report** called for tougher control of MPs after the investigation into how much MPs earn from **'outside interests'**. MPs are not allowed to take gifts or money from people without telling Parliament. Already a **register of members' interests** has been set up and MPs must report money or gifts received.

  For instance, Tony Blair receives sponsorship from the union, TGWU, while Conservative MP Kenneth Baker is an adviser to the large chemical company ICI.

- **MPs pay:** at a time when workers in Britain are getting very low wage rises, Britain's MPs voted for a 26% pay rise in July 1996. Tony Blair, leader of the Opposition, stated that he did not want the pay rise, as criticism rose over it. Nurses were one group of workers who complained about the MPs' pay rise, as many of them will get under 2% increase this year.

Figure 1M   Influences on MPs

House of Commons

Divisions, Committees, Debates, Private Member's Bills, Questions

Pressure Groups

Bills, Questions, Debate

Personal Interests

Votes of Conscience, Committees

Constituency Issues

Local interests, Representations, Questions, Debates, Local galas/fetes, Constituency meetings

SALARY OF MPs (July 1996)

Year	MP	Prime Minister (John Major)	Leader of the Opposition (Tony Blair)
1995	£34000	£84217	£64167
1996	£43000	£101557	£83332

Figure 1N Figures showing MPs' 26% pay rise

Other people were not so critical of the MPs' rise, as the following excerpts from the *Herald*, of 12 July 1996, show:

AGAINST

'Most people don't receive £180 per week as a wage. How can MPs justify this?'

James Elsby, TGWU

'It is not good for democracy if representatives become detached from the people they represent.'

Richard Leonard, STUC

FOR

'MPs are entitled to the rate for the job.'

Helen Liddell, MP

'If you want the best person for the job you have to pay the salary.'

Bill Walker, MP

QUESTIONS

1 Look at Figure 1M. What do you think is the most important influence on an MP? Explain your answer.
2 Why do you think that MPs should register if they get paid money or accept gifts?
3 Why were MPs' recent pay rises criticised?
4 Look at the different views on MPs' pay. Which do you agree with most?

What the MP does inside the House of Commons

An MP is involved in a number of activities when he is at the House of Commons. The main activity is the making of laws (**legislate**). MPs do this by taking part in **debates** and voting, and we can now see them do this on television.

When MPs are not taking part in a debate they have other tasks to carry out.

Select Committee

MPs look at Bills very closely. This is called **scrutinising**. MPs are appointed by their party to look at the work of one of the government departments. For example, Labour MP Tam Dalyell scrutinises the work of the Ministry of Defence.

Question Time

The government can be asked questions about its **policies** and activities by MPs. Questions can be written or oral.

Legislation

If an MP feels strongly about an issue, they may put their name forward to give them an opportunity to introduce a Private Member's Bill.

Lobbying

MPs meet people from their own constituency or other persons interested in a particular issue in the House of Commons Lobby. The MP might then contact a government department on behalf of this group, e.g. the recent Dunblane massacre led the constituents of Dunblane to lobby MPs for a law to control guns in Britain.

7

Voting

MPs are expected to vote with their political party but sometimes there are **back-bench revolts** when some MPs feel strongly about something, as Figure 1O from the *Economist* magazine shows.

LABOUR'S PAINS

Ten Labour MPs went against their leadership advice to abstain on the November Budget's tax cuts vote.

Dennis Skinner, Tony Benn, Jeremy Corbyn and Denzil Davies were among the Labour Rebels who defied the leadership. Mr Donald Dewar, Labour's Chief Whip, is expected to make a statement on the party unity.

Figure 1O   Labour's Pains

Source: Economist, 9 December 1995, abridged

Mr Donald Dewar has a number of options open to him, should he wish to use them against the Labour rebels mentioned. He could **withdraw the party whip** which means that the group are banned from the Parliamentary Labour Party for a period of time.

A second source of action open to Mr Dewar in more serious events could be the request for **deselection** of the MP. To do this the constituency party of an MP would be asked **not** to choose them as a **candidate** for the next election.

Life of MPs

Figure 1P   Adapted from the *Welcome to Labour* pamphlet

Most people's idea of Parliament comes from what they have seen on TV. But there is much more to being an MP than attending Prime Minister's Question Time. Hilary Armstrong – Labour MP for North West Durham – says that for her, work back home in her constituency is the most important part of her job.

'It is folk at home who make sure that I know how the laws the government passes in London affect them,' she says. 'They tell me what it really means to be unemployed, to have to queue for hours in casualty, or what will happen if they have an open cast coal mine next to their village. They keep my feet on the ground.'

Her job as an MP means a lot of commuting from her home in Durham to a flat in London. It means having two of everything – from two word processors and filing systems, down to two sets of cutlery in her two kitchen drawers.

'There is a lot of ritual in Parliament. You'd be forgiven for not understanding how it works,' she explains.

New laws are generally mentioned in the **Queen's Speech** at the beginning of the Parliamentary session in November. The government uses this opportunity to outline its plans for the year.

Then the relevant minister will publish a **Bill**. The formal introduction of the Bill into Parliament is called the **First Reading**. Some time later, a debate takes place, called the **Second Reading**, where government and opposition parties argue and a full vote takes place.

The Bill then goes to its **Committee stage**. The Committee stage can, confusingly, involve every MP, in which case the House is tied up for weeks in a series of votes. The Bill is then taken back to the floor of the House of Commons for a **Report Stage**, immediately followed by a **Third Reading**. This is the last vote in the Commons on the Bill. Should it pass, it then goes to the House of Lords, and goes through a similar series of stages. The Lords will frequently revise a Bill again, but there are limits as to what they can do. If the government does not like what the Lords have done, then it may seek to overturn their decisions again in the Commons, before the Bill goes to the Queen for **Royal Assent**, when it becomes an **Act of Parliament**.

While they are engaged in all this detailed work MPs still, of course, have all their constituency work to do.

'We can ask Ministers questions, and try to get them to take action on certain cases,' explains Hilary Armstrong. 'But in the end, our power is limited by the fact that the Tories are in government, and we are not.

'That's what makes it even more vital that we do all we can to win the next (1997) election.'

Defecting

If an MP loses belief in their political party they might 'defect' to another political party. Recently, Conservative Alan Howarth defected to Labour, and Emma Nicholson defected to the Liberal Democrats.

Figure 1Q   Emma Nicholson

QUESTIONS

1 Describe an MP's duties in your own words.
2 What can a Whip do to discipline an MP?
3 Why might an MP defect to another party?

Working in the Constituency

An example of an MP working in the constituency is Sam Galbraith, Labour MP for Strathkelvin and Bearsden.

Mr Galbraith's constituency is on the outskirts of Glasgow and he represents a mixture of constituents from traditional Conservative areas such as the wealthy suburbs of Milngarie and Bearsden, to the Labour voters in Strathkelvin.

Prior to becoming an MP, Mr Galbraith was a well-known neurosurgeon and was involved in politics through the Scottish Campaign for Nuclear Disarmament (CND). As a surgeon, Mr Galbraith is well qualified to speak about the problems affecting hospitals in Britain. He also provides his local constituents with help if problems occur.

**Figure 1R
Sam Galbraith,
Labour MP for
Strathkelvin and
Bearsden**

Recently a situation arose where a local girl was accepted to an English university but she had only four days to accept the offer. However, the Scottish Office, which gives grants for higher education, refused the necessary grant. Without this money she wouldn't have been able to afford to go to the university. Mr Galbraith was able to solve this problem for the girl after phoning the government ministers in charge of the Scottish Office.

Mr Galbraith described an average day at the House of Commons.

9.00 a.m.   I arrive at my office in the House of Commons and attend to work that is involved with being an MP.

1.00–2.30 p.m.   Lunch and informal meetings with MPs or other people to discuss Parliamentary matters.

2.30–at least 10.30 p.m.   The House of Commons starts at 2.30 p.m. and this involves debates in the Chamber, in Committees or other meetings. This can go on until at least 10.30 p.m. and often well into the night.

Figure 1S   A day in the life of Sam Galbraith

Source: Abridged

9

Mr Galbraith's average day shows that the life of an MP is quite a hectic one, yet many people put themselves forward as candidates at each election. On many occasions the candidates fail to be elected, but at other times the candidates don't get as far as the Parliamentary elections, as Mike Watson MP found out.

QUESTION

1 Describe an MP's day in your own words.

The MP: A Job for Life?

**Figure 1T
Mike Watson**

**Figure 1U
Mohammed Sarwar**

There is a government department which looks at the size of constituencies throughout the UK to see if they are too big or too small compared to other constituencies. This is called the **Boundary Commission**.

In 1996 the Boundary Commission made the decision that Glasgow had too many constituencies and that the number of MPs should be reduced from 11 to 10. The Commission decided that the Glasgow Central constituency would be split between Glasgow Govan and Glasgow Shettleston in the 1997 general election so Mike Watson, the Labour MP who represented it, would have to find another constituency.

At about the same time another Glasgow constituency, at Govan, became vacant and needed a Labour candidate to fight the next general election. Mr Watson put himself forward for this seat, but so did local Asian businessman, Mohammad Sarwar, who had support amongst the large Asian population. It was decided that both Mr Watson and Mr Sarwar should take part in a selection contest.

In the contest Mr Watson won by one vote after 50 votes were disqualified under Labour Party rules. However, Mr Sarwar protested that many of the people disqualified did not have English as their first language and were his supporters. A re-run of the election was demanded and the Labour Party leadership agreed.

Mr Sarwar became Scotland's first Asian MP in May 1997.

Mr Watson now has to look elsewhere for the opportunity to continue as a Labour MP. If he is not successful he will lose his job as an MP at the 1997 general election. His wife, Lorraine, works with him as his secretary and they both stand to lose about £60000 per year, which includes expenses and allowances.

QUESTIONS

1 How did Mike Watson MP lose his seat?
2 How would this affect his family?
3 Why might the election of Mohammed Sarwar be a 'first for Scotland'?

How Representative is the House of Commons?

Women in politics

The British population is 51% female and 49% male. In 1992, just under 10% of MPs were women. In 1997 this increased, but only to 18%. Is this fair?

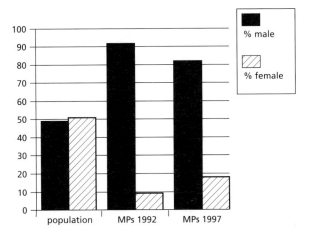

Figure 1V   Percentage of men and women elected at the 1992 and 1997 general elections

In almost every other European country, except Belgium, Portugal, Greece and France, a large number of MPs are women. In Sweden and Finland 40% of MPs are female.

Why are there so few women MPs?

Women face the same difficulties in politics as they would in any other job. Some of the reasons for this include:
- bringing up a family;
- running the home;
- lack of contacts to help them get into politics;
- amount of time required to be a politician means less time with their family;
- the centre of British politics is London and this is too far away for most women who wish to continue family commitments;
- women tend to be less well paid than men and politics can be expensive;
- selection committees tend to be mostly made up of a majority of men.

The Labour Party wants to increase the number of women in politics and has introduced **positive discrimination** to try to improve the chances for women in politics. They want 40% of Labour candidates to be women at the next general election. All-women shortlists of candidates were introduced. This meant that the successful candidate would have to be a woman. But a recent court decision has said that this is not legal.

In Scotland the Scottish Constitutional Convention proposes that women make up 50% of the members of a Scottish Parliament.

Ethnic minorities

In the 1992 general election only six black or Asian MPs were elected – 5 Labour MPs; 1 Conservative MP. In a number of 'safe' constituencies, the Asian/black candidates were not elected to Parliament; for example, Conservative John Taylor lost Cheltenham to the Liberal Democrat candidate.

Why do the Asian/black candidates find it so difficult to be chosen as candidates for the Labour, Conservative or Liberal Democratic Parties?

If the political system represented the numbers of the blacks/Asians in the British population, there would be 30 black/Asian MPs.

Political parties do not select the black/Asian candidates because of **institutionalised** racist practices.

There has to be a way to increase the number of black MPs and allow black people to become fully involved in all political parties, so that they can play a bigger part in society.

Figure 1W

Source: Herald,
11 November 1995, abridged

One person who has an opinion on this is Neelam Bakshi who was a regional councillor on Strathclyde Regional Council before the new councils were set up in April 1996.

Scotland has quite a large ethnic population but no black or Asian MP. This situation may change after the general election as Mohammed Sarwar has been chosen as the Labour candidate in the Govan constituency of Glasgow. It is believed that Mr Sarwar will become the first Scottish Asian MP because Labour has a good record in Govan and there is a large ethnic population in this constituency.

The Scottish Nationalist Party (SNP) has also chosen an Asian candidate to 'fight' for the Shettleston constituency.

The SNP has tried to bring the ethnic minorities into the political system. As well as selecting Asian candidates for election they have set up **Scots Asians for Independence**. The following extract from the *Herald* reports on the launch of this group (see Figure 1X).

> Bashir Ahmed received a standing ovation as he launched the Scots Asians for Independence group at the SNP conference.
>
> Many Asians have relations who fought for independence in their homelands and won. Here in Scotland the fight still goes on.
>
> The SNP leader, Alex Salmond, said that the group would create support for Scottish Independence amongst the Asian Community.

Figure 1X Source: Herald, 22 September 1995, abridged

In February 1997, three more prominent members of the Asian community joined the SNP. One was Mr Abdul Majeed, a leading member of the Conservative Party, Mr Adil Bhatti, a leading member of the Labour Party and Mr Haji Mohammed Sadiq, a Labour Party supporter and past vice-president of Glasgow Central Mosque.

QUESTIONS

1 What criticism can be made of the low number of women MPs in Britain?
2 What special difficulties do women face in becoming MPs?
3 How many women MPs would there be in a Scottish Parliament?
4 According to Neelam Bakshi, how many black and Asian MPs should there be?
5 How has the SNP sought to attract the ethnic minority vote?

The British Electoral System

Britain's electoral system is very simple. A candidate in an election who receives more votes than any of the other candidates is the winner of the constituency. The political party in a general election which wins most constituencies in the whole of Britain becomes the government until the next election.

The name given to the British voting method is the **simple majority**, better known as **'first past the post'**.

At present there are 659 constituencies in Britain, and if one political party wins more than 330 of these it will have more seats than *all of the other parties* together. In this case the party will form a **majority** government.

If a political party wins more seats than any other single party, but less than 330, it will form a **minority** government. This means that if all the other parties' seats are added together, they would have more seats in Parliament than the government.

'Safe' and 'marginal' seats

'Safe seats' are constituencies where an MP has won a large majority of votes over his nearest rival at the election. A 'marginal seat' is one where the MP has won a small majority over rivals at the election. Marginal seats could be lost at the next election. Political parties will try hardest to win these seats.

SAFE SEAT

Glasgow Provan

Jimmy Wray, Labour	15885
Alexandra McRae, SNP	5182
Andrew Rosindell, Conservative	1865
Charles Bell, Liberal Democrats	948

MARGINAL SEAT

Ayr

Phil Gallie, Conservative	22172
Alastair Osborne, Labour	22087
Barbara Mullin, SNP	5949
John Boss, Liberal Democrats	4067
Others (Natural Law Party)	132

Figure 1Y   Examples of safe and marginal seats

In the marginal seat the political parties will aim to win support from the voters who have not made up their minds which party to vote for. This type of voter is called a **floating voter**. To win a general election the political parties hope to do two things:

- win over the floating voters to their party;
- win the marginal seats.

Swings from One Party to Another

The Staffordshire South-East 'By-election' (A **by-election** occurs when an MP dies, or resigns from his seat.) The *Herald* on 13 April 1996 produced the result of this by-election in quite a complicated way but it shows the swing from Conservative to Labour (see Figure 1Z).

The result from Staffordshire South-East reduced the Conservative Party's majority over all other parties in the House of Commons to one, and introduces the possibility of the government losing important debates. It could also lead to the government calling a general election early, something it might not want to do.

The timing of general elections

The government wants to be re-elected at a general election, and the Opposition parties want to be elected to run the country. It is important that the government picks the right time to call a general election – a time when their standing is good in the eyes of the voters.

The following list shows factors that are important when calling a general election.

- The **feel good factor**. If people believe they are better off under the government, this will affect how they vote.
- The **economy**. If unemployment is low or falling this could affect working-class voters.
- **Taxes**. Voters do not like increases in tax or mortgage rates.
- How well the government is doing. For example, are they carrying out the promises they made in the manifesto and how well they are doing this?

Result

STAFFORDSHIRE SOUTH EAST: Lab gain from Con Brian Jenkins (Lab) 26,155 (60.22%, +22.05%); Jimmy James (Con) 12,393 (28.53%, -22.13%;) Ms Jennette Davy (LD) 2,042 (4.70%, -4.92%); Andrew Smith (UK Independence) 1,272 (2.78%); Lord David Sutch (Official Monster Raving Loony Party) 506 (1.17%); Ms Sharron Edwards (National Democrat) 358 (0.82%); Steven Mountford (Liberal) 332 (0.76%); Leslie Tucker (Churchill Conservative) 123 (0.28%); News Bunny (The Official News Bunny Party) 85 (0.20%); Neville Samuelson (Daily Loonylugs Earing Up The World) 80 (0.18%); Frederick Sandy (Action Against Crime Life Means Life) 53 (0.12%); David Lucas (Natural Law Party) 53 (0.12%); Alan Wood (Democratic Restoration of the Death Penalty) 45 (0.10%); Lab maj 13,762 (31.69%); 22.09% swing Con to Lab Electorate 72,116; Turnout 43,431 (60.22%, -21.84%) 1992: Con maj 7192 (12.49%) -Turnout 57,603 (82.06%) Lightbown (Con) 29,180 (50.66%); Jenkins (Lab) 21,988 (38.17%); Penlington (LD) 5,540 (9.62%); Taylor (Soc Dem) 895 (1.55%).

Figure 1Z   *Source: Herald, 13 April 1996*

Figure 1AA

Source: Herald,
13 April 1996

In April 1996 the *Herald* stated that 1 May 1997 was the last date for a General Election – they were right (Figure 1AA).

One way in which the people express their views about how well the government is doing is through **opinion polls**, like the example in Figure 1BB.

	Now	Jul	Jun	May	Gen Elec
Labour	51	51	54	53	39
SNP	23	25	24	23	22
Lib-Dem	10	9	8	9	13
Con	15	15	12	13	26
Greens	1	–	–	1	1

The poll was taken among 1029 people in 40 constituencies between 25 and 30 July 1996. The figures may not add up to 100% because of the effects of rounding up or down. It excludes 17% of respondents who refused to indicate their preference, did not intend to vote or were undecided.

Figure 1BB

The poll shows that the Conservatives were not doing very well as far as public opinion is concerned. Labour MPs had been very careful not to criticise Tony Blair as this could reduce the lead that Labour has over the Conservatives in the polls as the public does not like to see 'splits' within political parties.

QUESTIONS

1 What is the name given to the British method of voting?
2 How many constituencies are there in Britain?
3 What is meant by a minority government?
4 Explain the terms 'safe seat' and 'marginal seat'.
5 What is a floating voter?
6 Why are they important?
7 Why are swings in voting important?
8 What are the main influences on how people vote?
9 What do opinion polls tell us?
10 How might they influence when an election is called?

Is our Electoral System Fair?

The results from the 1992 general election show that the Conservative and Labour Parties do better from the first past the post system than other parties (see Figure 1CC).

Political party	% of votes	% of seats
Conservatives	41.9	51.6
Labour	34.4	41.6
Liberal Democrats	17.8	3.07
Others	3.6	3.69

Figure 1CC

From the table we can see that the winning Conservative Party only received 41.9% of the votes which means that 58.1% of the voters did not vote for them, yet the Conservative Party became the government with 51.6% of seats.

The reasons for this situation arising are listed below.

• Constituencies are of different sizes and have different numbers of voters. In Scotland we can see this by looking at three constituencies (see Figure 1DD).

Constituency	Number of voters
Gordon	81097
Caithness and Sutherland	31173
Western Isles	23015

Figure 1DD   Different constituencies have different numbers of voters

- The Conservative and Labour Parties are better organised and have more money than other parties, so they contest most constituencies.
- Liberal Democrat supporters are spread throughout Britain, whereas Labour and Conservative supporters are concentrated in certain areas of the country. Figure 1EE gives an idea of how many votes it takes to elect an MP from different major parties.

Political party	Votes required to elect an MP
Conservatives	42000
Labour	42804
Liberal Democrats	304000
Others	

Figure 1EE

This situation of the party which becomes the government having less than half of the voters supporting them also occurs in the constituency elections. The examples in Figure 1FF help to illustrate this point.

STRATHKELVIN & BEARSDEN (1992)

Party	MP	Votes gained
Labour	Sam Galbraith	21267
Conservative	Michael Hirst	18105
SNP	Tom Chalmers	6275
Liberal Democrats	Barbara Waterfield	4585

Total votes cast – 50,232

Majority	3162
% of votes	42.3%
% who didn't vote for Sam Galbraith	57.7%

ARGYLL & BUTE

Party	MP	Votes gained
Liberal Democrats	Ray Mickie	12739
Conservative	John Corrie	10117
Labour	Desmonde Brown	4946
SNP	Neil MacCormick	8689

Total votes cast – 36,541

Majority	2622
% of votes	34.8%
% who didn't vote for Ray Mickie	65.2%

Figure 1FF

Figure 1FF shows that in both the constituencies the majority of voters did not support the winner of the seat. In Ray Mickie's case, just over one-third of the voters chose her as their MP.

QUESTIONS

1 Which political parties might describe first past the post as unfair?
2 What criticisms might they make?
3 Look at the results in Strathkelvin and Argyll & Bute (Figure 1FF). Why might Michael Hirst have reason for complaint at not becoming an MP?

Alternative Voting Systems

For over 20 years now there has been talk of introducing a new, more fair, system of elections. A form of **proportional representation** (PR) has been suggested. The introduction of PR would remove the problem of candidates and parties being elected by a minority of voters.

In PR a political party would have the same proportion of seats at Parliament as they had voters. For example, a party receiving one-third of the votes is likely to receive one-third of the seats in the House of Commons.

One type of PR is called the **National Party List System**. The **electorate** (the people who vote) would vote for a political party, not a candidate. The results shown in Figure 1GG may be produced.

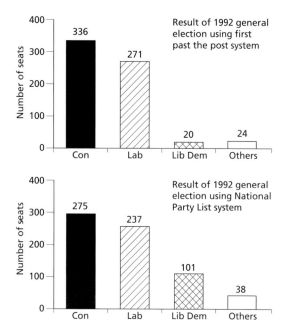

Figure 1GG

The bar charts show that under the National Party System the Liberal Democrats and Others would do better, with the Conservatives and Labour being worse off.

Another form of PR is the **Single Transferable Vote System** (STV). Under STV Britain would have:

• larger constituencies;
• multi-member constituencies, i.e. political parties would put forward more than one candidate for each constituency;
• candidates listed in order of preference.

STV is criticised as being a very complicated form of PR.

The third type of PR is the **Alternative Voting System** (AV). This would mean only a little change to our present system but it would mean that the electorate would get two votes.

Again, voters list candidates in order of preference, e.g. 1, 2, 3, 4, and so on. A candidate has to get 50% of the **'first preference votes'** to get elected, i.e. more than 50% of the voters would have to mark him/her down as their number one choice on their ballot paper. Candidates who get very low votes have their second place votes redistributed until successful candidates are elected.

Glasgow Provan AV Sample Ballot Paper
Place 1 against preferred choice of candidate.
Place 2 against next preferred choice of candidate.

Candidate	Party	Vote
Charles Bell	Liberal Democrats	
Alexander McRae	SNP	
Andrew Rosindell	Conservative	
James Wray	Labour	

Figure 1HH

The sample AV paper in Figure 1HH gives an idea of how a possible ballot paper would look if that form of PR was introduced.

It has been suggested that should Britain change the electoral system, the STV system is the likely form that would be used.

Advantages and disadvantages of PR

As with our present first past the post system there are reasons why PR would be good for Britain, but it may also cause some problems.

Advantages of first past the post:
• cheap to organise and run;
• simple, so easily understood by the electorate;
• results are known quickly – by early morning/next day;
• British people are accustomed to it.

Advantages of PR:
• all votes would count. No wasted votes;
• fairer allocation of seats;

- no big swings in policy when there is a change in government;
- more representation for smaller parties allows different views in Parliament.

But PR has its critics and they state that, among other things, it is very complicated and voters would have difficulty understanding how it works. In addition, **coalitions** between parties to gain power might mean that manifesto promises are broken.

QUESTIONS

1 What is the name of the voting system which could replace first past the post?

2 Look at Figure 1GG. If the Party List System was introduced, which political parties might be the winners and which might be the losers?

3 What are the main advantages and disadvantages of PR?

The Labour and Conservative Parties Compared

Until 1979 both Labour and the Conservatives had a form of agreement about the way in which Britain should be governed. This type of agreement is called a **consensus**.

Since 1979, however, the two major political parties have held different views on the running of the country in several major areas.

Margaret Thatcher was elected Prime Minister in 1979 and her ideas become known as Thatcherism.

The differences between the Conservatives and Labour politicians can be summarised into a table (see Figure 1II).

CONSERVATIVES	LABOUR
Taxation	**Taxation**
Low taxes so that those in work should be rewarded for their efforts. A tax level of 20 pence in the pound is many Conservatives' aim. Increases in VAT have led to criticism, especially of VAT on fuel.	In the past, higher taxes have been charged to pay for public services. Tony Blair's Labour Party wants to be the party of low taxes.

 **Chancellor of the Exchequer Kenneth Clarke**

 **Shadow Chancellor Gordon Brown**

Health	**Health**
Reform of the NHS began in 1980s with: • introduction of **market forces**; • boosting of private healthcare;	Labour wants extra money to be put into the National Health Service (NHS) and are very critical of Conservative changes to the NHS.

CONSERVATIVES continued

Health continued

- GP fundholding;
- privatising of non-medical services;
- setting up of hospital trusts.

The Economy

The Conservatives are continuing with **privatisation**, e.g. the railways most recently. They also want:

- to avoid the **single European currency**;
- low inflation and interest rates;
- tax cuts;
- to control government spending;
- to privatise parts of the Welfare State.

Employment

The Conservatives believe that more jobs will be made when British companies become more **competitive**, and through low interest rates. They think that trade unions have caused high wages that companies can't afford.

Measures include:

- Youth Training places for 16–17-year-olds not in work or education;
- Training for Work available to all unemployed;
- Job Plan Workshops for those unemployed for over one year;
- Workwise courses for 18–24-year-olds to get them back to work;
- Jobseekers' Allowance which will try to make the unemployed look harder for jobs.

The Constitution

Conservatives want to keep it as it is:

- they oppose a Scottish Parliament;
- don't want more power to the European Union;
- support an assembly for Northern Ireland.

LABOUR continued

Health continued

They want to reduce hospital waiting lists and cut NHS red tape.

The Economy

Under Tony Blair the Labour Party's approach to the economy has changed. New Labour policies include:

- no commitment to de-privatisation;
- build a 'stakeholder economy' where workers and managers sit down together to make decisions about company policy;
- a low-taxation party;
- improving the infrastructure;
- adopting the Social Chapter of the European Union.

Employment

Labour thinks that the Government should put more money into British industry to **modernise** it. Labour wants to raise standards in education, and keep inflation and interest rates low to help create work.

Their policies to create jobs include:

- Target 2000 which ensures that training and education is available to all youngsters;
- jobs with a private employer for six months with employers getting £60 per week, but they must give one day off per week for training;
- a job on the **'environment workforce'** which is part of the **citizen's service**;
- a job with a **voluntary sector employer**. They will receive a wage equivalent to benefit, plus a fixed sum for six months;
- tax rebates for employers who hire someone who has been unemployed for over two years.

The Constitution

- Set up a Scottish Parliament although the 'two question' referendum has caused problems;
- reform of the House of Lords;
- possible reform of the electoral system.

18

Figure 1ll Labour and Conservative policies compared

QUESTIONS

1 What are the main differences between the Conservative and Labour Parties on:

a Health Service;

b employment;

c taxation?

Political Change in Britain

Traditional views of the policies of the British political parties place them into three political categories, as shown in Figure 1JJ.

Since 1979 the Conservatives have moved more towards the **right wing** and have tried to reduce the effects that Socialism had upon Britain. Margaret Thatcher's policies made such great changes to British society that this period became known as the **Thatcher Revolution**. Some of the most dramatic changes involved the following:

* sales of council houses to tenants;
* privatisation;
* reducing the power of the unions;
* reducing local government's spending;
* reducing inflation.

So successful was Thatcherism and the Conservative Party's move to the **right** that the voters re-elected Margaret Thatcher twice, in 1983 and 1987, and John Major once, in 1992.

Left Wing	**Centre**	**Right Wing**
⬇	⬇	⬇
LABOUR	LIBERAL DEMOCRAT	CONSERVATIVE
⬇	⬇	⬇
Socialism	**Social Democracy**	**Capitalism**
⬇	⬇	⬇
More industries controlled by the government	Mixed economy	Privatisation
⬇	⬇	⬇
Higher welfare spending with higher taxes to pay for this	Higher taxes than Conservatives	Low taxes
	⬇	⬇
⬇	Spending on health and education by Government	Private education
Comprehensive education		⬇
	⬇	Small Welfare State
⬇	Freedom for individuals to decide about their future	⬇
Support for unions		Law and order
		⬇
		Strong Army
		⬇
		Reduce union power

Figure 1JJ The policies of the three main parties

Figure 1KK Mrs Thatcher and John Major

The Labour Party, having lost four general elections in a row, realised that left-wing policies wouldn't get them elected. A change in policy was necessary.

Figure 1LL   Problems for Tony Blair

New Labour

In 1994 Tony Blair was elected as leader of the Labour Party, after the sudden death of John Smith. Since that time there has been a shift in the policies of the Labour Party towards the **right**. These include:
* lower taxes;
* low inflation;
* no return to universal comprehensive education;
* introduction of the Social Chapter;
* end of Clause 4 (Clause 4 was a commitment by the old-style Labour to nationalise industries);
* no re-nationalisation because it would cost too much;
* a Scottish Assembly;
* no major changes to Conservative anti-union laws.

'New Labour is neither old left or new right, for neither remotely corresponds to the nature of the challenges facing us. Instead we offer a new way ahead, that leads from the centre, but is profoundly radical in the changes it promises.'

Figure 1MM   *Source: New Labour New Life for Scotland pamphlet, 1996*

QUESTIONS

1 What were the main policies of the Thatcher Revolution?
2 How has New Labour changed Labour Party policy towards the right?

Scottish Local Government

Local government is in charge of many services that are provided at a local level. The system is based upon which services are best provided at local level by local people and those which are better organised at a more regional level.

Prior to 1 April 1996 services were provided mainly by the District and the Regional levels of local government and included:

District Council
* Housing;
* Libraries and Recreation;
* Parks;
* Refuse collection;
* Registration of Birth, Deaths and Marriages.

Regional Council
* Education;
* Social Work;
* Fire Service;
* Police;
* Roads and Lighting
* Water.

There were some local government areas in which services were not divided between the

District Council and the Regional Council, e.g. the Island Councils in Orkneys, Shetlands and Western Isles were unitary councils.

From 1975 to 1996 there were:

- nine Regional Councils (*Strathclyde being the largest*);
- 53 District Councils;
- three Island Councils.

The representatives of the District and Regional Councils were called **councillors**. The District Councillor would represent an area called a **ward**, which is similar to a constituency but much smaller. Regional Councillors represented areas which covered a number of wards.

The end of two-tier local government

Local government was called two-tier because it had two levels, the District and the Regional.

The Conservative government felt that there were too many councils and it was a waste of the taxpayers' money. The Conservatives also felt that they could be difficult to control because many councils were controlled by Labour Party councillors. It was decided that a new type of local government should be introduced and on 1 April 1996 the **new councils** came into being.

The map in Figure 1NN and the list of new councils show that there are now 32 councils.

The new councils are called **unitary authorities** because they provide most of the services that were provided by the District and Regional Councils. There are some differences however:

- Water services and sewerage are now run by water authorities;
- Police and Fire Services are organised by Joint Boards;
- Children's Panel is now run by the Scottish Office.

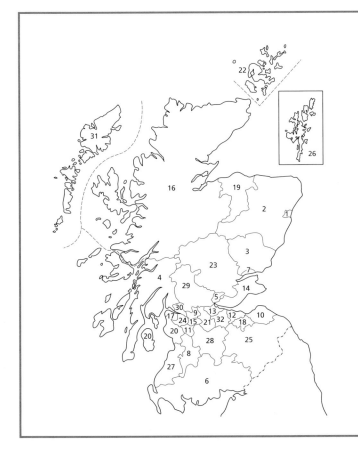

Figure 1NN   The 32 new councils

New councils – 1 April 1996

1. Aberdeen City Council
2. Aberdeenshire Council
3. Angus Council
4. Argyll & Bute Council
5. Clackmannanshire
6. Dumfries & Galloway
7. Dundee City
8. East Ayrshire
9. East Dunbartonshire
10. East Lothian
11. East Renfrewshire
12. City of Edinburgh
13. Falkirk
14. Fife
15. City of Glasgow
16. Highlands
17. Inverclyde
18. Midlothian
19. Moray
20. North Ayrshire
21. N Lanarkshire
22. Orkney Islands
23. Perthshire & Kinross
24. Renfrewshire
25. Borders
26. Shetlands
27. South Ayrshire
28. S Lanarkshire
29. Stirling
30. W Dunbarton
31. Western Isles
32. West Lothian

QUESTIONS

1 Describe local government before 1 April 1996.
2 Why did the Conservatives change local government in Scotland?
3 How many new councils were created on 1 April 1996?
4 What services do local councils no longer have direct control of?

Conflict Between Local and Central Government

Local government is run by the same set of political parties as **central government**. It provides services at the local level. To do this it has to raise money from the local residents, in the form of **council tax**, but most of the money (86%) comes from central government.

The political parties try to gain support of the voters at **council elections** by offering a **manifesto** containing promises of improving local services, such as housing or sports facilities. At the local council elections there is a lot of competition between candidates to get elected as a councillor.

Despite the Conservative Party being in government and running the Scottish Office prior to May 1997, it does not do well in the local council elections. For example, Figure 1OO shows the number of Conservative councillors in Scotland prior to and after 1 April 1996, when the new councils were set up.

	Number of council seats (Regional & District)	Conservative councillors	% of total
Before 1.4.96	1611	230	14.2%
After 1.4.96	1760	82	7%

Figure 1OO   Council seats before and after 1 April 1996

Before the introduction of the new councils the Conservative Party controlled only four District Councils:
- Eastwood (near Glasgow);
- Kyle and Carrick (Ayrshire);
- Perth and Kinross (Perthshire);
- Aberdeen.

After the new council elections the areas of Eastwood (now part of East Renfrewshire) and Kyle & Carrick (South Ayrshire) showed two different pictures.

East Renfrewshire Council 1996
POLITICAL COMPOSITION OF THE COUNCIL:

CONSERVATIVE	9
LABOUR	8
LIBERAL DEMOCRAT	2
RESIDENTS' ASSOCIATION	1

South Ayrshire Council 1996
POLITICAL COMPOSITION OF THE COUNCIL:

LABOUR	21
CONSERVATIVE	4

City of Glasgow 1996
POLITICAL COMPOSITION OF THE COUNCIL:

LABOUR	77
CONSERVATIVE	3
LIBERAL DEMOCRAT	1
SCOTTISH NATIONAL PARTY	1
SCOTTISH MILITANT LABOUR	1

Figure 1PP   Results of the new council elections for three areas

Some critics of the **reform of local government** claimed that the new councils were brought in by the Conservatives to try to improve their standing in local government. The information in Figure 1PP showed that this turned out much differently from what they expected. The *Herald* of 7 April 1995 had the following comment about the Conservative Party's standing after the elections to the new councils.

'Conservatives wake up this morning after their worst nightmare in Scottish local elections.'

'Annihilation in Scottish elections.'

'Conservatives left without control of a single council in Scotland.'

Figure 1QQ   *Source: Herald, 7 April 1995, abridged*

The Labour Party did very well from the new council elections. Figure 1RR shows how the parties fared in the elections.

Political party	Number of councils in their control
Labour	20
Conservatives	0
SNP	3
Liberal Democrats	0
Independent	4

Figure 1RR

What do councillors do?

Councillors represent wards and they run services on behalf of the people who live in them. Councils employ different types of workers to deliver the services, for example:

Type of service	Employee
Education	Teachers, janitors, clerical and cleaning staff.
Social work	Social workers.
Roads	Road engineers, skilled workers and labourers.
Housing	Clerical housing staff and repair workers.
Cleansing	Refuse workers.

Figure 1SS   Different types of council employees

The councillors are involved in making sure that things which affect our everyday lives are provided. In return for their time they are paid an **allowance**, because being a councillor is not a full-time job, like that of an MP. The average allowance is about £3000 per year but councillors can also claim expenses for travel on council business and for food.

The work of a councillor is usually done on committees, where decisions are taken for all services, e.g. the Education Committee discusses and makes decisions on educational matters. There are also meetings involving the councillors of the individual political parties, called **group meetings**, where **policy decisions** are made in line with the national party's view on the running of local government. As in the House of Commons, councillors vote with their political party.

Figure 1TT
Councillor Hugh Henry

Also, as in the House of Commons, the leader of the biggest political party in the council becomes the **Council Leader**. (Figure 1TT shows Councillor Hugh Henry who is the Council Leader in Labour-controlled Renfrewshire Council.)

Councillors hold **surgeries** where local constituents who have a problem with a local service can go along to ask for help. The times and places of the surgeries, or the names and addresses of councillors, are usually published in the local newspaper. Examples of this are shown in Figure 1UU, again for the Renfrewshire Council.

RENFREWSHIRE COUNCIL **Councillor's Surgery** GLENBURN SOUTH (WARD 9) Councillor **Richard Vassie** is available for the interview of his constituents at Langcraigs Primary School, Glenfield Road, Glenburn, Paisley Wednesday, 14th August, 1996 from 6.30 p.m. – 7.30 p.m.	RENFREWSHIRE COUNCIL **Councillor's Surgery** HUNTERHILL (WARD 14) Councillor **Paul Mack** is available for the interview of his constituents at Lylesland Church Hall on Tuesday, 13th August, 1996 from 6.30 p.m. - 8.00 p.m.	

Ward 15, Lochfield, John McGurk, 68 Southwold Road, Paisley (Lib Dem). Tel: 0141-883 6120.

Ward 16, Seedhill, Iain Hogg, 87 Marchfield Avenue, Paisley (Lab). Tel: 0141-848 1947.

Ward 17, Barshaw and Hawkhead, Cecilia Lawson, 27 Ben Lui Drive, Paisley (SNP). Tel: 0141-887 0531.

Figure 1UU Different ways of advertising surgeries

By living in the area which they represent, the councillors are likely to have more dealings with their constituents as they go about their daily activities, like meeting at the shops or at the park. Often councillors hold unofficial surgeries by listening to the local people talking about their problems or complaining about local services. This is an important part of the local councillor's job, as they are only involved part-time in their official duties.

Council elections are held every four years, as are by-elections (see Figure 1VV).

Labour by-election win

LABOUR last night safely retained its Toryglen seat in a Glasgow City Council by-election, but its majority was markedly reduced.

The contest was caused by the death of Councillor Hugh McKenna. He had a majority of 1255 in the elections of just over a year ago. On that occasion it was a straight Labour-SNP contest.

However, yesterday Labour faced four opponents and significant support seemed to be diverted to Rosie Kane, the candidate put forward by the recently formed Scottish Socialist Alliance.

The result was: James Burke (Lab) 948; J M Byrne (SNP) 375; R Kane (SSA) 315; W J Thomas (Con) 36; R Stewart (Lib Dem) 19; Lab Maj: 573. Turnout: 37%.

Figure 1VV

Paying for Local Government Services

The cost of providing local services is expensive. The central government in London believes that this cost should be controlled by both local and central government and they have introduced a way to do this.

The Scottish Office in Edinburgh tries to

make sure that the government's rules on local government spending are followed.

If a council tries to spend more on services than the amount set by the government, the Scottish Office can impose a limit on it. This is called **capping**. In this way the government controls spending on local services.

The money to be spent on local services is raised by taxing the people who live in the area. If the council wants to offer a better service to the local population it will raise the local tax to pay for this. In the past raising the money caused many problems as it was the wealthier constituents who had to pay the higher taxes, called **rates**, which were based upon the size of house that they lived in.

To make the local tax system fairer, the Conservative Government introduced the **Poll Tax**. Under this system everyone in the local area would pay the same amount of money, regardless of how well off or poor they were. The introduction of the Poll Tax caused an uproar in many parts of Scotland where some people were too poor to pay it. Many people refused to pay it and some even ended up having their household belongings seized by Sheriff's Officers and sold to pay off the Poll Tax.

One campaigner against the Poll Tax, Glasgow Councillor Tommy Sheridan, was put in prison for refusing to pay a fine.

More recently, after the failure of the Poll Tax, the government introduced the **Council Tax**. The amount that people pay for this local tax is based on the value of their house. Houses of similar types are placed in a 'band' (there are eight of these) and the higher the band, the more tax the person pays.

Band A	up to £27000
Band B	£27000 to £35000
Band C	£35000 to £45000
Band D	£45000 to £58000
Band E	£58000 to £80000
Band F	£80000 to £106000
Band G	£106000 to £212000
Band H	over £212000

Companies in a local area also pay a tax, called **business rates**, but these don't go straight to the local council to pay for services. All business rates go to the Scottish Office which shares them out among all of the Scottish Councils. The more people living in a council area, the more money the area receives from the Scottish Office.

The transfer of business rates to the Scottish Office has been criticised by councils which have a lot of businesses because money is taken from them and given to other areas with a small number of businesses. Glasgow, for example, has a large number of businesses **but** also many problems in the local area. Yet money is transferred from Glasgow to other areas with fewer problems. As a result of this policy, Glasgow lost £50 million in 1997/98 and had to make even bigger cuts in services. The articles in Figure 1XX are examples of what

Figure 1WW
Tommy Sheridan

TIGHTENING THE COUNCIL PURSE STRINGS

The squeeze on council spending has forced a rethink on the way that the lolly is splashed about. Like on grants for 'summer outings'.

A whole list of applications landed on the South Area management committee. Carnwadric Tiny Tots, wanted more than £1000 for a four day stay at Butlins. Their own contribution amounted to £120.

continued . . .

25

continued ...

Crossmyloof Lunch Club wanted £500 to supplement their own £70 for their annual trip to Oban. St Luke's senior citizens needed £500 (own share £90) for a day out to Ayr. The list went on.

New rules are being introduced, which will put limits on the level of council grants and with clubs being told to raise a bigger slice of the cash themselves.

POOLING A FAST ONE?

Whiteinch councillor Heather Ritchie claims local kids are being muscled out of Scotstoun Leisure Centre during the school holidays.

It costs them £1.30 a swim, even when they scramble to get the cash, they are apt to find the 'pool full' notice is flashing.

The facilities are apparently bursting at the seams from the overspill from closures in the surrounding areas such as Whiteinch.

Councillor Ritchie is now protesting to parks officials that something must be done before the summer is over.

Figure 1XX   *Source: Glaswegian, 18 July 1996*

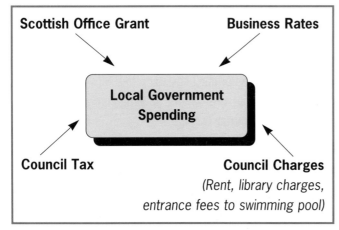

Figure 1YY   Sources of council spending money

happens when **cuts** on local government cash are made.

The councils have little real control over the amount of money they need to spend on local services. Council tax only amounts to about 14% of the money that is needed. The money for the spending comes from a number of sources, as shown in Figure 1YY.

QUESTIONS

1 How does the government control what councils spend?
2 Why did many people oppose the Poll Tax?
3 Why might cities like Glasgow and Dundee complain about how the business rate is distributed to other council areas?
4 Look at the articles in Figure 1XX. Explain in your own words how cuts in council services affect people living in these areas.
5 How much of local government spending comes from the Council Tax?

Constitutional Issues

Quangos are bodies set up by the government to run some public services. Members are not elected to their position. They are appointed by a government minister and can only be removed from their position by government. They are also paid a salary for their services. It is not necessary for them to have any formal qualifications for the job.

Quangos include:
• the new Water Authorities (see Figure 1ZZ);
• Scottish Homes;
• Scottish Enterprise;
• NHS trusts;
• colleges of further education.

26

WEST OF SCOTLAND WATER AUTHORITY

419 Balmore Road, Glasgow G22 6NU
Tel: 0141-355 5333 Fax: 0141-355 5146
Emergency Telephone: 0345 700 800
(for water and sewerage services)

Chief Executive – *Ernest Chambers*
Chair – *John Jameson OBE*

Board Members
Norman Berry
Councillor Mungo Bryson
Sir Robert Easton CBE
John Goodwin
David Gray
Peter Kennedy
Councillor Billy Petrie OBE
Councillor Robert Reid
Councillor Leslie Rosin
Councillor Ian Young

Figure 1ZZ   An advert for a new water authority

Just less than half of all the money that the Scottish Office receives is controlled by these quangos. The fact that they control so much of Scotland's money and are not elected to power, so cannot be held responsible to the voters, has caused concern.

Paisley North MP Irene Adams had this to say about quangos:

'There are 1500 **elected** members of the New Councils at present and by next year there would be 5000 **unelected** Quango members.'

Figure 1AAA   *Source: Herald, 18 March 1995*

Another critic, Mr Jenkins, a former editor of *The Times*, said:

'The packing of health and education quangos by wives of Conservative MPs was causing concern.'

Figure 1BBB   *Source: The Times, 18 January 1995, abridged*

The *Observer* newspaper also expressed concern over the quangos:

'In Britain there are over 5000 quangos run by over 60,000 members. They control over one-third of government expenditure.

Only 11% of quangos hold public meetings to explain their work. Council meetings are public in contrast. People have no say either directly or through their elected representatives.'

Figure 1CCC   *Source: Observer, 14 July 1996*

The *Scottish Trade Union Review* had the following to say about quangos, headed '**No Low Pay For Quango Cats**'.

'Only three ministers publish details of what they pay the quango cats. Fifteen others avoid this. The Scottish Office simply ignore the matter in their Annual Report.'

Figure 1DDD   *Source: Scottish Low Pay Unit in Scottish Trade Union Review, May–June 1996*

What is revealed is that although few people know who is employed in the quangos and what they are paid, information is available on the pay of a few quango cats:

- Sir Brian Shaw, chairman of the London Port Authority, received £150000 for 36 days' work, i.e. £4000 per day
- Sir Colin Walker receives £13000 per year for 21 days' work

- Lord Bellwin receives £27380 a year for two days' work per week.

The Scottish Secretary responded to the critics of the quangos by saying:

> 'The dedication and expertise of those appointed represent an important contribution to public life in Scotland, and make public services more efficient.'

Figure 1EEE   *Source: Herald, 18 January 1995*

QUESTIONS

1 What are quangos?
2 Make a list of some of the quangos in Scotland.
3 What criticism does Irene Adams make of quangos?
4 What other criticisms are made of quangos?
5 How does the Scottish Secretary defend them?

The Scottish Dimension

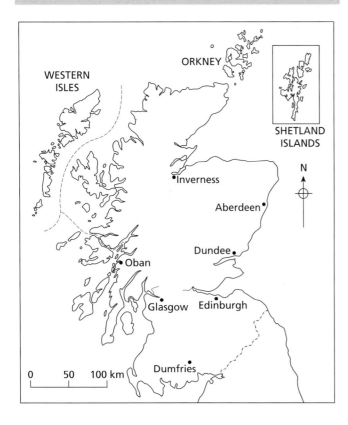

Figure 1FFF   Map of Scotland

For some time now there has been an interest by many Scots for some type of self-rule for Scotland. Some Scottish political parties and other groups feel that Scottish interests would be looked after much better if there was a Scottish Parliament.

Some other groups, including the Conservative Party, feel that Scottish interests are best looked after by a British Parliament.

Background to recent push for devolution

On 1 March 1979 a vote was taken in Scotland on whether or not self-rule should be introduced. Figure 1GGG shows the results of this **referendum**.

Those in favour (Yes)	Those against (No)
1230937	1153502

Figure 1GGG

The election of the Conservative Government in 1979 ended any possibility for devolution. The Conservatives were the party in power in Britain but there was little support for them in Scotland. This fall in support for the Conservatives continued into the 1980s and caused the situation known as the **Doomsday Scenario** to arise.

This refers to the situation in 1987. If the Conservative Party won the election and their support in Scotland fell, then there wouldn't be enough Scottish Conservative MPs to run the Scottish Office. English Conservative MPs would have to be brought in to look after Scottish interests.

The Conservative Party did win the 1987 general election and English MPs were used to look at Scottish-only issues. Many Scots who had not voted for a Scottish Parliament in 1979 began to change their minds as the Conservative Party had very little support in Scotland.

28

The Scottish Constitutional Convention

The Constitutional Convention was set up in 1988 to look at ways in which self-rule could be achieved for Scotland.

Figure 1HHH

SCOTTISH PARLIAMENT

Groups for	Groups against
Labour Party	Conservative Party
Liberal Democrats	Scottish businessmen
Churches	*(majority of)*
Trade Unions	
SNP *(only if full independence)*	

Figure 1III   Groups for and against a Scottish Parliament

In 1993, the Scottish Convention set out their suggestions for a Scottish Parliament:
- 129 Scottish MPs;
- fair representation of women and men;
- responsibility for education, health, law, employment/training, transport, environment and planning;
- **'Tartan Tax'** of 3 pence in the pound;
- budget from Westminster.

Michael Forsyth, the Conservative Secretary of State for Scotland, mounted a campaign against a Scottish Parliament, especially the 'tartan tax'.

**Figure 1JJJ
Michael Forsyth**

In response, Tony Blair announced in June 1996 that a future Labour government would hold a referendum made up of two questions, one on support for a Parliament in Scotland and the other on the 'tartan tax'. Many Labour Party members, including MPs, criticised this decision. Figure 1KKK shows a meeting of Scottish MPs who believe that there should only be one question.

Figure 1KKK

However, the Labour Party has already started campaigning for a new Scottish Parliament as Figure 1LLL shows.

Figure 1LLL

The Government's reaction/response

The Conservative Party said that the number of Scottish MPs in the House of Commons should be reduced to 57 if there was a Scottish Parliament. They put forward their own plans for Scotland:

- more meetings of the Scottish Grand Committee (all 72 Scottish MPs meet to discuss Scottish matters);
- more power to Scottish local government;
- more say by local government on how their money is spent.

The Conservatives claim that the tartan tax would mean that the Scottish taxpayers would pay higher taxes than the rest of the UK.

QUESTIONS

1 Why do the Conservatives oppose a Scottish Parliament?
2 What was the result of the 1979 referendum?
3 What criticisms are made of the way Scotland is governed?
4 Which groups support a Scottish Parliament?
5 Describe the Scottish Constitutional Convention's proposals in your own words.
6 How has the Conservative Party responded to these proposals?

Britain and the European Union

Figure 1MMM   The European Union

The UK became a member of the European Economic Community (EEC) in 1973. Many people opposed membership. Members of the same political party were also split on membership. In 1975, the Labour Government held a referendum to ask whether Britain should remain in the EEC (as the EU was then called). The British people voted to stay in the EEC but opposition was still strong.

Since Britain's entry to the EEC/EU a number of policies have been introduced to bring all of the members closer together. These are:

- **1985** Plan for a **European Single Market** to be introduced. This would create one large market for the products of member-countries and give the EU greater power over the parliaments of member countries.
- **1987** European Single Market introduced.
- **1991 Maastricht Treaty** proposed to bring member countries closer together through closer financial and political ties. Apart from the Social Chapter and single currency this was agreed by the British government in 1992.

British political parties and the EU

There are also different views within the same party. The following gives some idea of these differences:

Conservative Party: closer ties with Europe are good for Britain but some Conservative MPs are against the Maastricht Treaty. This group within the Conservative Party are called **Euro-sceptics**.

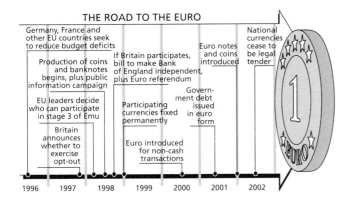

THE ROAD TO THE EURO

Germany, France and other EU countries seek to reduce budget deficits

Production of coins and banknotes begins, plus public information campaign

EU leaders decide who can participate in stage 3 of Emu

Britain announces whether to exercise opt-out

If Britain participates, bill to make Bank of England independent, plus Euro referendum

Participating currencies fixed permanently

Euro introduced for non-cash transactions

Euro notes and coins introduced

Government debt issued in euro form

National currencies cease to be legal tender

1996 1997 1998 1999 2000 2001 2002

Figure 1NNN

Different views of Conservative MPs can be seen from the following reports in the newspaper:

Michael Portillo

'Single currency would mean giving up the government of Britain.'

Source: *Herald*, 13 February 1995

Jonathan Aitken

'I don't want to see a single currency, period.'

Source: *Herald*, 13 February 1995

Kenneth Clarke

'I will not be silenced on Europe . . . joining the single currency should not be ruled out now.'

Source: Abridged, *Herald*, 16 February 1995

Figure 1OOO   Some Conservative MPs' views on a single European currency

David Heathcoat Amory said about his decision to leave the Cabinet: 'Joining a single currency would be disastrous, politically and economically.'

Labour Party: wants closer ties to Europe and a single currency. But there are a number of MPs and MEPs who don't want close ties with Europe.

'If the UK joins a single currency, economic power will be transferred to European bankers beyond our control. Public expenditure cuts would result affecting schools, housing and community care. Job losses would occur.'

Figure 1PPP   Statement of 70 Labour MPs and MEPs
                    Source: The Single Currency
                    Labour Programme, *abridged*

Liberal Democrats: want Britain to remain in Europe but they would like to see a **federal system** set up where all nations would have control over their own affairs, but the European Parliament would have power in European matters.

SNP: wants Scotland to go it alone in Europe as a member in its own right, not as part of the UK. This explains the SNP slogan: **'Independence in Europe'**.

QUESTIONS

1 When did Britain become a member of the European Community?
2 What are the main policies to bring member states together?
3 Who are the Euro-sceptics?
4 What evidence is there of differences of opinion on Europe within the Conservative Party?
5 What evidence is there that not all Labour MPs are in favour of a single currency?
6 Describe the Liberal Democrats' and SNP's policies on Europe.

31

Britain is a **representative democracy** which has evolved over the centuries. The term democracy implies that power lies in the hands of the people.

It is of course impossible for a country the size of Britain to have a political system where the individual wishes of all the people are taken into account over every decision.

Instead people vote for representatives who usually belong to political parties. These political parties aim to get the support of voters and win elections.

The political parties can only win elections if they aim to represent the political opinions of as many people as possible. They compete with the other political parties to win the support of the people at any particular point in time.

This is known as the **electoral system**.

In Britain people can **participate** in the electoral system by voting for the following types of **representatives: the Member of Parliament (MP); the local councillor; the Member of the European Parliament (MEP)**.

One might get the impression that the British people are well 'represented' and that Britain is the finest democracy in the world.

However, a government can be elected for a term of office lasting no longer than five years. In addition, since 1945, no British government has been supported by more than 50% of the voting population.

Constitutional Monarchy

Britain is a representative democracy, but it is also a **constitutional monarchy**.

This means that the country is governed by ministers in the name of the **Queen**, who is the Head of State.

All Bills passed by Parliament can only become laws if they receive **Royal Assent**, which means they must be approved by the Queen.

The Queen could, in theory, act like the American President and stop Bills becoming laws. Unlike the President she is not elected!

The separation of powers

Separate bodies (organs of government) are given the roles of making laws, governing the country and deciding on how laws affect individuals and groups.

The three organs of government are the:

- **legislature**, commonly known as Parliament (the House of Commons and the House of Lords);
- the **executive** (the Cabinet and government ministers); and finally
- the **judiciary** (the courts) which safeguard the rights of the individual.

Q UESTIONS

1 What does the term democracy mean?
2 What is the name given to the way the British people participate in choosing elected representatives?
3 Name three types of representatives which the British people can choose?
4 What evidence is there that Britain might not be truly a democracy?
5 What are the three organs of British government known as?
6 What are the names of the two houses which make up the legislature?

Figure 1.1   The Houses of Parliament

32

How a Government Bill is made

The idea for a new piece of legislation may come from a variety of places.

It could come from one of the following:

- the party **manifesto**;
- interest groups, e.g. Child Poverty Action Group, Help the Aged;
- professional bodies, e.g. British Medical Association, the Law Society;
- government departments.

Types of Bill

There are three types of Bill.

Government Bills and **Private Member's Bills** are both general Bills, in that they relate to matters of general concern, and must be introduced by an MP or a Peer.

There are also **Public Bills** which deal with issues affecting a specific individual or group.

Private Member's Bills (PMBs) are drafted by individual MPs whose names are drawn out of a hat to get debating time. Only those PMBs with government backing have any chance of being passed.

The idea for a Bill is outlined in a **Green Paper** for consultation with interest groups, MPs and other government departments.

After this a **White Paper**, detailing the government's intentions in the Bill, is published. The Bill is then **drafted** after it has received Cabinet approval.

The Bill in Parliament

There are important stages and procedures which proposed legislation must go through before a Bill can actually become law.

First reading   Here the Bill is introduced to let MPs know about it. There is no debate.

Second reading   The main principle of the Bill is debated by MPs and a **vote** or division takes place. MPs file through two main **division lobbies**. If there are more ayes than noes then the Bill proceeds to the next stage.

continued . . .

continued . . .

Committee stage   A clause-by-clause scrutiny takes place by a **Standing Committee**. The government has an in-built majority and amendments to the Bill can take place.

Report stage   Any amendments are considered by MPs who wish to contribute to the debate.

Guillotine   The government may cut short a Bill's proceedings by using a 'guillotine motion' which orders that one or more stages of a Bill are completed by a certain date.

Third reading   The final version is debated and voted on. Once a Bill has passed its third reading in the House of Commons, it goes to the House of Lords.

It passes through the same stages as it did in the Commons. The Lords vote on amendments and these amendments are incorporated into the Bill.

The Bill then passes back to the Commons to discuss changes made by the Lords.

Royal assent   The Royal Assent is given by the Lord Commissioners on behalf of the monarch.

The Bill then becomes law and goes in the **Statute book**.

Figure 1.2   The stages of legislation

QUESTIONS

1 From what sources are proposals for a Bill likely to come?

2 Explain what happens in the following stages:
   a **second reading**;
   b **Committee stage**;
   c **third reading**.

3 What built-in safety device does the government have at the Committee stage?

Organisation of Government

The British Parliament is said to be **bicameral** which means it is made up of two chambers.

33

The **House of Commons** is an elected chamber of 659 MPs.

The **House of Lords** is an unelected chamber of some 1200 **peers**. Some sit there because they are appointed by the government for life. They are known as **life peers**.

There are those who sit in the Lords because they are **hereditary peers** – their title is passed on to them through the inheritance principle, e.g. from a father or uncle.

The Executive

The government is the body of ministers responsible for running the country, chosen from the political party which wins the most seats in the general election.

About 100 of the present Labour MPs in the Commons are in the government. The most senior of these government ministers are in the **Cabinet**. The leader of the Cabinet, and therefore of the government, is the **Prime Minister**.

The Judiciary

This consists of the judges and the courts. They are formally separate from Parliament and the government and are responsible for interpreting British and European law and protecting the rights of the individual.

They can also come into conflict with the executive. If a member of the government acts illegally, then the courts will say so. For example, in March 1996 the Home Secretary, Michael Howard, was found to have illegally deported asylum seekers before they could properly put their case.

However, the government can also exercise power over the judiciary. It appoints senior members of the judiciary, e.g. the Attorney-General, Sir Nicholas Lyell and the Solicitor-General, Sir Derek Spencer. The Home Secretary in England and Wales and the Scottish Secretary in Scotland also have an influence on the appointment of judges in other courts.

What is the function of the legislature?

The legislature consists of two houses, namely the Commons and the Lords. These two chambers are where the real work of government goes on.

The House of Commons is more important than the House of Lords as it is the (elected) representative chamber.

Q U E S T I O N S

1 What does the term bicameral mean?
2 Explain the difference between those who sit in the House of Commons and those in the House of Lords?
3 What evidence is there to suggest that the Lords is undemocratic?
4 Explain the difference between the two types of peer.
5 What is the executive?
6 What are the most senior members of the government commonly called?
7 Find out who holds the following key posts:
  a Education Secretary;
  b Foreign Secretary;
  c Home Secretary;
  d Health Secretary.
8 What is the role of the judiciary and what evidence is there to suggest that they are not totally independent of the government?

The House of Commons

The political party which wins the majority of seats in the Commons following a general election usually forms the **government**. There are 659 MPs in the Commons. Each MP is elected to represent a **constituency**. The 1992 and 1997 **General Election** results were as follows:

	1992	1997
Conservative	336	165
Labour	271	419
Liberal Democrat	20	46
Official Unionist	9	10
Plaid Cymru	4	4
SDLP	4	3
SNP	3	6
Democratic Unionist	3	2
Popular Unionist	1	1
Sinn Fein	0	2
Independent	0	1
Total	651	659

Figure 1.3   1992 and 1997 general election results

34

As you can see from Figure 1.4, in 1992 the Conservative Party had more seats than all the other parties put together. This is called an **overall majority**.

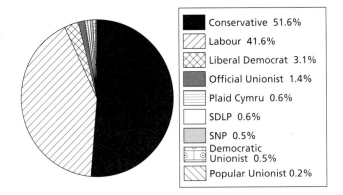

■	Conservative 51.6%
⧄	Labour 41.6%
⧆	Liberal Democrat 3.1%
▨	Official Unionist 1.4%
▤	Plaid Cymru 0.6%
□	SDLP 0.6%
▥	SNP 0.5%
	Democratic Unionist 0.5%
⧄	Popular Unionist 0.2%

Figure 1.4   1992 general election results

The Conservative Party, with an overall majority, formed the government as it was the party with the most seats. The Labour Party came second and became the official **Opposition Party** in the House.

All the other parties who won seats can sit in the Opposition side of the House. The House is divided up into government and opposition. On the one side there is the governing party and on the other side, the opposition parties.

When there is a vote in the House of Commons, it is called a **division**. Instead of MPs voting by putting up their hands or pressing a buzzer, their votes are counted by them filing out of the House of Commons into what are called **the Division lobbies**. There is one lobby for the Ayes and one for the Noes.

The votes are counted by **tellers** who inform the **Speaker** (who acts like a chairperson), whose job it is to announce the result. MPs' votes are also registered in **Hansard** which is the official record of everything which is said and decided by the House of Commons.

The front benches

If you look at Figure 1.5 you will see the composition of the House. The **front benches** on either side consist of the Cabinet and their opposite numbers in the **Shadow Cabinet**.

Each member of the Cabinet, e.g. Michael Howard, the Home Secretary, has an opposite number in the Shadow Cabinet, e.g. Jack Straw, the

Shadow Home Secretary, whose job is to keep their opposite number 'on their toes'.

If Labour was to win the next election, it is more than likely that Shadow Cabinet members would become members of the new Cabinet.

Figure 1.5   The House of Commons chamber

The back benches

Put quite simply, all those MPs who are neither in the government nor the opposition front bench sit on the back benches on either side. Back-bench MPs who belong to the government party sit behind the government front benches. Opposition back-benchers sit behind the Opposition front-benchers.

In theory the ordinary MP has a lot of freedom to vote according to how their conscience dictates. But in reality ordinary MPs usually vote the way their party leader wants.

QUESTIONS

1 Why is the Commons considered to be the more important of the two houses?
2 How is the government formed?
3 Which party is the official opposition?
4 What is a vote in the House of Commons called?
5 In your own words describe how MPs' votes are counted and registered.
6 What is the role of the Shadow Cabinet?
7 What are back-benchers?

The Whip System

As stated earlier, MPs usually vote along party lines. Each political party has a **Chief Whip** whose job is to make sure the MPs in that party vote the way the leadership wants them to. The Chief Whip has the help of other Whips to help do the job.

Whips play an important part in the everyday work of Parliament.

Whips issue notices of important Divisions (votes) in the House of Commons. These notices are also called 'whips'. They have information which is underlined to show how important the party leaders think MPs' attendance is.

- *One line whip*

  Lets MPs know that a vote will take place.
- *Two line whip*

  Lets MPs know that they should attend unless they have made an arrangement with another 'opposite' MP not to attend. This is called a pair. The Whip's office must approve this.
- *Three line whip*

  MPs must attend.

Whips also put other pressures on MPs to vote the way the party leaders want them to.

In the debate over the **Maastricht Treaty**, government Whips were accused of using every trick at their disposal to make sure Tory Euro-rebels voted for the Bill.

Some MPs accused the Whips of threatening to tell embarrassing stories about the MP's personal lives to the newspapers if they didn't vote with the government.

Likewise, in March 1996, Labour Whips were ordered to prevent 25 or so Labour MPs voting against a renewal of the Prevention of Terrorism Act.

Tony Blair, the Labour leader, wanted to demonstrate that a future Labour government would not be soft on terrorism.

This issue was important for another reason. This was the first time since 1983 that Labour had not opposed its renewal.

Pressures on an MP

The back-bench MP has various other pressures put upon them. They have to do a fine balancing act between the interests of various competing groups. Study Figure 1.6 carefully.

House of Commons
Divisions, Committees, Private Member's Bills, Questions

Personal Interests
Votes of Conscience, Committees

Constituency Issues
Local interests, Representations, Questions, Debates, Local galas/fetes, Constituency meetings

Pressure Groups
Bills, Questions, Debates

Figure 1.6   Influences on MPs

In some instances an MP may have to take a crucial decision and vote according to their conscience and maybe against their party.

For example, in 1992 Michael Heseltine announced the closure of coal mines as part of the government's energy programme. One of the pits earmarked for closure was in the constituency of a Conservative MP, Elizabeth Peacock. She had to take the crucial decision whether or not to support the Conservative government and her own party on this issue, or her constituents.

Just a Job?

In recent years the behaviour of our elected representatives has come in for much criticism.

Many ordinary MPs have outside interests and their annual salary of £43000 per year may be small in comparison to the money they might receive from these interests.

Many MPs act as paid consultants to pressure groups and various business interests. An MP is not supposed to accept money or gifts from third parties without declaring them in the **register of members' interests**.

Ken Livingstone and Tony Blair (Labour) are both sponsored by the TGWU. Kenneth Baker (Conservative) is parliamentary adviser to ICI plc. Tony Banks (Labour) advises the London Beekeepers Association and receives 12 pots of honey a year.

The **Nolan Report** into ethics in public service calls for a much tougher system for controlling MPs' outside interests.

Q UESTIONS

1 What is the function of the party Whips?
2 Give two examples of the Whips at work.
3 Which do you think are the most important influences on an MP?
4 What arguments might be put forward for MPs having to declare all their interests?

In July 1996, MPs voted themselves a 26% pay increase, raising ordinary MPs' salaries from £34000 to £43000.

The Prime Minister received a rise from £84217 to £101557. The Leader of the Opposition's pay rose from £64167 to £83332.

These increases in MPs' pay were widely criticised by trade unions, particularly those representing low-paid workers. MPs defended their actions.

Look at Figure 1.7 from the *Herald*, 12 July 1996, and answer the questions which follow.

> 'Many people throughout the country will be asking themselves how can MPs justify such an increase of approximately £180 per week when most people do not receive this as a weekly income.'

Figure 1.7a   *James Elsbey, Scottish Secretary, Transport and General Workers' Union*

> 'There was a real danger that MPs would increasingly lead different lifestyles from the people they represent and become more divorced from the realities of everyday life. That is not good for representative democracy.'

Figure 1.7b   *Richard Leonard, Assistant Secretary, Scottish Trades Union Congress*

> 'I think MPs are entitled to the rate for the job.'

Figure 1.7c   *Helen Liddell, Labour MP, Monklands East*

> 'If you want people of quality and calibre then you have to pay the salary that will recruit and retain them. My constituents believe I try to do always what's right. I expect they will recognise that I don't do this for Bill Walker, but I believe it is right for Westminster.'

Figure 1.7d   *Bill Walker, Conservative MP, Tayside North*

> 'The package for the first time brings MPs' pay to a level greater in real terms than when I first entered parliament 30 years ago.'

Figure 1.7e   *Robert Maclennan, Liberal Democrat MP, Caithness and Sutherland*

Q UESTIONS

1 How much did MPs vote to increase their pay by?
2 What criticisms do the trade unionists make of the pay increases?
3 How does each of the MPs suggest that their pay was too low before the increase?
4 'That is not good for representative democracy.' (See Figure 1.7b.) Give arguments for and against the MPs' pay increases.

E XTENSION QUESTIONS

1 Look at Figure 1.8. What message is it trying to get across?

Figure 1.8   *Source: Guardian, 7 November 1995*

What the MP does inside the House of Commons

One of the main roles of the House of Commons is to **legislate** (to make laws).

The role of the MP inside the House of Commons is varied. In theory they can vote in any way they wish. However, the whip system restricts their individual freedom.

Usually we think of MPs taking part in **debates** in the chamber of the House of Commons because this is how we see them on television.

However, MPs have other roles which are not as visible.

Scrutinising

One of the MP's tasks is to scrutinise Bills and the government's actions. This means that they have to look at these very closely and critically. A bit like Evaluation!

They can join a **Standing Committee** to scrutinise a Bill in detail.

They can put their name forward to join a **Select Committee** which scrutinises the work of the major government departments, e.g. Education and Employment.

They can ask questions of government ministers at **Question Time**. These questions are usually written or oral.

Promoting legislation

An MP may feel so strongly about a particular issue that they put their name forward to give them the opportunity to introduce a Private Member's Bill, e.g. **Domestic Violence Bill 1995**.

Lobbying

The MP will also meet lobbyists in the Commons **lobby**. They are usually constituents who want to see their local MP over a particular issue or grievance, e.g. a major factory closure.

The MP in turn might lobby a government minister to influence government policy on behalf of their constituents.

Many large companies and pressure groups now employ professional lobbyists whose job it is to meet MPs and try to persuade them to act on their behalf.

The Nolan Committee was set up after the 'Cash for Questions scandal'. It was discovered that two MPs had been paid £1000 each to ask questions in the House on behalf of a private company.

QUESTIONS

1 Give five examples of how an MP takes part in the legislative process.
2 What are the main differences between a Select Committee and a Standing Committee?
3 What are the two ways of tabling a question to a government minister?
4 What opportunity exists for the ordinary back-bench MP to introduce legislation?
5 What does the term 'lobbying of parliament' mean?
6 Why might there be concerns about the activities of professional lobbyists?

Voting

The most powerful weapon at the MP's disposal is the vote. Despite all the pressure on them used by the Whips, they can make their protest felt through abstaining or even voting with the opposition.

This is called a **back-bench revolt**.

If MPs vote against their leader's wishes they can have **the whip** withdrawn from them. This means that they no longer belong to the Parliamentary Party (MPs belonging to one political party in the House of Commons). It's a bit like being expelled from a club.

This can be very dangerous for an MP, as the party leader will put pressure on that MP's constituency party not to support them at the next election.

MPs can also **refuse the whip**. This means that they will vote the way they want to and ignore the instructions of their party's whips.

MPs don't need to resign their seats if they disagree with the party to which they belong. Some MPs argue that they are personally elected by the voters in their constituencies, not just because they are members of a political party.

Two Tory MPs have recently defected to other parties. Alan Howarth joined Labour and Emma Nicholson joined the Liberal Democrats.

QUESTIONS

1 Give examples of how an MP can show displeasure with their party.
2 Which two recent examples are a worrying trend for the Conservatives?

Life of MPs

**Figure 1.9
Helen Liddel, MP**

Read the article in Figure 1.10 and answer the questions which follow.

Helen Liddell, Labour MP for Monklands, makes the point that people often have the wrong idea about what being an MP is like.

'The job is totally different from what people think it to be.

'You are part social worker, part media performer, part organiser and a very large part peripatetic wanderer.'

Helen Liddell became an MP after the death of Labour leader, John Smith. Before this she had 20 years' experience in Labour party politics and she originally came from the constituency.

'An MP's life is very hectic, but I enjoy it,' she says. Away from London, Helen enjoys meeting constituents at her local surgeries. 'It gives me tremendous satisfaction when I can be of help to people.'

Although you don't need any qualifications to become an MP an interest in politics is useful, but commitment is essential.

'People should be aware of what they are taking on,' she says. 'It's more than a job. It's a way of life and you have to be prepared for disruption within the family.

'Although you are in the media spotlight it can be a very solitary job. The travelling and the hours can be appalling.

continued . . .

Juggling commitments between work and family is very difficult.'

Being away from home five days a week, Helen, a mother of two, is fortunate in having Margaret, her childminder and housekeeper of 20 years, who is an important person in keeping the Liddell household afloat.

Could it be that behind every successful woman there is another doing the housework?

Helen Liddell is front-bench spokesperson with 10 portfolios including agriculture, education and tourism.

Helen finds organising her diary a nightmare. Indeed, when her phone rings she sometimes pretends not to be in!

Figure 1.10   *Source: Herald, 28 May 1996, abridged*

QUESTIONS

1 Which constituency does Helen Liddell represent?
2 What factors were important in her being selected to stand as a Labour candidate?
3 What aspects of her work give her satisfaction?
4 What quality does she see as being essential?
5 How can the MP's job be a lonely one?
6 Give examples of the areas Helen Liddell is responsible for.

Working in the Constituency

Figure 1.11 is an extract from a letter sent by a school pupil to Sam Galbraith, Labour MP for Strathkelvin and Bearsden, and his replies to the questions.

Dear Mr Galbraith,

I am doing a Modern Studies Investigation into the work of an MP. I would be very grateful if you could give me your thoughts on the following matters.

• What made you become an MP?

Reply: I became an MP because I was unhappy with the way our society was moving and felt changes had to be made. I want a fairer and more just society in which everyone can reach their potential. I feel I could achieve this by being in a position of power and influencing events.

continued . . .

continued . . .

- What are your views on the NHS and do you think enough money is being spent on it?

Reply: The NHS is one of the country's assets. It delivers health care efficiently, effectively and fairly. At the moment it is experiencing unnecessary bureaucratic changes which will not solve its problems. The government should increase its resources and direct the money to those who need it.

- Do you find the working hours of your job long and very tiring and do you spend much time with your family and friends?

Reply: Yes, I do find the hours long and I do not get as much time as I would like to spend with my family and friends.

- Can you give me an example of how you have recently helped your constituents?

Reply: I have recently intervened with a bank on behalf of a local company, thus ensuring their future and jobs for their employees who are my constituents.

There was also a case where a young student had won a place at a university in England and she had four days to accept the placement. She was very much looking forward to starting her course. However, the Scottish Office had refused her a student grant and because of her family circumstances it would have been impossible for her to afford the course. After several phone calls to government ministers I was able to resolve the matter.

- How do you spend an average working day in Parliament?

Reply: I arrive in Parliament by 9.00 a.m. and stay there until 1.00 p.m., remain there over lunch, then perhaps attend an informal meeting.

I start work in the chamber at 2.30 p.m. and after that work through, either in the Chamber or in Committee, or at other meetings, until at least 10.30 p.m. in the evening, and often well into the night.

Figure 1.11

Before Sam Galbraith became an MP he was one of Scotland's most well-known neurosurgeons and a leading member of Scottish CND.

He defeated Michael Hirst, the sitting Conservative MP, in a constituency which contains some of the highest earners in Scotland (Bearsden and Milngavie) who traditionally voted Conservative or Liberal Democrat, as well as the solidly Labour voters in Strathkelvin and Bearsden.

QUESTIONS

1 Why did Sam Galbraith decide to become an MP?
2 How does he criticise the government over its NHS policy?
3 Give an example of how this MP helped his constituents with their problems.
4 What evidence is there that the MP's job is a demanding one?
5 Find out who your MP is and draw up a list of questions you might want to ask him. Remember to show the letter to your teacher before posting.

The MP: A Job for Life?

The job of an MP is not a job for life as it used to be 20 or so years ago.

Labour MP, Mike Watson, was recently rejected as the Labour candidate for the Govan constituency. He went from being a well-respected trade-union-sponsored constituency MP for Glasgow Central, which he won in a difficult by-election, to a person now looking for a job.

The **Boundary Commission**, a government body which looks at the size of constituencies, decided that Glasgow had too many MPs for the size of its population. The number of Glasgow's constituencies was reduced from eleven to ten.

Mr Watson then had to find a seat to contest at the next general election.

The sitting Govan MP, Ian Davidson, won the selection contest of the Pollok constituency which he will contest at the next election. So the Govan seat became available.

Mr Watson had to contest the selection of the Govan constituency against local Labour councillor, Mohammed Sarwar, a wealthy Glasgow businessman who had the support of the area's large Asian party membership.

Mr Sarwar 'lost' the first ballot by one vote after 50 votes were disqualified under Labour Party rules. Mr Sarwar's supporters claimed that many of the people were disqualified because they did not have

English as a first language and were Sarwar supporters. They demanded a re-run.

The re-run of the contest led to Mr Sarwar winning by an 82-vote majority. Mr Watson was surprised at the scale of the defeat and he remarked that those party members who said they were going to pick him clearly did not.

He further remarked that the ethnic minority vote was able to outvote the traditional trade union vote.

Mr Watson has his wife Lorraine as part of his parliamentary team. She is his full-time secretary and together they earn around £60000 plus expenses and allowances.

Figure 1.12   Mike Watson, left and Mohammed Sarwar, right

Mr Sarwar had the chance of becoming Scotland's first Asian MP at the next general election. He has been a local councillor and has been very successful doing the job.

Mr Watson, it is believed by some, is owed a huge debt by the Labour Party for winning Glasgow Central and halting the rise of the SNP.

Before entering parliament, Mike Watson was a regional union organiser for Manufacturing, Scientific and Finance Trade Union (MSF). He commented 'I don't know what the future holds for me. I still have a contribution to make, but I am not jumping ship or any nonsense like that. I will take a

bit of time to consider what to do, to consider what is best for myself and Lorraine.'

Mr Watson said that he might write a book about the whole episode.

How Representative is the House of Commons?

Look at Figures 1.13a and b:

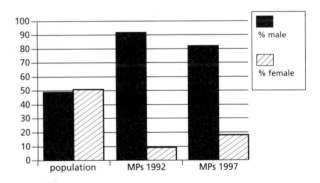

Figure 1.13a   MPs elected at the 1992 and 1997 general elections by gender

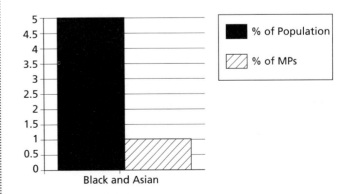

Figure 1.13b   MPs elected at the 1992 general election by race

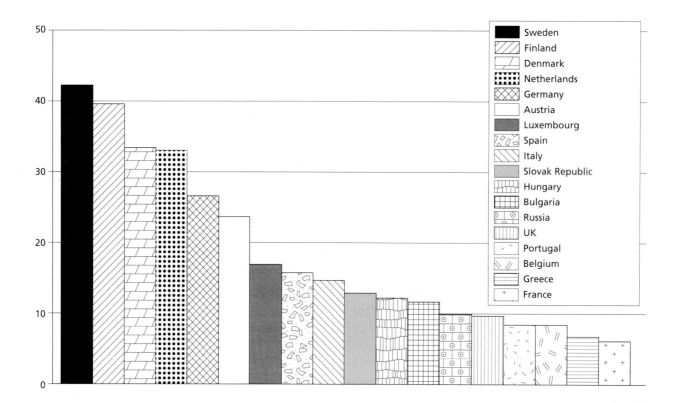

Figure 1.13c   Women as a percentage of MPs in national parliaments

Source: European Parliament Research Division

It is clear to see that there is still under-representation of women and ethnic minorities in parliament.

As the table shows, female representation in Britain remains lower than in many other national legislatures in Europe. Less than 10% of British MPs are women. This compares unfavourably with every country in western Europe, except Belgium, Portugal, Greece, and France.

This contrasts strongly with the Scandinavian democracies, where around 40% of the Swedish and Finnish representation in parliament is female.

In the UK, there have been 163 women MPs between 1918 and 1992 compared with almost 4000 men.

At the current rate of growth it would take about 200 years to achieve equal representation for women in the UK parliament.

Figure 1.14
Source: Irene Oldfather, a researcher and writer specialising in European affairs, Herald, 12 April 1995, abridged

The Labour Party has introduced **positive discrimination** to ensure more women are chosen as parliamentary candidates. All-women shortlists were introduced so that up to 40% of all candidates representing Labour at the next general election would be women.

This was recently challenged in the courts and found to be illegal.

Proposals agreed at the Scottish Constitutional Convention for a Scottish Assembly would seek to ensure that 50% of members of a Scottish Parliament would be women.

Why so few women?

Women suffer the same disadvantages in politics as they would in any other job. Domestic responsibilities and family duties hold women back. Those who succeed in politics build up a network of contacts at an early stage in their career. Often these contacts are made at political party meetings and activities which are held in the evenings.

Many women who marry and have families will miss out on this network.

Other reasons given for fewer women in the House of Commons are:

- the working hours of the House of Commons

restrict the amount of time MPs can have with their families. Irene Adams, MP for Paisley North, commented, 'I only entered politics when I was 42, because I wanted time with my family.'

- London (the centre of British politics) is too far away for most women to be able to maintain a political career *and* family commitments. Women are more involved in local government. 22% of local councillors in Scotland are women, compared with less than 10% of women in the House of Commons (increased to 18% in 1997).
- Becoming a candidate involves giving up a lot of time and money travelling to constituencies, meeting party activists and trying to win their support. Women are still generally lower paid than men and have less time and money.

The selection committees of the major parties also tend to be male-dominated because of this and are less likely to choose a female candidate for 'winnable' seats.

Dr Elizabeth Vallance, a leading researcher into women and politics, has stated 'women are selected mainly for hopeless and marginal seats'.

Why so few ethnic minorities?

At the 1992 general election there were five black or Asian MPs elected for the Labour Party. The Conservatives had one successful Asian candidate in Niranjan Deva.

John Taylor, a black Conservative candidate, lost in Cheltenham, a solid Conservative seat, although he was supported by John Major. The local constituency partly opposed him. The white Liberal Democrat victor campaigned as 'the local candidate'.

It is extremely difficult for black and Asian candidates to be selected for the major parties. When they are selected it is usually in areas where there is a large black or Asian electorate.

In Scotland, the fight to win support of the ethnic minority community gained importance following the contest for the Labour candidature for the new Govan seat at the 1997 general election.

In June 1996 Mohammed Sarwar was finally selected by Govan constituency Labour Party to fight the 'winnable' Labour seat at the next general election. In 1997, he became Scotland's first Asian MP.

If our Parliament was representative of the numbers of black people throughout the UK, we would have more than 30 black MPs, and half would be women. On a purely numerical basis, Scotland would have one black MP.

The major issue is whether black people are entitled to have a voice in this country's decision-making process. If so, and I believe we do, why are black people not being selected and elected in seats up and down the country – in all parties?

We cannot escape one conclusion, which is that all political parties, reflecting society itself, have institutionalised racist practices.

The solution is not just to increase the number of black MPs and share the burden, but also to enable black people to participate fully in all political parties so that attitudes, policies and practices reflect the demands of a fair society, and society itself does not limit black people's aspirations and achievements.

Figure 1.15   *Source: Neelam Bakshi,*
Labour Regional Councillor for Summerston/Maryhill,
Herald, 11 November 1995, abridged

One of the most emotional standing ovations seen at the SNP conference came when a founder of a new organisation bringing people of Asian origin into the party said what independence meant to him.

Mr Bashir Ahmed launched a new group called **Scots Asians for Independence**. He told the conference that it was often assumed that Asians would automatically vote Labour but his own experience suggested otherwise.

'Many of us and our fathers and grandfathers have first-hand experience of the struggle for independence,' he said to widespread applause.

'Their struggle against colonialism came when country after country won freedom, but here in Scotland the struggle still goes on.'

SNP leader Alex Salmond said he was confident the creation of the group would create wider support for Scottish independence among Asians who lived here.

Figure 1.16   *Source: Herald, 22 September 1995*

Scotland's ethnic minority community has traditionally voted Labour, although Liberal Democrat and Conservative ethnic minority candidates have also been selected for local

43

authority elections. The SNP has also selected an Asian candidate to fight the election in Glasgow Shettleston.

QUESTIONS

1 Look at Figures 1.13a and 1.13b. What evidence is there to support the view that women and ethnic minorities are badly represented in the House of Commons?
2 Look at Figure 1.13c and Figure 1.14 by Irene Oldfather. To what extent are British women poorly represented in comparison to those in Europe?
3 What efforts have the Labour Party and the Scottish Constitutional Convention made to ensure greater female representation?
4 Suggest three reasons why women are poorly represented in British politics.
5 What evidence is there that the major political parties 'play safe' when it comes to selecting black or Asian candidates?
6 According to Neelam Bakshi, why are there fewer black and Asian MPs?
7 What indications are there that political parties in Scotland are responding to demands for fairer representation of blacks and Asians?

The British Electoral System

The British electoral system is the subject of much debate. It is relatively simple and easy to operate. It is known as the **simple majority** or the **first past the post system**.

There are 659 seats in the Commons. The candidates who are elected to represent these **constituencies** simply have to get more votes than the other candidates to win the seat.

The political party with the most seats usually forms the government. If a party wins 330 seats or more it will form a **majority** government.

If a political party wins the most seats in the Commons but has fewer than 330 seats it will be a **minority** government and it may have to rely on other political parties to get its legislation passed.

Safe seats

Each of the current 659 constituencies are contested in a general election. Many of the constituencies are held by MPs with very large majorities. They have very little chance of losing their seat. See Figure 1.17.

Glasgow, Provan

Jimmy Wray Labour	15885
Alexandra McRae SNP	5182
Andrew Rosindell Conservative	1865
Charles Bell Liberal Democrat	948

Figure 1.17   Example of a safe seat

Jimmy Wray, the Labour Party candidate, had a majority of 10703, that is 10703 votes more than the candidate who came second.

Marginal seats

These are constituencies where the winning candidate at the last election had a very small majority. They could possibly lose the seat next time around. See Figure 1.18.

Ayr

Phil Gallie Conservative	22172
Alastair Osborne Labour	22087
Barbara Mullin SNP	5949
John Boss Liberal Democrat	4067
Others (Natural Law Party)	132

Figure 1.18   Example of a marginal seat

Phil Gallie, the Conservative candidate, had a majority of only 85. His seat was one of the most marginal in Scotland.

Michael Forsyth, the Scottish Secretary and MP for Stirling, had a majority of only 703. His seat was a key Labour target at the last two elections.

Marginal constituencies are very important to any political party hoping to win an election. It is these constituencies that the major political parties concentrate on winning. The definition of a **marginal** seat is one where it would take a small swing of 6% for it to be won or lost.

Marginal seats may change hands from one election to the next. The electorate do not appear to have set political preferences. Many of these voters who change their minds and vote at the last minute are known as **floating voters**.

In the UK there are reckoned to be 60 key marginals. Early victory in these marginals makes it more than likely that that party is going to win the election.

Look at Figure 1.19 and answer the questions which follow.

The computer-aided survey by Labour has taken into account the new boundaries of all the 659 seats which will make up Britain's next parliament.

The exercise is particularly poor reading for Ayr Conservative MP, Phil Gallie. Labour says that boundary changes there already mean that Ayr would be a Labour seat, and that there is no requirement of a swing from Conservative to Labour for the party to win it.

According to the Labour research, boundary changes alone would take Mr Forsyth's majority in Stirling, currently 703, down to 423, leaving Labour only a target of a 0.3% swing from Conservative to win it.

Labour claims that, under the new boundaries, it will have to take 55 seats from the Conservatives to win an overall majority – and that requires only a swing from Tory to Labour of 4.5%.

Figure 1.19   *Source: Herald, 4 August 1995*

QUESTIONS

1 What is the name given to the UK electoral system?
2 Explain how a political party is elected to government.
3 Why is it important that a party wins an overall majority in the Commons?
4 Explain the difference between a safe seat and a marginal seat.
5 Why do the main political parties concentrate on marginal seats at election time?
6 Who are floating voters and why are they important to the election outcome?
7 How many seats will there be in the new parliament?
8 How could the boundary changes affect Phil Gallie?
9 How much of a swing would Labour need to win the key marginals?

By-elections

A by-election takes place when an MP dies, retires or resigns. By-elections are very dangerous for an unpopular government. The Conservatives have not won a by-election since 1989.

The April 1996 by-election in Staffordshire South East after the death of Tory MP Sir David Lightbown (majority 7192) produced the following result, with a massive 22% swing to Labour.

Brian Jenkins Labour		26155
Jimmy James Conservative		12393
Jeanette Davy Liberal Democrat		2042

The seat was a former Conservative safe seat. Labour managed to capture it from the Conservatives who had previously held it with an 7192 majority.

Figure 1.20

A leading firm of actuaries – Lane, Clark, and Peacock – predicted there were likely to be four more Tory deaths during 1996. If correct, the prediction would wipe out Mr Major's majority.

Another Conservative MP, David Ashby, lost a costly libel action. It was suggested that he was helped financially by rich Conservatives to prevent him being declared bankrupt. If declared bankrupt he would have to quit the Commons.

The Conservatives would have had to defend a majority of only 979 in his Leicestershire North West constituency.

The timing of general elections

The timing of a general election is crucial to both the party in government and the main opposition party which hopes to win it.

There are several factors which influence the timing of general elections.

- The state of the economy is very important. If people feel they are prospering under the party in power, then the **feel good factor** is very important.
- Unemployment ceased to be an important issue (particularly in middle-class marginals) in the 1980s because it mainly affected the working

classes. In the 1990s unemployment began to affect the middle classes and the 'fear of unemployment' began to become an issue for them.

- Tax increases, whether direct or indirect, are very important.

The competence of a political party in office is important. Look at Figure 1.21 which shows an **opinion poll** of support for the main UK political parties conducted by the *Guardian/ICM*.

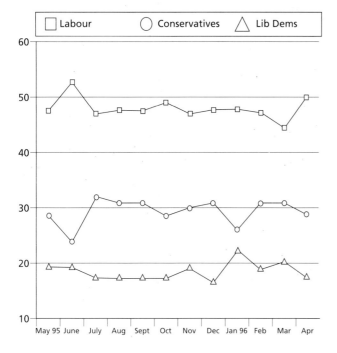

Figure 1.21   Opinion poll example

The Conservatives were trailing badly in the polls in 1996. If Labour was to maintain this lead it would almost certainly win the 1997 general election.

QUESTIONS

1 What evidence is there that by-elections are dangerous to unpopular governments?
2 What effect could the deaths of Conservative MPs have on John Major's majority?
3 Why was it suggested that rich Conservatives supported David Ashby?
4 What factors influence the timing of a general election?
5 In which two months did Labour show its biggest lead over the Conservatives? (See Figure 1.21.)

Is our Electoral System Fair?

If you look at the election results in Figure 1.22 you will notice that some parties do better from the first past the post system than others.

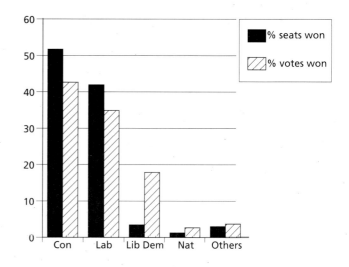

Figure 1.22   1992 general election results

The first past the post system produces results where the winning party has a majority of seats in the House of Commons, yet gets only a minority of support in the country.

This situation comes about through various reasons:

- Constituencies are not all the same size and consequently have different sizes of electorate. For instance, Gordon constituency has 81097 electors while the Caithness and Sutherland has 31173 and the Western Isles has only 23015.
- The Labour and Conservative parties are well-organised party machines with plenty of money to contest all the constituencies.
- Third parties, e.g. the Liberal Democrats, have their support diluted because, although they won a respectable 6 million votes in the 1992 general election, these votes were spread throughout the whole of Britain. In many constituencies they were squeezed into third place.

In the 1992 general election it took on average 42000 votes to elect a Conservative MP, 42804 votes to elect a Labour MP, 304000 votes to elect a Liberal Democrat MP.

It is also worth noting that if we analyse an election result at constituency level there is also the situation where a candidate wins the seat because they have the most votes, but they may only have a minority percentage of the total votes cast. Look at the example in Figure 1.23.

Strathkelvin & Bearsden

Labour	Sam Galbraith	21267
Conservative	Michael Hirst	18105
SNP	Tom Chalmers	6275
Liberal Democrat	Barbara Waterfield	4585

Figure 1.23

Now compare the results of Strathkelvin & Bearsden with those of Argyll & Bute (see Figure 1.24).

Argyll & Bute

Liberal Democrat	Ray Mickie	12739
Conservative	John Corrie	10117
Labour	Desmonde Brown	4946
SNP	Neil MacCormick	8689

Figure 1.24

Q UESTIONS

1 Which party did best out of the first past the post system in the 1992 general election?
2 Which party did worst out of the first past the post system in the 1992 general election?
3 Why might some people complain about the different sizes of constituencies?
4 What complaint might Michael Hirst have about losing Strathkelvin & Bearsden?

Alternative Voting Systems

It is commonly accepted that if another type of election system was to be introduced into Britain it would be some form of **Proportional Representation (PR)**.

There are various types of PR system. One simple form is the **National Party List** system.

Under this system the parties would produce a list of candidates and the electorate would vote for the party not the candidate.

If a party were to win 30% of the vote cast, then the first 30% (195) candidates on that party's **national list** would be elected to the House of Commons.

The 1992 general election result might have looked something like this (see Figure 1.25):

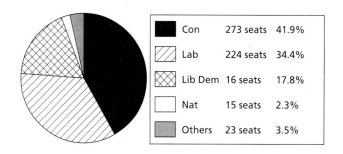

	Con	273 seats	41.9%
	Lab	224 seats	34.4%
	Lib Dem	16 seats	17.8%
	Nat	15 seats	2.3%
	Others	23 seats	3.5%

Figure 1.25

Another form of proportional representation is the **Single Transferable Vote (STV)**. This system is widely used on the continent. Under STV it is likely that Britain would be divided into **multi-member** constituencies.

Each party would field three or four or more candidates per constituency. Voters would then select candidates in order of preference.

If we use the example of the six Edinburgh constituencies at the 1992 general election, we can see that the ballot paper itself would have a lot more names on it.

Figure 1.28 is a list of the candidates for the six Edinburgh seats standing for the main parties. It shows what a ballot paper might be like under STV.

In 1992, using first past the post four Labour MPs and two Conservative MPs were elected. They were:

Malcolm Chisholm	Lab	13790
Alistair Darling	Lab	15189
Nigel Griffiths	Lab	18484
James D.-Hamilton	Con	18701
Malcolm Rifkind	Con	18128
Gavin Strang	Lab	15446

Figure 1.26

Interestingly, three unsuccessful candidates did better (in the wrong constituencies) than some of the successful candidates. They were:

47

Donald Gorrie	Lib Dem	17192
Struan Stevenson	Con	14309
Marc Lazarowicz	Lab	13838

Figure 1.27

BALLOT PAPER EDINBURGH CONSTITUENCY

Candidate	Party	Vote
Hillary Campbell	Lib Dem	
Kathleen Caskie	SNP	
Malcolm Chisholm	Lab	
Alistair Darling	Lab	
Lynn Devine	SNP	
Graham Farmer	Green	
Donald Gorrie	Lib Dem	
Nigel Griffiths	Lab	
James D.-Hamilton	Con	
Robin Harper	Green	
Linda Hendry	Green	
Fiona Hyslop	SNP	
Irene Kitson	Lab	
Roger Knox	SNP	
Marc Lazarowicz	Lab	
Bob McCreadie	Lib Dem	
Donald McKinney	SNP	
Paul Martin	Con	
Andrew Myles	Lib Dem	
Malcolm Rifkind	Con	
Mohammed B. A. Rizvi	Con	
Devin Scobie	Lib Dem	
Keith Smith	Lib Dem	
Struan Stevenson	Con	
Gavin Strang	Lab	
Graham Sutherland	SNP	
Kenneth Ward	Con	

Figure 1.28   Candidates for the six Edinburgh seats

Under STV, this result would have been very different.

In the new 'Edinburgh constituency', there are six candidates to be elected. The formula used to find the **quota** (the number of votes you need to get elected) is as follows:

$$\frac{\text{Number of votes cast}}{\text{Number of seats}+1} + 1$$

This works out at:

$$\frac{246567}{6+1} + 1$$

Which makes the quota 35224 + 1.

None of the candidates in 1992 got more than the quota.

The voters' **second preference votes** would then be distributed until six candidates reach the quota.

Supposing only one candidate was elected on the first count; that candidate's **surplus votes** would be distributed until a second and third candidate were elected, and so on.

The theory is that no votes are wasted and every candidate's vote is used, even those eliminated on the first count.

It is also suggested that successful candidates are likely to have more support in the communities they are expected to serve, and that the best MPs are elected, no matter what their party.

On the other hand, it would be impossible to predict how voters would respond to a completely different electoral system, where second and first preference votes are used.

Some might get confused and only vote for those at the top of the ballot paper, or, if they are skilful electors, may only vote for those they definitely want and not use all their possible preferences. Therefore it is impossible to predict who would have won in Edinburgh under STV.

The alternative vote

This system is not a form of PR. In this system the UK would keep the existing 659 constituencies but voters would vote in order of preference, e.g. 1, 2, 3, 4 and so on.

A candidate has to receive 50% of the **first preference votes** to get elected.

If no candidate receives 50% of the first preference vote, then the bottom candidate is eliminated and their vote shared out amongst the other candidates until one candidate receives 50% of the vote. Figure 1.29 is an example.

Robert Green	Con	14467
William Grey	Lab	12329
May Brown	Lib Dem	11631

Figure 1.29

Advantages of PR	The disadvantages of PR
• Every vote would count, producing seats in proportion to the votes cast • It would get rid of the system at present where votes are wasted. • It might still be fairer to third parties, e.g. Liberal Democrats. • It would likely produce **coalition** governments with **centrist** policies. • Coalitions enjoying majority support might be more beneficial to the country in terms of continuity in policy. • Coalitions can be stable and effective. • There is a desire for change in the country.	• Only the National List system would ensure exact proportionality and every vote would not necessarily count, e.g. different sizes of constituencies. • It would not be fairer to voters as smaller parties might hold the balance of power and might become 'king makers'. • Governments would be likely to be formed after post-election deals between the various parties. • It would be difficult to ensure accountability of multi-party coalitions. • Coalitions can easily break up if one or more of the parties fall out with each other. • There is popular support for the present system, so why change it?

Figure 1.30

No candidate received 50% of the votes cast so May Brown is eliminated and her votes are redistributed.

Of the 11631 votes Brown got, 7890 second preference votes went to Green and 3741 went to Grey. Green's total now becomes 22357 and Grey's total becomes 16070. Green is now elected MP for that seat.

One major advantage of the **AV** system is that the MP gets more than half the choice of the voters in that constituency, unlike the present system.

QUESTIONS

1 Under headings list the benefits and difficulties which might arise using different types of electoral system.
2 Decide which system you think is the best and give reasons for your answer.

INVESTIGATION

1 Find out each political party's views on electoral reform and why they support either keeping the first past the post system or adopting a particular type of PR.
2 Find out what the proposals are for electing a Scottish Parliament. In what ways might they change how politicians operate?

3 Find out about the electoral systems in a number of different countries. In what ways can they lead to a better system of representation and government than the British system, and in what ways do they lead to problems?
4 Make a balanced argument, using examples for **and** against electoral reform.

Labour and Conservative Parties Compared

Between 1945 and 1979 there was a degree of **consensus** (broad agreement) between the major political parties on the key social, economic and political issues.

Both major parties supported the idea that the interests of Britain would best be served by having a **mixed economy**. This meant that the economy would be run by both the government (public sector) and the private sector.

In the public sector, the government owns and provides Welfare, Education and health services. The major utilities such as gas, water, electricity, coal mining, steel are owned by the state on behalf of the nation.

In the private sector, individuals or groups of individuals own and control industry and make profits.

Both Conservatives and Labour supported the public sector and the private sector was allowed to flourish alongside it.

The failure of consensus

In the years from the end of the war to the last Labour government in 1979, Britain's economy underwent a massive transformation.

High unemployment and economic stagnation were blamed on an inefficient public sector by those on the **right** of the political spectrum. They saw Britain dominated by trade unions who were holding the country to ransom with excessive pay demands.

The **left**, however, saw it differently. They said Britain's poor economic performance was due to the private sector which had failed to invest in industry, thus making Britain less competitive.

The 1979 general election

It was this event more than any other in the post-war period which saw a radical departure from consensus politics. Margaret Thatcher was elected during a period when trade unions had become unpopular.

The **social contract** between Labour and the unions had collapsed in the **winter of discontent**.

The Conservatives promised the electorate a radical agenda. They argued that they would rid Britain of socialism. They said that 'the state interfered too much in people's lives'. The Conservatives promised the electorate increased choice in everything from housing to health.

There have been four election victories for the Conservatives in the last 18 years. Listed on the next few pages are some of the main policy differences of the two main parties which contain some of the issues on which the 1997 general election will be fought.

Q U E S T I O N S

1 What is meant by the term 'mixed economy'?
2 Why was the election of Mrs Thatcher in 1979 a radical departure from consensus politics?

Taxation

Figure 1.31 Conservative double whammy poster from 1992 election

Figure 1.32 Labour poster indicating tax rises since the 1992 general election

Conservatives

It is this issue more than any other which costs a political party votes at election time.

The Conservatives have traditionally been seen as the party of low taxation. High taxes, they argue, act as a disincentive to work.

Those who earn more money would then have a greater proportion to spend as they choose.

The Conservatives believe that lower taxes should reward hard work and entrepreneurship.

The wealth created at the very top of society by savings through tax cuts would then 'trickle down' to the less-well-off members of society.

Recent increases in Value Added Tax (tax on spending) has had a greater effect on the poorer sections of society.

The ultimate aim of the Conservatives is to reduce basic rate of income tax from 25% to 20%.

Kenneth Clarke, the Chancellor of the Exchequer, argued on the other hand that tax cuts would only come if there were savings on what the government spent.

Some Conservatives like John Redwood, argue for major cut-backs in public expenditure to finance tax cuts.

Labour

This issue still haunts the Labour party after the 1992 election. Labour promised that they would increase taxes for those earning over £21000 and only the richest 10–20% would have to pay extra.

This ignored those higher earners in the key marginals in the south east and the Midlands.

This new prosperous generation would have to be persuaded to vote Labour before they would have any chance of winning an election.

The Conservatives and their supporters in the press dubbed it **'Labour's tax bombshell'**.

Labour has always believed that the taxation system was the best way to redistribute the wealth of the country.

The more a person earned the more they should pay.

Taxation would fund the Welfare State and all the services it provides.

Tony Blair is all too aware of the problem of the tax issue. He prefers not to talk in terms of figures until much closer to the election.

It is worth noting that New Labour now argue that they are the party of low taxation and that people are worse off under the Conservatives.

Figure 1.33

Employment and unemployment

Conservatives

The Conservatives have always argued that Britain will not experience higher employment until it becomes more competitive with its major trading partners.

They have further argued that too-high wage increases fuel inflation, causing further unemployment.

Interest rates have been used by the government to keep the cost of borrowing high. This in turn will reduce inflation.

However, as firms need to borrow money to invest in technology and manpower they will not do so when interest rates are high.

The government at present has a mixture of schemes designed to get people back to work.

Youth Training

Guaranteed place for all 16–17-year-olds not in work or education. Since 1988 benefit has been withdrawn from almost all 16–17-year-olds.

Labour

Labour has always stressed the need for more investment and training to improve the competitiveness of British industry. They have not pledged to bring down interest rates to make it easier for industry to borrow. Labour have recently talked of four new opportunities.

Employment

Employers taking on a long-term person under 25 will get a £60 per week rebate for 6 months. Employers must provide approved in-work-training one day a week, or day release.

The Voluntary Sector Option

Voluntary organisations will be able to provide opportunities to pay a wage equivalent to benefit, plus a fixed sum, for 6 months. Employers would have to provide the same training facilities as a private employer.

continued . . .

continued . . .

Conservatives

Training for Work
A mixture of training and work experience delivered by Training Enterprise Councils, available to all unemployed.

Job Plan workshops
Individual assessments for those unemployed for over a year. There is also a one-week course in job-seeking skills.

1-2-1 scheme
For those 18–24-year-olds who refuse offers of help after one year of unemployment. A series of six interviews which might lead to Workwise (see below). Claimants will be guided through a job search programme. If they do not attend, benefit will be suspended.

Workwise
A four-week remotivational course for 18–24-year-olds in need of intensive help.

Sanctions
From October 1996 the Jobseeker's Allowance will be introduced. The unemployed can be directed to a specific course of action to make themselves more employable.

Labour

Full-time education
Young people without basic educational qualifications will have the option to study full-time on an approved education training course. They will be able to keep their benefit, thus relaxing the 16-hour rule which prevents the unemployed from retraining.

An Environmental Task Force
Young people will have an option of a place on this task force, working alongside the proposed Citizen's Service initiative. They will get a wage equivalent to their benefit plus a fixed sum for six months. They will also get day release leading to a vocational qualification.

Windfall tax
Labour proposes a £3billion tax on the privatised utilities to help create jobs and provide training places for 16–25-year-olds.

Sanctions
Anyone under 25 refusing one of the four options will lose 40% benefit after one month.

Figure 1.34

Health

Conservatives
The party under John Major has pressed ahead with the health service reforms started under Mrs Thatcher.

These reforms have introduced 'market forces' into the health service. Hospitals and GP practices can now 'opt out' of local health authority control.

The system is designed to make the health service more efficient and to give the health professionals more autonomy as to how their money will be spent.

The government claims they are spending more on health than ever before.

Future building of hospitals and large health care projects should be financed by the Private Finance Initiative which would mean private firms building hospitals and leasing them (for rent) to the NHS or Trusts.

Figure 1.35

Labour
The Labour Party has accused the government of creating a 'two-tier' health service where the patients of opted-out GP fund-holders receive quicker medical attention than the patients of those doctors who have not opted out.

There is further criticism of these reforms because hospital wards have closed when funds have run out. The government reply to this criticism is that this is due to hospital mismanagement.

After the 1992 general election both parties have been reluctant to use the health service as a means of scoring points. Labour used the 'tale of Jenny's ear' in their pre-election broadcasts. This highlighted the differences in the speed of treatment for two patients with a similar complaint.

One was an NHS patient, the other the patient of an opted-out fund-holder.

Labour was criticised for using the 'pain and suffering of a small girl' to get its message across.

The economy

Conservatives	Labour
The Conservatives are to continue with their **privatisation** policies, especially of the railways. There have been 32 Citizen's Charters introduced to improve the performance of public services and industries. Britain is to maintain an opt-out on a European Single Currency. The government has promised to bring public spending below 40% of **GDP** (the total amount of a country's wealth produced in one year). The government has further highlighted its desire to move towards a basic 20% tax rate. There will also be a step-by-step privatisation of the Welfare State.	The move to the right under Tony Blair has meant that the party has had to ditch some of its traditional policies. Labour was previously in favour of a programme of **de-privatisation** but such a programme would be too costly. Tony Blair has now talked in terms of a **stakeholder society** where workers sit on consultative committees, take part in decision making and employee share ownership. New Labour supports the European Single Currency but entry only when the time is right. They have pledged no tax rises except possibly for the super rich. They have a plan to bring down the £80 billion Welfare State programme by a welfare-to-work package.

Figure 1.36

53

The constitution

Conservatives	Labour
The Conservatives want to keep the British constitution largely unchanged. Michael Forsyth, the Scottish Secretary, has increased the number of Scottish Grand Committees, which consist of all the Scottish MPs, being held in Scotland. Government ministers are also invited to address the Scottish Grand Committee when it is sitting in Scotland. The Conservatives oppose a Scottish Parliament and have used the slogan 'tartan tax' to describe the proposal to give the Scottish Parliament the power to increase income tax in Scotland. They want to fend off greater powers from Brussels. In particular, the Conservatives want to reduce the power the European Court has over UK law. In Northern Ireland, they propose the setting up of an elected assembly while at the same time attacking Labour for the break up of the UK.	A future Labour government would introduce a Scottish Parliament within three years of election, with tax-raising powers. It also proposes the setting up of a Welsh assembly. In June 1995, Tony Blair announced that a Labour Government would introduce a referendum on a Scottish Parliament. This would ask two questions. The first would be about support for a Parliament. The second would be on its tax-raising powers. Labour also proposes to remove the voting rights of hereditary peers. Labour is keen to be seen as the party which champions freedom and individual rights, and they have proposed a Freedom of Information Act. Labour has also proposed to tackle the anomalies of the election system by holding a **referendum** on proportional representation.

Figure 1.37

QUESTIONS

1 What is the reasoning behind the Tories' taxation policy?
2 What is the 'trickle down' effect?
3 Why do you think that an increase in VAT would hit the poor the worst?
4 Why is Labour cautious over its tax policy?
5 Why are high interest rates both good and bad for the economy?
6 Choose one Conservative and Labour employment scheme and compare them.
7 In what ways have market forces been introduced to the health service?
8 What are the main Labour criticisms of the Tory health reforms?
9 Compare and contrast Labour and Conservative policies on:
   a privatisation;
   b European currency.
10 In what sense does Labour propose to change the constitution?
11 How did Labour respond to the Conservative's 'tartan tax' slogan?

Political Change in Britain

The traditional view

- British politics has traditionally been viewed as the politics of right and left.
- The Conservatives are regarded as the main right-wing political party.
- The Labour Party is regarded as the main left-wing political party.
- The Liberal Democrats are regarded as being in the centre.
- And the Nationalists contain supporters of right and left.

Traditionally those **left wing** supported **socialism** and felt that the state was the best means to ensure a fairer society whether through high taxes on the rich, comprehensive education for all, support for the Welfare State and nationalised industries.

Those on the left blamed inequalities in society for crime and believed that nationalism led to wars where the workers were the ones to suffer.

Those on the **right** believe in **capitalism** and feel that the state should have nothing or very little to do with people's lives, and that there should be lower taxes. They believe that individuals should look after their own education, health and welfare through savings, and that private ownership is best way to run the economy.

They tend to be tough on such issues as law and order and tend to be fiercely patriotic.

Those in the **centre** take the view that society and the people in it have their interests best served by a government which controls the economy but also gives the individual the opportunity to determine their own future.

In Britain the political spectrum has changed radically in the last 20 years.

The Conservatives were elected in 1979 and have moved radically to the right.

Mrs Thatcher once remarked that she did not believe in such a thing as society and that she was determined to rid Britain of socialism.

Margaret Thatcher's revolution changed British society. Her most popular policies included the privatisation of much council housing and nationalised utilities.

Highly skilled, unionised, manual workers had been amongst the strongest supporters of the Labour Party.

Many of these better-paid manual workers lived in marginal constituencies in the south-east and Midlands of England. Margaret Thatcher's policies meant they were able to buy the best council houses for which they had paid high rents to live in. They became home owners, were able to get credit more easily and made profits from buying shares in privatised industries.

Privatisation created many more property owners, whom Margaret Thatcher believed would vote for the party of property owners – the Conservative Party.

Margaret Thatcher was the longest-serving Prime Minister this century. She and her successor, John Major, were successful in four general elections.

The Labour Party suffered four consecutive electoral defeats under three different leaders.

Many in the Labour Party leadership believed that Britain's electorate have moved to the right and if Labour were to win, then their left-wing policies would have to change.

Case Study: New Labour New Right

After Neil Kinnock's defeat in 1992, he was replaced by John Smith. John Smith died in 1994 and Tony Blair was elected as Labour leader.

Under Tony Blair, Labour has shifted to the right. He believed that Labour's traditional policies were outdated and had cost them dearly in terms of electoral defeats.

The Labour Party constitution was changed so that **Clause 4**, which called for socialist economic policies, was dropped.

Study the policy changes from the 1992 Labour General Election Manifesto below:

Tax

Traditional policy

Higher tax for the rich at 50p in the £.

New Labour

This has now been dropped as Tony Blair is aware that he has to win the votes of 'middle England' who might oppose higher taxes.

National minimum wage

Traditional policy

Set at half the average male earnings rising to two-thirds of average male earnings (£4.26 per hour).

New Labour

Now the level will be decided by a Low Pay Unit. The shift has occurred because Labour does not want to frighten business and thinks that employers should be consulted first.

Comprehensive education

Traditional policy

All state schools to be brought back under democratically elected local government control.

New Labour

Their status can only change with a ballot of the parents.

Private education

Traditional policy

In the area of private schools, VAT should be charged on school fees, private schools to lose their charitable status and the assisted places scheme (government support for private education) to be abolished.

New Labour

This suggestion has now been dropped. Private finance will be encouraged to refurbish state schools.

**Figure 1.38
Tony Blair, leader of the Labour Party**

Employees' rights

Traditional policy

There should be a **charter of rights** for all workers, full- and part-time.

New Labour

Await the outcome of a Lords' decision on unfair dismissal.

Trade unions

Traditional policy

Individuals should have the legal right to be represented by a trade union.

New Labour

Employers should recognise unions where the majority vote for it. Tory laws on picketing are to stay and sacked strikers can appeal to an industrial tribunal.

Privatisation

Traditional policy

Some of the previously nationalised industries, now privatised, should be re-nationalised.

New Labour

This is too expensive.

55

Scottish Local Government

Local government delivers many of the key services on which the public depends. These include:

- education;
- social work;
- council housing;
- fire service;
- police;
- refuse collection;
- water and sewerage;
- parks;
- consumer protection;
- libraries and recreation facilities;
- roads;
- registration of Births and Marriages.

Before April 1996

Until April 1996, Scottish Local Government consisted of nine Regional Councils, three Island Authorities and 53 District Councils.

Local government is run by elected councillors representing **wards** which tend to be much smaller than parliamentary constituencies.

The delivery of these essential services was divided between Regional and District Councils, so that:

- Regional Councils delivered the larger strategic services like education, social work, fire, police, water and sewerage and roads;
- District Councils delivered services which could be better managed at a more local level, such as council housing, libraries, parks and refuse collection.

The three Island Authorities delivered all the services.

The Conservative government argued that these councils were too bureaucratic and having two tiers of local government, Regional and District, wasted taxpayers' money needlessly.

Opponents of this view argue that it is largely because the councils were Labour controlled that these changes have come about.

They suggested that local government reorganisation should come about only after the election of a Scottish Parliament.

The New Councils

There are now 29 single-tier Unitary Authorities, and three Island Authorities.

Look at Figure 1.39 and find out which authority you live in.

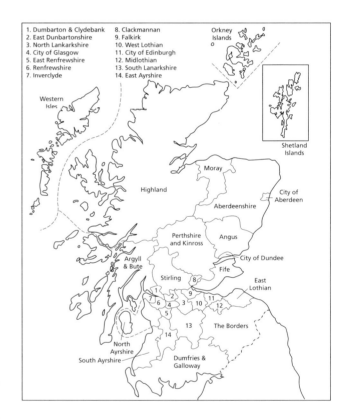

Figure 1.39 Scottish Local Government
Source: The Scottish Office

These Unitary Authorities now control almost all of the services previously run by Regions and Districts separately with the exception that:

Water services have been split up into three different Scottish area boards, to be run by people appointed by the government (see Quangos);

Fire Services and the Police are run by a number of councils working together;

The Children's Panel System and Trunk Roads are now run by the Scottish Office.

56

Conflict between Local and Central Government

Local government in Scotland is run by elected councillors and delivers services. This means that it is run by politicians and spends money.

Critics of the government's local government reforms claimed that the new council borders were deliberately drawn (gerrymandered) to ensure that the Conservatives won control of some of the new unitary authorities.

Conservatives wake up this morning after their worst nightmare: annihilation in the Scottish local elections, a disaster at the polls which saw them lose control of even their flagship council in East Renfrewshire.

Scotland is left without a single Tory administration among the 29 single-tier authorities which will take over local government a year from now.

Labour will have more than half of all council seats. They control 20 councils, including Glasgow; the SNP three; the Highlands are Independent; and four councils are hung. Argyll and Bute declares today [Independent control]. Fife is a Tory-free zone, with not a single Conservative councillor, but it has two Communists.

Labour dominated with a 44.4% share of the vote. SNP achieved 26.5%, the Conservatives took 11.25% and the Liberal Democrats had 9.75%.

Figure 1.40   *Source:* Herald, 7 April 1995

Before reorganisation, the Conservative Party had only 230 Regional and District Councillors (14%) out of a total of 1611. It controlled only four District Councils: Eastwood, Kyle and Carrick, Perth and Kinross and Aberdeen.

After local government elections in April 1995, the Conservatives had only 82 councillors (7% of the total) and controlled no councils at all.

QUESTIONS

1 Copy the map in Figure 1.39 into your notebook. Using the information above and different coloured pencils to help you make a key, colour in the new authorities to make a 'Political Landscape of Scotland'.
2 Why did critics of the government claim the new authorities were 'gerrymandered'?
3 What councils did the Conservatives control before reorganisation and after?

What do councillors do?

Councillors are elected to run local services on our behalf. They are also employers of workers who deliver the services, like teachers, social workers, roads workers and refuse collectors.

Councillors are not paid like MPs. Instead, they keep their full-time jobs and are paid an allowance which is about £3000 per year on average. They are also paid expenses for any travelling they do on council business.

Like MPs, councillors take decisions which affect our everyday lives. These decisions are taken at Council committee meetings which are open to the public and reported in the local press. They are usually held every six weeks. For instance, decisions about education are taken at Education Committee meetings, Social Work decisions are taken at Social Work Committee meetings.

In addition, councillors attend meetings of their political group on the council. These 'group meetings' are held to decide the policy of each political party to any decisions which the councillors have to make. Like the House of Commons, councillors usually vote on party lines.

Councillors also hold surgeries where they are available to meet constituents and try to help them with any problems to do with council services.

Councillors are local politicians and usually live in the area which they serve. Times of their surgeries, their names and addresses, and telephone numbers are also published in the local press. Living locally, they are also more likely to meet people in the streets, in shops and hold 'unofficial surgeries' when they are stopped with complaints from local residents.

57

QUESTIONS

1 Compare councillors to MPs. Draw up a list of similarities and differences.
2 In what ways are councillors likely to meet their constituents more often than MPs?
3 Do you think that councillors should have to give up their full-time jobs and be paid a wage like MPs?
4 Find out the name of your local councillor and write them a letter asking about what they do.

Paying for Local Government Services

Local government's job is to deliver services to the local area. These services cost money.

Since 1979, Conservative governments have sought to control public expenditure, which is the total amount spent by central and local government.

Now, the Scottish Office has the power to set a limit on the total amount that each council is allowed to spend. This is called **capping**.

The government also introduced the **Poll Tax** to stop councils forcing the better off to pay for improved services. Everyone living in a council area would pay the same amount of money no matter how well off or how poor they were.

The Poll Tax failed and the government introduced the **Council Tax** to replace it. Now people pay a local tax based on the value of their house.

Houses are grouped in bands and the tax is the same for everyone within that particular band in that council area.

The bands are given in Figure 1.41.

Band A	up to £27000
Band B	£27000 to £35000
Band C	£35000 to £45000
Band D	£45000 to £58000
Band E	£58000 to £80000
Band F	£80000 to £106000
Band G	£106000 to £212000
Band H	over £212000

Figure 1.41 Band valuation of property

In 1988, the government also removed local authorities' control over **business rates**. Those are local taxes which businesses pay for services. The business rate is now controlled by the Scottish Office.

The business rate is collected by local government, transferred to the Scottish Office and then redistributed to councils on the basis of the number of people living in that council's area.

This means that areas with a large number of businesses effectively transfer money to areas with fewer businesses.

In practice this means that Glasgow and the larger cities' business rates are transferred to other areas.

One of the results of this is that cities with a higher proportion of poorer people, but with more businesses, transfer money to the suburbs where people are better off, but have fewer business rate payers.

Councils only now have real control over a very small amount of the money which they need to spend on services. They have control over charges such as rents for council housing or library fines!

Council Tax only amounts to about 14% of the money which councils spend. The rest of the money

The Scottish Secretary claimed Scottish councils were being treated 'very favourably' and there was no need for cuts in front-line services or excessive council tax increases.

He had improved on last year's plans by £106m. Government support for council spending would total £5400m.

Mr Forsyth said that the amount the government thinks councils need to spend on services and debt charges was 1.75% higher than in the current year. Councils' total income from grant and business rates would rise by 2.62%.

However, Convention of Scottish Local Authority leaders said the settlement went nowhere near meeting the 3.2% rate of inflation, nor the fact that councils would have to find more than £200m of additional spending for government initiatives.

Cosla disagreed totally, and warned of council tax rises and the need for 'savage' cuts in services.

Figure 1.42a   *Source: Herald, 29 November 1995*

Glasgow City Council is facing the prospect of cuts of £43million and the loss of over 1000 jobs. Dundee faces cuts of £14.8million, Edinburgh up to £40million and Aberdeen £24million. Council Tax bills will rise by an average of 13%.

Figure 1.42b   *Source:* Labour Research, *April 1996*

spent on services comes either from grants from the Scottish Office or the business rate which is also controlled by government.

Look at the two articles in Figure 1.42a and b and answer the questions below.

QUESTIONS

1 What is the control the Scottish Office has on council spending called?
2 How is a person's council tax worked out? Ask your parent or guardian what your council tax band is.
3 How have government changes to the way the business rate is organised hit cities badly?
4 Which areas face the largest cuts in services?
5 Study Figure 1.42 closely. Draw up a table listing the increases which local councils are getting and the increases they say they need.

  Using the information, say whether you agree with Michael Forsyth or Cosla leaders.

Case Study

The new councils were faced with making cut-backs in services. Education is the most expensive service provided by local authorities.

Look at Figures 1.43 to 1.47 and answer the questions which follow.

Closure of schools, old folk's homes, swimming pools and libraries are included in £40.7million cuts and 1200 job losses being proposed to ease Glasgow's budget crisis. This is still £5m short of a Scottish Office capping limit of £807.

  Councillor Gordon MacDairmid said, 'Even if we achieve all the savings, Council Tax bills will have to go up by 36%.'

Figure 1.43   *Source:* Herald, *2 February 1996*

Figure 1.44   On 24 February 1996, teachers, parents and children took part in a demonstration in Edinburgh organised by the teachers' trade union, the EIS. 40000 took part in Scotland's largest demonstration in living memory.

Figure 1.45   The doors of Glasgow City Council Chambers were firmly locked against all comers yesterday. The danger came from around 60 mums, dads and their children protesting against the closure of a school.

Source: Herald, *19 April 1996*

59

'Parents gathered in Glasgow City Halls last night to mark the campaign against plans to close 22 schools. In the past few weeks, there have been scores of individual demos. If they vote to shut the schools, we'll be sitting in the schools preventing them from putting the padlocks on in the first place.'

Figure 1.46　　　*Source: Herald, 5 April 1996*

Glasgow's ruling Labour group opted out of risking further political damage yesterday.

Having halved its original hit list of 22 schools after an emotionally charged Labour group meeting on Monday, Labour councillors found they had no stomach for the closure of St Gerard's RC Secondary and three other primaries.

From an initial savings target of £2.4million, they are now left with savings of only £545,000.

Meanwhile about 30 parents and pupils began an occupation of a school still threatened with closure.

Figure 1.47　　　*Source: Herald, 18 May 1996*

Q UESTIONS

1 In what way does the Edinburgh demonstration show that people regard education as one of the most important issues affecting Scotland?
2 What did Glasgow Council plan to do to make savings?
3 How do we know that this would still not be enough to meet Scottish Office targets?
4 List the ways that parents responded to the plans to close their children's schools.
5 How were the parents successful?
6 What effects did this have on the planned savings?
7 What might councils like Glasgow have to do if they could not make savings through closing schools?
8 Find out how your local services have been affected by recent cuts.

Constitutional Issues

Quangos

Quasi-autonomous-non-governmental organisations (**quangos**) are bodies set up by the government to run public services.

Quangos control 40% of the Scottish Office budget.

Members of quangos are not elected. They are appointed by the government minister responsible and can only be removed by the government minister.

Unlike councillors, members of quangos are paid for their services.

It is a growth industry. There will be 5000 of them employed next year, and they will earn anything from £4000 part-time to £40000 if they fancy taking the chair.

The other accusation is that quangos are stacked full of Tory loyalists.

Figure 1.48　　　*Source: Herald, 18 January 1995*

Quangos in Scotland include:
• the new Water Authorities;
• Scottish Homes;
• Scottish Enterprise;
• Local Enterprise Councils;
• NHS Trusts;
• further education colleges.

Look at Figures 1.49–1.52 and answer the questions which follow.

According to MP Irene Adams there would be 1500 elected members in the Scottish unitary authorities. But she added that there would be at least 5000 unelected quango members by next year.

The Labour Party claims Government-appointed representatives on quangos will control more public expenditure than the 32 unitary authorities in Scotland.

Figure 1.49　　　*Source: Herald, 18 March 1995*

The Scottish Secretary counters the quango-bashers. 'The dedication and expertise of those appointed by him represent an important contribution to public life in Scotland, and they have helped make the provision of public services more efficient.'

Figure 1.50　　　*Source: Herald, 18 January 1995*

In evidence to the Nolan Committee on Standards in Public Life, Mr Jenkins, former Editor of *The Times*, said 'The packing of health and education quangos by the wives of Tory MPs had caused widespread disquiet. Many people find it offensive.'

Figure 1.51   *Source: The Times, 18 January 1995*

In the UK there are at least 5750 quangos run by 66000 members (three times the number of local councillors).

By the end of 1995 they controlled government spending amounting to £60.4billion – 35% of government expenditure.

Unlike local council meetings which are public, only 11% of quangos hold meetings to explain their work to the general public.

According to a report by Democratic Audit, entitled 'The Untouchables', 'People have no say either directly or through their elected representatives. They cannot call quango members to account or replace them. They rarely even know who they are.

If the Conservatives win the next election all of Britain's schools will be taken out of local authority control and run by a government-appointed quango, the Schools Funding Agency.

This will remove 40% of local government funding and revive the idea of abolishing local government altogether.

Ministers have repeatedly refused to publish a register of quangos and their members' business and political interests.'

Figure 1.52   *Source: Observer, 14 July 1996, abridged*

QUESTIONS

1 What does 'quango' stand for?
2 What areas of public spending are these quangos responsible for?
3 How much public money do they spend each year?
4 List the criticisms made of quangos.
5 How does the Scottish Secretary defend quangos?

The Scottish Dimension

The demand for greater self-rule for Scotland has grown in recent years. The Conservative government has argued that the interests of the Scottish people would be better served by Scotland remaining in the United Kingdom.

The Labour Party, Liberal Democrats, STUC and other parties in the Scottish Constitutional Convention have committed themselves to some form of **devolved** assembly, thus giving the Scottish people a greater say in their own affairs.

The Scottish Nationalists want full independence under their slogan 'Independence in Europe'.

Background

In 1979, the Scottish people voted in favour of a devolved assembly in a referendum. However, the majority was not big enough for the proposals to go ahead.

As a result, the SNP withdrew their support for the minority Labour Government and a general election was called.

The election of the Conservatives in 1979 and 1983 effectively killed off any chance of a devolved assembly for Scotland. Throughout the 1980s Conservative support in Scotland declined.

Before the 1987 general election there was a talk of a **doomsday scenario** if a UK Conservative government was returned for a third time.

Under the doomsday scenario falling support for the Conservatives in Scotland would lead to there being insufficient Scottish Conservative MPs to fill the Ministerial offices in the Scottish Office.

This would lead to a constitutional crisis as the Scottish Office would not be able to operate properly.

After 1987 there was a slight increase in support for the SNP. This was evident in their 1988 by-election victory at Govan.

As well as this many Labour party supporters in Scotland were now beginning to feel that the UK Labour Party was not taking their demands for a devolved assembly seriously.

English Conservative MPs were also more often being used to increase the government's support during Scottish business in Parliament.

The Constitutional Convention

This body was set up in 1988 and it represented a broad range of organisations which favoured some type of self-government for Scotland.

They included the Labour Party, the Liberal Democrats and the Communist Party, the Scottish Trade Union Congress, the Churches and other organisations. The Conservatives did not take part as they opposed devolution. The SNP boycotted the Convention because they favour full independence.

Convention proposals

The organisations represented in the Scottish Constitutional Convention agreed their final proposals for a Scottish Parliament in October 1995.

These are:
- there will be 129 Scottish MPs made up from constituencies and party list systems to ensure a fair representation of women and men;
- each voter will have two votes: one for a constituency member, the other for a local party list of additional members;
- the proposed Parliament will be responsible for education, health, law, employment and training, transport, environment and planning;
- Westminster would still continue to regulate with regard to foreign affairs, defence, immigration, and social security;
- the new Parliament could also vary income tax by 3 pence in the pound;
- the new Parliament will have a fixed budget from Westminster.

In June 1996 Tony Blair, the Labour leader announced that a new Labour Government would hold a referendum before it introduced legislation which would ask two questions; the first on support for a parliament, the second on support for tax-varying powers.

The government's response

The Conservatives have always advocated that if Scotland got devolution the number of Scottish MPs at Westminster would have to be reduced (from 72 to 57) so that the number of Scottish MPs was proportionate to the size of Scotland's population.

The Conservatives' view is that devolution would be the first step towards independence and the break-up of the UK.

The government has responded with the following proposals:
- **The Scottish Grand Committee** which is made up of all 72 MPs will meet more often throughout Scotland, with greater attendance of senior government ministers.
- Important bills could be passed without going to committee and added on to UK legislation.
- The Committee will not actually vote on legislation but record the debate.
- Powers taken from local government will be handed back.
- Councils will be given a bigger say in how they should spend their budgets.

The Conservatives also attacked plans to give the assembly tax-varying powers. Michael Forsyth claimed that this would lead to a 'tartan tax' and that Scottish taxpayers would pay higher taxes than the rest of the UK.

QUESTIONS

1 In your own words explain the 'doomsday scenario'.
2 How did the demand for greater self-rule in Scotland come about?
3 Which groups support the Scottish Constitutional Convention?
4 Why did the Conservatives and SNP refuse to take part in the Convention?
5 In a short paragraph summarise the main Convention proposals.
6 Which political party would be hurt most if the number of Scottish MPs were reduced to 57?
7 How will the government's proposals improve government in Scotland?
8 How does Tony Blair's proposal for a two-question referendum deal with Michael Forsyth's claims that a Scottish Assembly would lead to a tartan tax?

Study Figure 1.53a and b and answer the questions which follow.

THE WEST LOTHIAN QUESTION

'For how long will English constituencies and English honourable members tolerate not just 71 Scots, 36 Welsh and a number of Ulstermen but at least 119 Honourable Members from Scotland, Wales and Northern Ireland exercising an important, and probably often decisive, effect on English politics while they themselves have no say in the same matters in Scotland, Wales and Ireland? Such a situation cannot endure for long.'

Figure 1.53a   *Tam Dalyell, MP for West Lothian, 14 November 1977*

THE WEST LOTHIAN ANSWER

'What about the strange position of English MPs? Why should they be stopped from voting on Scottish or Welsh affairs when Scottish and Welsh MPs may vote on English affairs.

This is the so-called Lothian Question. It is less complicated than it sounds. The same situation was tolerated in the case of Northern Ireland MPs between 1920 and 1972.'

Figure 1.53b   *Adapted from Ferdinand Mount, 'Homage to Caledonia', Times Literary Supplement, 1 August 1995*

Q UESTIONS

1 What is the West Lothian question?
2 In what ways does the answer:
   a **deal with the problem satisfactorily?**
   b **not deal with the problem satisfactorily?**

Britain and the European Union

Britain has been a member of the European Community since 1973 (now called the European Union).

In 1973, the European Economic Community consisted of nine member states including the United Kingdom.

As you can see from Figure 1.54, the EEC has slowly expanded and on 1 January 1995 Sweden,

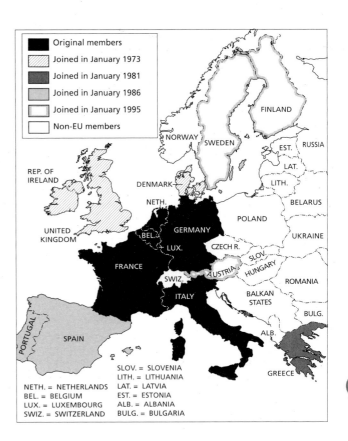

Figure 1.54   The EU member states

Source: Politics Review

63

Finland and Austria joined the European Union.

Britain's membership has always caused problems for both major parties.

As far back as 1975, the then Labour PM, Harold Wilson, ordered a referendum asking the British people whether or not they wanted to remain members of the EEC. The Labour Party was divided on this issue and many people regarded that the EEC threatened the sovereignty of the British Parliament.

The result was a two to one victory for remaining membership. Nevertheless, opposition remained strong.

Closer European Union

In 1985, the European Commission published plans for a **European Single Market**. This aimed to create one European market for all Community members' products and increased the power of the Community over national parliaments.

The Single European Act which was passed by the British Parliament came into effect in July 1987.

In December 1991 John Major, the British Prime Minister, put Britain's signature to the **Maastricht Treaty** which aimed to bring about 'an even closer European Union'. This would be done by bringing about greater European monetary and political integration.

It was agreed by the British Parliament in 1992.

Party politics and European Union

Within both major political parties there are divisions on the way forward for Britain and the European Union. The Liberal Democrats support a 'Federal Europe'. The SNP supports 'Independence in Europe'.

Within the Conservative Party those who are against the Maastricht Treaty are called **Euro-sceptics**.

The Labour Party is divided between **New Labour** which favours closer European Union and a single European currency, and **Old Labour** which believes that the rules on moving towards a single currency would force a future Labour government to cut public expenditure by £18billion.

QUESTIONS

1 When did Britain join the European Community?
2 Describe how membership has grown since 1975.
3 How did Harold Wilson try to solve problems within the Labour Party over membership?
4 What were the aims of the Single Market and the Maastricht Treaty?
5 How are the two main parties divided on Europe?

Different views on the European Union

The Conservative Government has suffered more from divisions over Europe than the Labour Party.

In November 1994 John Major withdrew the Whip from 8 MPs. Nicholas Body, another Euro-sceptic, refused the Whip in protest. As Major's majority fell, the Whip had to be restored to the nine Euro-rebels in April 1995.

Look at Figures 1.55–1.59 and answer the questions which follow.

Employment Secretary Mr Portillo: 'A single currency would mean giving up the government of the UK.'

Welsh Secretary John Redwood intervened: 'It is not just an economic issue. It is a very big constitutional issue as well.'

Number 2 at the Treasury, Mr Jonathan Aitken, another hardliner: 'I don't want to see a single currency, period. I would hesitate for an eternity before I came out and said that I would vote for a single currency.'

Figure 1.55   Source: Herald, *13 February 1995*

The Chancellor of the Exchequer, Mr Kenneth Clarke, says today that he will not be silenced on Europe.

His insistence on making the case for closer European unity and giving favourable consideration to the idea of a single European currency will heighten tensions within the Tory Party.

He said that while the conditions under which Britain might enter a single currency needed to be clarified, joining should not be ruled out now.

Figure 1.56   Source: Herald, *16 February 1995*

Unveiling the document, A People's Europe, Mr Cook declared it was time for Britain to take a constructive approach to the EU and attacked the Tories' negative attitude.

The document spells out Labour policies on Europe in a bid to show how advantageous the EU is to British people's lives, but the Shadow Foreign Secretary denied Labour would support a federal European superstate.

'The Europe we seek is an association of free member states sharing common interests, not surrendering sovereignty,' Mr Cook said.

On single currency, Labour would sign up only if British industry was able to compete effectively and there was true economic convergence across Europe. However, it stressed this must only be with the consent of the British people, gained through a general election or a referendum.

Figure 1.57   Source: Herald, *2 August 1996*

'I am leaving because I can no longer support the government's policy towards the European Union. This policy is not working. In particular, I am convinced that joining a single currency would be disastrous, both politically and economically.'

Figure 1.58 *Source: Extract from resignation letter of David Heathcoat-Amory, Paymaster General in John Major's Cabinet, 22 July 1996*

'If the UK is forced into a single currency, all effective economic power will be transferred from an elected government to European bankers, beyond our control.

The first casualty would be public expenditure cuts of £18billion.

Spending cuts – on schools, housing, community care – and job losses would be inevitable.'

Figure 1.59 *Source: Extract from the Single Currency Axing Labour's Programme backed by over 70 Labour MPs and MEPs, 21 July 1996*

QUESTIONS

1 Why was John Major forced to restore the Whip to the Euro-rebels?
2 What evidence is there that there are divisions within John Major's Cabinet?
3 What is New Labour's policy on Europe?
4 How do these differ from the pamphlet issued by the 70 Labour MPs and MEPs?

Participation in a Democracy

Getting Involved in Politics

Many people in Britain are involved in politics in one way or other. This is called **political participation**. For example, most of the people who are **eligible** to vote in an area, those who are over 18 years old, are listed in the **electoral register**.

Some people do not register to vote in an area for different reasons, some of which are listed here:

- People who have recently moved into a new home in a new constituency.
- Some persons did not register while the Poll Tax was in operation to avoid paying it.
- Some people don't support any of the

Figure 2A Labour party membership application form

political parties and others feel that the parties do nothing for them. Many poor people don't vote.

- People who are ill may not register to vote. Every house receives a form to fill in each year and they have to list all the persons staying, at that time, in their house. This is to ensure that the electoral register is kept up to date.

Political party membership

Figure 2A shows an example of the Labour Party application form.

All political parties try to attract new members. Application forms are available from the parties. At times a political party will run a **recruitment campaign** to attract new members, like the recent Labour Party campaign which increased its membership by 7000 to 20,000.

One group of society which has been targeted by the political parties is the young

voters, 18–34-year-olds. Many of them have lost faith in the political system and prefer not to vote.

A report published in 1993 warns of:

> 'the danger of young people being cut-off from the rest of society because of unemployment and home-lessness'

Figure 2B *Source: Demos 1995*

All political parties have youth sections which cater for the young voter.

QUESTIONS

1 What is political participation?
2 Which people are listed in the electoral register?
3 List the reasons why some people over 18 may not be able to vote in an area.
4 Name one way that a political party may try to attract new members.
5 How successful was a recent Labour Party campaign?
6 Why do political parties target young people?
7 According to the *Demos* report (Figure 2B), why don't some young people vote?

Participation in elections

To vote a person has to be:
• over 18 years of age;
• living in Britain;
• registered to vote;
• living outside Britain for less than 20 years.
Some people are not allowed to vote at an election, including the following:
• prisoners;
• members of the House of Lords;
• people in mental institutions;
• people who have not registered in their electoral constituency.

Election day

• **Polling stations** stay open from 7.00 a.m.–10.00 p.m. See Figure 2C.

Figure 2C

• Voters bring **polling cards** and their name is checked off the election register.
• The voter is given a **ballot paper**.

Figure 2D *Source: Sociology Alive, Stephen Moore, Stanley Thornes, 1992*

67

- The voter goes into **polling booth** and puts a **X** against the candidate of their choice.
- The voter folds the ballot paper and puts it into the sealed **ballot box**.

Figure 2E

- After 10.00 p.m. all ballot boxes are taken to a central location where they are counted.
- After counting the ballot papers, the winner is announced.

Non-voters

Figure 2F shows the percentage of the population in different age groups who were not registered to vote (excluding under-18s).

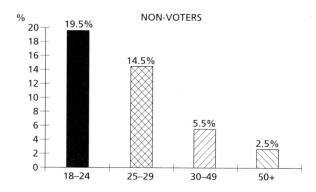

Figure 2F

Many young people appear not to be interested in voting at elections, but are involved in **single issue campaigns** such as the M77 motorway through Pollok Estate in Glasgow or the Animal Rights Campaign.

In such campaigns different methods of **protest** could be used. A recent Radio One poll on the different ways of protesting and should they be used produced the following results.

	Definitely should be allowed	Probably should be allowed	Probably should not be allowed	Definitely should not be allowed	Don't know
Signing petitions	88	11	–	1	1
Publishing pamphlets	67	26	4	2	1
Demonstrations	54	36	5	3	–
Going on strike	44	37	11	7	2
Occupying buildings	9	22	35	31	4
Protests likely to lead to injury	1	3	10	85	2
Damaging buildings or property	1	1	10	88	1

Figure 2G   Support for ways of protesting, per cent

Source: BBC Radio One, 1995

QUESTIONS

1 Which groups are not allowed to vote?
2 Describe the procedure for voting in your own words.
3 Using the statistics in Figure 2F, what evidence is there that young people are the most 'switched off' by politics?
4 What type of political activity appeals to some young people?
5 According to the Radio One poll, what are the four most popular methods of protesting?

Pressure Groups

Pressure groups are groups of people who try to influence the government or other public bodies by contacting MPs or other important people to put forward their views at Westminster. There are two types of pressure group.

The sectional pressure groups

- These are normally professional like British Medical Association, or occupational.
- Their aims are to protect their members' interests and future development.

One important pressure group is the Confederation of British Industry (CBI) which acts for British companies. This group was important in getting laws introduced which reduced the power of the trade unions in the 1980s.

Figure 2H shows Michael Heseltine, the deputy Prime Minister and Conservative MP, speaking at the CBI conference in November 1995.

Figure 2H

Figure 2I   SKAT (Skye and Kyle Against Tolls) protests about tolls on the Skye bridge

SHELTER TAKE THE ROOF OFF HOMELESS PROJECT

By Derek Alexander

A leading homeless charity has hit out at plans to open a new hostel in the city.

Shelter have lodged concerns over a bid by Glasgow's new homeless magazine, Streetlife, to renovate a derelict building into a stay over centre for rough sleepers.

They reckon funds raised from their sales should be injected into other emergency services for the city's spiralling homeless population.

A Shelter spokeswoman said: 'I don't think that opening a new institution for the homeless is the answer to the problem.

'It is only human to react to a problem where there is an obvious need for help.

'But The Great Eastern hostel is now being phased out which shows institutions have had their day.'

She added: 'A befriending service or a drop in centre would be a better alternative for them to work on.'

Streetlife magazine will launch in Glasgow later this month.

They hope to raise £1.2m to revamp an abandoned hotel in the city centre.

A spokesman for Streetlife said: 'It won't be simply another hostel. It'll be a 24 hour emergency centre.

'We hope that it will be an asset for all the homeless people currently struggling to survive on Glasgow's streets.

'There will be a section for accommodation because not a night has gone by in my three years' experience in working with the homeless that we haven't been approached for this.

'We will also be training people to prepare them for moving back into permanent accommodation.

'We have plans to start work on a 59 bedroomed hotel in Queen Street, but it's early days yet, we still have to raise about £1m.'

Figure 2J   *Source: Glaswegian, 18 April 1996*

Promotional pressure groups

These types of pressure groups are interested mainly in a social cause and gaining publicity for it. Environmental protection groups have been active in recent years, such as **Greenpeace**, **Friends of the Earth**, and various Animal Rights Groups. One Scottish pressure group is SKAT (Skye and Kyle Against Tolls). SKAT, see Figure 2I, protests about tolls on the Skye Bridge and has support from the local community, the SNP and some Scottish MPs.

Shelter is a UK-wide pressure group which campaigns on behalf of the **homeless**. Figure 2J from the *Glaswegian* newspaper gives an idea of the project/work Shelter is involved in.

QUESTIONS

1 List the different types of pressure group and give examples of their activities.
2 Why are SKAT protesting?
3 What types of problems does Shelter get involved in?

Membership of pressure groups

In recent years the membership of pressure groups has increased quite quickly, especially for environmental groups like Friends of the Earth. Figure 2K shows the increase in pressure groups to present-day levels.

Group	Membership in year	Membership now
Friends of the Earth	1000 in 1971	116000
Greenpeace	30000 in 1981	411000
Royal Society for the Protection of Birds (RSPB)	98000 in 1971	850000

Figure 2K   Green pressure groups

How governments use pressure groups

Governments are often in contact with pressure groups to find out their views of policy. In this way the pressure group is able to provide a government with up-to-date information on their views. These can be very useful. The British Medical Association was consulted by the Conservative government before they set about reforming the National Health Service. However, this did not stop the medical profession from criticising the reform of the NHS.

Criticisms of Pressure Groups

The name given to the activity carried out by pressure groups at Parliament is called **lobbying**, i.e. speaking to MPs in the Lobby of Parliament to try to get them to put forward the group's ideas on a particular topic.

There are a number of ways that an MP might be able to influence Parliament:
- by the introduction of a **Private Member's Bill**; or
- by asking questions at Question Time.

In addition, some pressure groups **sponsor** MPs. Dennis Skinner, for example, is sponsored by the National Union of Mineworkers (NUM) and Tony Blair by the Transport and General Workers' Union (TGWU). It is the job of the MP to forward the interests of their 'sponsor' in the House of Commons.

Recently there has been criticism of the way that some MPs use their power in Parliament. In 1994, two MPs were suspended for accepting payment to ask questions.

As a result of the abuse of their position by some MPs, an investigation was set up, known as the Nolan Enquiry, into MPs' income from other sources, apart from their jobs. There is now a **Code of Practice** and MPs must let Parliament know of their interests.

QUESTIONS

1 Which environmental pressure groups have shown the biggest increase in membership?
2 Give an example of a way the government and pressure groups work together.
3 Explain what is meant by 'lobbying MPs'.
4 Why do trade unions sponsor some MPs?
5 Why was the Nolan Committee set up?

Other Pressure Groups

Mass media consists of the newspapers, television, radio and any other sources which can reach a wide audience. Mass media has the power to reach many people with a point of view, and to influence them.

Conservative	Labour
News of the World	Daily Mirror
The Times	Sunday Mirror
The Sunday Times	The Sun
The Express	Daily Record
Sunday Express	The People
Daily Star	The Independent
Daily Mail	Independent on Sunday
Mail on Sunday	The Guardian
	Sunday Observer
	Morning Star

Figure 2L   Who supports who

Newspapers are important in politics and they try to influence their readers towards one political view and against another. It is possible to list the major newspapers according to the political party whose views they support (see Figure 2L).

Some newspaper companies have an interest in television and radio companies, for example Rupert Murdoch, owner of the *Sun, News of the World, The Times* and *Sunday Times* and Sky TV.

One example of the power of newspaper in politics was the *Sun*'s headlines after the 1992 general election:

'It was the Sun wot won it.'

Neil Kinnock, the leader of the Labour Party at that time, believed that the *Sun* was a major influence in Labour's defeat.

The *Sun* has now switched to the Labour Party from Conservative for the 1997 General Election.

QUESTIONS

1 What is the mass media?
2 Look at the list of newspapers which support the different political parties (Figure 2K). Try to find out the circulation of these newspapers and suggest which party gets most newspaper support.

Participation in a Democracy

Getting Involved in Politics

Registration

Each local council is responsible for collecting information for the **Electoral Register**.

This is a list of all the people in the constituency who are **eligible** to vote at the next election. If anyone is nearly 18 years of age, it also contains the date of birth of that person. If the election takes place after their eighteenth birthday, they are able to vote.

Once a year each household receives a form which they must fill in. They must give the names of all the people living at that address. It is important that people should fill this in because otherwise they might lose their right to vote.

Non-registration

One in three people moves between registers and one in five 17–25-year-olds is not a registered voter. The biggest reason given by young people before the last election for not registering was fear of having to pay the **Poll Tax**.

Non-voting

10 million people didn't bother to vote at the last general election. This was because they couldn't be bothered, they didn't support any of the parties or candidates standing, or that their party had no chance of winning. Surveys show that the largest group of non-voters are the poor who feel that the political parties do nothing for them!

Joining a political party

Each of the major political parties has a youth section whose task is to attract new members. It is important to attract the young voters as they are the generation of tomorrow.

If you wish to join a political party you can contact their party HQ. Labour has increased its membership from 14000 to 20000. The Conservatives claim to have 350,000 members.

Voting at elections

In Britain, voting takes place for an electorate who must be over 18 years of age, resident in Britain and registered to vote.

In 1983 the Conservative government allowed UK residents who have been living abroad for less than 20 years to vote in British elections. Now all political parties try to win the support of those citizens.

Certain people are excluded from voting such as prisoners, members of the House of Lords and people in mental institutions. Homeless people, with no fixed address were excluded until recently.

Voting day

On election day polling booths stay open from 7.00 a.m. until 10.00 p.m. The voter enters the polling station where their name is crossed off the electoral register after they produce their polling card. This is designed to avoid impersonation and people voting more than once.

Each voter is then given a ballot paper and they enter the polling booth where they simply put a cross beside the candidate of their choice. They then put the ballot paper into the ballot box. At the close of voting the ballot boxes are taken away to a central location and counted.

Attracting the young voter

The M power campaign emphasises the importance of voter registration. They argue that it is important for young people to vote as they will become increasingly isolated from the political process if they fail to take up their right to vote in elections.

Charter 88, a political pressure group, has argued that all political parties are to blame for young people feeling isolated from politics.

In September 1995 Demos, the independent think-tank, published a report about 18–34-year-olds in Britain today. It warned of the dangers of young people becoming cut off from the rest of society and turning into a class of 'underwolves': people who have become angry at their **alienation** (exclusion) from society, caused by unemployment and homelessness.

At present the government spends 1.2p per elector on voter registration, while failure to register could bring a fine of £1000.

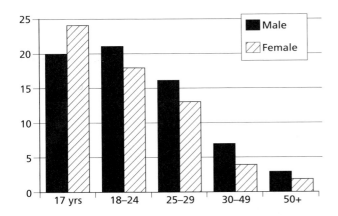

Figure 2.1　　　*Source:* Education Guardian, *24 October 1995 (OPCS)*

However, while many young people would appear not to be interested in many of the main political parties, they have become more involved in single issue campaigns such as those against new motorways or for animal rights.

A recent poll by Radio 1 produced the results shown in Figure 2.2.

	Definitely should be allowed	Probably should be allowed	Probably should not be allowed	Definitely should not be allowed	Don't know
Signing petitions	88	11	–	1	1
Publishing pamphlets	67	26	4	2	1
Demonstrations	54	36	5	3	–
Going on strike	44	37	11	7	2
Occupying buildings	9	22	35	31	4
Protests likely to lead to injury	1	3	10	85	2
Damaging buildings or property	1	1	10	88	1

Figure 2.2　Support for ways of protesting, per cent　　　*Source: BBC Radio 1*

Pressure Groups

Pressure groups are groups who seek to exert influence on government or public bodies. There are two types of pressure group.

Sectional

These are mainly based upon occupations and take in a wide variety of industries and professions ranging from the Confederation of British Industry (CBI) to the British Medical Association (BMA).

They exist to protect the interests of their members and to advance their cause.

Figure 2.3 John Major addresses the CBI

In the 1980s, the CBI had a very strong influence on Conservative Government policy regarding the economy and trade unions.

In the 1970s, the Trades Union Congress (TUC) had a very strong influence on the Labour Government in trying to promote the interests of trade union members.

Promotional

These groups are concerned with promoting particular social causes and to gaining publicity for such causes.

Figure 2.4 Motorway protesters campaigning against the M77 which will bypass a rich residential area, pass close to a working class area and cut through a park

Such groups range from Help the Aged and the Child Poverty Action Group to environmental pressure groups such as Greenpeace and the Noise Abatement Society.

Environmental pressure groups have been very prominent in recent years. Recent cases involve the building of new motorways and dumping oil rigs at sea.

The main environmental groups can be divided up into four types.

- The animal protection movement which has recently featured in the protests against the export of live animals to the continent.
- The amenity movement who are concerned with the protection of the landscape.
- The anti-roads movement which has featured in protests against road building, e.g. Newbury bypass and the M77 in Glasgow.
- Broad-based organisations with a wide concern, such as Friends of the Earth (FoE) and Greenpeace.

Pressure groups develop their power and influence in a number of ways.

Recruiting membership

Environmental pressure groups have been very successful in recent years in increasing their membership. FoE went from 1000 members in 1971 to 116000 in 1992.

Greenpeace has increased from 30000 members in 1981 to 411000 in 1992.

The Royal Society for the Protection of Birds has increased from 98000 in 1971 to 850000 in 1992.

Being consulted by government

Governments regularly consult with outside agencies with regard to policy.

In recent years health service reforms have been criticised by members of the medical profession despite earlier consultations with the BMA.

The Law Society was consulted before the 1994 Criminal Justice Bill was drafted.

Lobbying Parliament

Parliament is also the place where pressure groups can make themselves heard.

In recent years back-bench MPs have attempted

to introduce Private Member's Bills (PMBs) promoting a certain cause, e.g. outlawing blood sports.

Private legislation by David Alton, MP, sought to reduce the time limit for abortions. This received the active support of the Society for the Protection of the Unborn Child (SPUC).

Professional parliamentary lobbyists are paid by some firms and pressure groups and operate within the Palace of Westminster in attempts to win the support of MPs.

Sponsoring MPs

Many MPs are sponsored by outside interests such as business firms and trade unions, and they are employed as consultants or directors.

QUESTIONS

1 Look at Figures 2.3 and 2.4. What do they tell you about the way different types of pressure group operate?
2 Explain the difference between the two types of pressure group.
3 Name one pressure group which has influenced both major parties.
4 Divide your page into two headings, **promotional** and **sectional**. Put the following groups under each heading; Institute of Chartered Accountants; The Conservation Society; Howard League for Penal Reform; Association of University Lecturers; Engineering Employers' Federation; The British Dental Association; The Royal Automobile Club.
5 Name the four types of environmental pressure group and give recent examples of their work.
6 What evidence is there that these environmental pressure groups are becoming more popular?
7 In what ways do pressure groups use our elected representatives?

Criticisms of Pressure Groups

Paying MPs

There have been recent criticisms of the way some MPs use **parliamentary privilege** (their powers in Parliament). In August 1994, two MPs were suspended for asking questions of a government minister for which they had been paid.

All MPs must now disclose business interests and payments in relation to their work as MPs.

Other criticisms

There are various criticisms of the way pressure groups operate. Some people say they are narrow-minded and operate purely out of self-interest. Others say that pressure groups are vital in a pluralist democracy where all shades of opinion should be heard and represented.

Look at Figures 2.4, 2.5, 2.6 and 2.7 and answer the questions which follow.

Wimpey, the construction company, is anxious to avoid confrontations with the anti-road protesters, many of whom are camped Greenham Common-like on the southern edge of Pollok Estate. This, however, is a vain hope.

The truth is those who want the M77 extension greatly outnumber those who don't.

It will improve the quality of life for thousands of Glasgow householders. It will increase the commercial and industrial potential of south-west Scotland, an area still smarting from one of the worst unemployment rates in the UK. It may even save lives.

Strathclyde estimates that in a 30-year period following the opening of the M77, there will be 3690 fewer accidents. The motorway, it says, will be seven times safer than the existing roads.

Strathclyde intends to take advantage of this situation to improve its public transport system, introducing bus-priority measures and cutting bus journeys into the city centre by as much as 10 minutes.

The M77 will also result in vastly improved prospects for economic development in Ayrshire. The Glasgow South link will make local industry far more accessible to Glasgow Airport, to the new Euro freight terminal at Mossend, Lanarkshire, and to the rest of Britain.

Councillor Charles Gordon, chairman of Strathclyde's roads and transportation committee, has little sympathy for the M77's detractors.

'The protesters have been very adept at getting attention for themselves but I don't think they are representative of local public opinion,' he said.

Figure 2.5   *Source:* Herald, *7 January 1995, abridged*

We are told that 'those who want the M77 extension greatly outnumber those who don't'. Evidence, please? The only known poll on the subject was conducted by the *Evening Times* in October, 1994, and its readers voted more than two to one against the road.

The suggestion that the M77 'will increase the commercial and industrial potential of south-west Scotland' is a sweeping claim which lacks factual substance. Authoritative studies have found no evidence of a positive relationship between road accessibility and economic performance.

As for the accident-cutting potential of the M77, the claimed 20% reduction takes no account of the new traffic which will be generated by the road. A sustainable alternative to the M77 – incorporating traffic calming, modest road building, and upgraded rail services – would yield substantially bigger safety benefits. Major traffic-calming initiatives elsewhere in the UK have cut accidents by up to 80%.

The case for the M77 is so flawed it is surely no surprise that opponents now feel obliged to resort to direct action to halt this discredited project.

Figure 2.6

Source: Herald,
12 January 1995, abridged letter

Beside the Barrhead road a new rash of signs splashed with stark messages proclaim to motorists that they are driving past 'Asthma Junction'.

Betty Campbell, a Corkerhill resident for 22 years, can see the motorway. It runs past her back garden and she says she cannot escape the noise of the diggers.

'People round here aren't the sort to lie in front of bulldozers, they are conventional. But the Corkerhill community has been squeezed in by the motorway and cut off from the park – it is a form of social apartheid.

'Not one house has had any noise insulation put in. We are in touch with lawyers to claim damages, not only for the losses they are suffering now but for all the losses they will suffer when the road is completed.'

Figure 2.7

Source: Herald,
24 September 1995, abridged

QUESTIONS

1 Do you support the actions of the protesters? Give reasons for your answer.
2 According to the article of the 7 January (Figure 2.5), what will be the main benefits of the motorway?
3 How does the letter of 12 January (Figure 2.6) seek to challenge these benefits?
4 What problems have the building of the motorway brought to the people of Corkerhill?
5 Using the sources given, and any additional information you can gather, make a balanced argument for or against the building of the motorway.

Look at the case study below and answer the questions which follow.

Case Study
Clydeside Action on Asbestos

Clydeside Action on Asbestos (CAA) was formed in 1983 as a support group for asbestos victims and their families. CAA helps their clients with claims for industrial related benefit (IDB) and other related benefits by giving advice and support at Medical and Special Appeal Tribunals. Further help is given in civil action against their employers for negligence. Here, CAA locates possible witnesses, does company searches and advises the client of each particular stage in the long process.

CAA has helped to change the law where it has affected asbestos disease victims. In 1993, it was successful in amending a law called the **Effect of Death on Damages (Scotland) Act**. This law did not allow claims for damages being heard in a Scottish court after the claimant had died. It enabled the defenders (the employers) to delay the case until after the claimant had died, so reducing the settlement drastically. The law was changed for good in April 1993.

CAA is presently involved in a campaign to amend the way the Compensation Recovery Unit (CRU) works. The CRU, which is part of the DSS, claims back any social security payments if a claimant succeeds in getting compensation from an employer. We think this is unfair.

Asbestos-related disease is killing more than all other occupational cancers combined and is expected to increase threefold by the year 2025, resulting in at least 10000 deaths each year. These deaths would still occur if asbestos were banned tomorrow, all being a result of past exposure. Therefore, the services of CAA will still be in demand in the years to come, a service run by asbestos victims for the relief and benefit of other victims and society as a whole.

Q UESTIONS

1 Who does Clydeside Action seek to help?
2 What kind of help does it give?
3 Explain how it has been successful in changing the law.
4 Do you agree with CAA's opinion on the CRU? Give reasons for your answer.
5 Why will CAA's work still be important in the future?

Other Pressure Groups

The **mass media** is a very influential group in British politics. Newspaper circulation (the number of newspapers sold) is higher in Britain than in most other European countries.

Newspapers are politically motivated and try to persuade the reading public to see their point of view, through their headlines, selection and presentation of stories and their editorials.

In the aftermath of the 1992 general election victory for the Conservatives, the *Sun* confidently claimed 'It was the *Sun* wot won it'. This was a reference to their headline on election day 'Would the last person to leave please turn out the lights'.

This was an obvious message to the public over Labour's policies and what would happen if they were elected.

Neil Kinnock, the defeated Labour leader, claimed that, 'If one out of 17 *Sun* readers had switched to Labour, Labour would have won the election'.

In 1997, the *Sun* switched to support Labour in the general election.

Below is a list of newspaper companies, UK national newspapers and the parties they usually support.

Conservative supporters

News International
(37% of national daily newspaper circulation)
News of the World
The Times
Sunday Times

United News and Media
The Express
Sunday Express
Daily Star

The Daily Mail and General Trust
Daily Mail
Mail on Sunday

Labour supporters

The Mirror Group
(24% of national daily newspaper circulation)
Daily Mirror
Sunday Mirror
Daily Record
The People
Independent
Independent on Sunday

News International
The Sun

Guardian Newspapers Limited
Guardian
Observer

People's Press Printing Society
Morning Star

Q UESTIONS

1 How do newspapers seek to influence their readers' political views?
2 Which political party do most newspapers support?
3 In what way did the *Sun* newspaper take credit for the Conservative victory in 1992?
4 How is this supported by Neil Kinnock's statement?
5 Choose two tabloid daily papers and compare their support for a political party.
6 How important might the *Sun*'s switch to Labour be?

78

What are Trade Unions?

Trade unions are groups of workers who join together to try to improve their working situation. Early unions, called **craft unions**, were made up of skilled workers and later as unskilled workers became organised **general unions** became popular. More recently office, shop and professional workers have organised what are called **white-collar unions**.

Since 1945 the major political parties have recognised the importance of trade unions to British industry but they have different ideas about what part the unions have to play in the making of industrial policy. At times the unions have been at odds with the government's policy and this has led to **industrial conflict**.

Advantages of being a trade union member
People join trade unions for many different reasons:

- **Pay:** unions can negotiate pay rates, paid holidays, bonuses and hourly rates;
- **Working conditions:** healthy and safe working conditions can be organised through union negotiation;
- **Job security:** job protection is a part of the union's responsibility;
- **Victimisation:** a union's strength is its unity and a case of one person being picked on brings support from all members;
- **Benefits:** ill workers can receive money from the union to see them through their illness. Some unions have holiday homes for retired members;
- **Legal matters:** lawyers are provided to represent members who need legal advice;

- **Political:** pressure can be applied to politicians through **lobbying**. Some unions sponsor MPs to present their view in Parliament.

Figure 3A   Dennis Skinner has shown support for the NUM

Most workers in Britain today are not members of trade unions. The following report from the *Financial Times* of 9 February 1996 claims this.

TRADE UNION MEMBERSHIP AT LOWEST LEVEL SINCE 1945

'The number of employees (workers) belonging to trade unions has fallen to the lowest level since the Second World War.

For the last 15 years there has been a decline in trade union membership but 1995 saw the third-biggest decline in over 25 years. There are now only 8.3 million trade union members compared with 13.3 million in 1979 – only one-third of the workforce.

The biggest decline is in the number of men. In 1994 male membership fell by 8.7%, while female membership rose by 1% in the same period.'

Figure 3B

Source: Financial Times,
9 February 1996, abridged

1 What are trade unions?
2 What are the advantages of joining a trade union?
3 Where has trade union membership fallen?
4 Where has it increased?

What are the reasons for joining a trade union?

The earlier newspaper report (Figure 3B) states that two-thirds of the working population are not members of a trade union and there are a number of reasons why this is the case:

- some well-paid workers don't see the need to join a union;
- some jobs are difficult to organise a union for, e.g. North Sea Oil workers, shop workers and home workers;
- workers in small family firms can negotiate for themselves;
- some workers are self-employed;
- some companies do not recognise trade unions.

Types of unions

There are four main types of trade union and they all offer their members similar benefits.

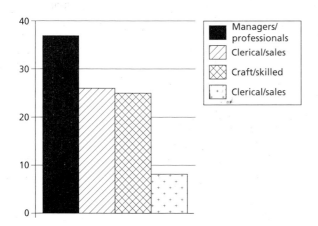

Figure 3C   Union membership by job type
Source: Labour Force Survey

The type of union is based upon the type of worker and the place of work, not the service given by the unions. See Figure 3D.

Type of Union	Membership Type
Craft Unions	Members are those who are employed in providing a skill, e.g. electricians, plumbers and engineers are some examples.
Industrial Unions	Organise workers in an industry regardless of the job that they do, e.g. National Union of Mineworkers (NUM).
General Unions	Members in all industries and all types of skill. The Transport and General Workers' Union is an example.
White-Collar Unions	Members are office workers, managers, professionals and civil servants. The Educational Institute of Scotland (EIS), Scotland's biggest teaching union, is an example.

Figure 3D   Types of unions

Trade union negotiations

Trade unions represent their members in negotiation with managers on pay and working conditions. Both sides sit down together to discuss the pay or conditions and try to reach an **agreement**. This is known as **collective bargaining**.

If agreement in the union–management talks is not reached there are a number of types of **industrial action** that can be taken to move the **dispute** on. Industrial action may lead to agreement being reached quite quickly or it may lead to a more serious rift between managers and unions.

79

Types of industrial action	What it involves	Effect
Work-to-rule	Workers only do what they are paid to do. E.g. no 'tidying up' after job is finished	• hits employers.
A 'go-slow'	Workers don't work at their normal rate	• hits production.
Overtime ban	Workers refuse to work overtime	• hits employers as production falls; • workers lose some money.
Token strike	Usually one day	• warning that union is not happy; • the company loses production; • workers lose pay.
Unofficial strike	Does not have union backing and breaks the law	• creates a bad 'public image' of the union; • workers lose pay
Official strike	By law a secret ballot must be taken to get an idea of the support for strike action	• costs the union money because of strike pay; • affects the production of the items being made by the strikers; • it is bad for worker and manager relations; • customers are lost; • strikers lose out on pay.

Figure 3E Types of industrial action

Although unofficial strike action or 'wildcat strikes' are quite uncommon, a recent example was the postmen's action in Edinburgh. The following headline and report from the *Herald* shows how this type of industrial action is used.

3000 POSTAL STAFF IN WILDCAT STRIKE

Mail in Edinburgh and Fife ground to a halt yesterday after 3000 postal workers walked out. The unofficial strike arose in a dispute over the planned sacking of a worker.

Communications Workers Union (CWU) official, Mr John Keggie, met with Royal Mail managers to sort out the problem. Later the postmen returned to work.

Figure 3F

Source: Herald,
27 July 1996, abridged

QUESTIONS

1 Why don't some workers join a trade union?
2 Look at Figure 3D. List the four different types of trade unions and say what groups of workers belong to each type of union.
3 What is collective bargaining?
4 What are the main types of industrial action?
5 Which two types of industrial action affect the employer, but not the workers' wages?
6 Explain why taking strike action might be the last thing workers would want to do?
7 Why did the post office workers walk out and how was the situation resolved?

Reductions in Trade Union Power

In the 1960s and 1970s the trade unions became very powerful in Britain. Both the Labour and Conservative Governments recognised the growing power of the unions and tried to do something to curb this.

Conservative Governments tried to introduce laws to reduce union power in the early 1970s but this had little effect when the miners went on strike in 1974. The Labour Government **repealed** the Conservatives' laws against trade unions in 1974 and tried to work with the unions under the **Social Contract** of 1976.

The Social Contract was an agreement between the Labour Government and the unions to keep wage increases low if the Government kept prices low.

By 1978 the unions felt that the Labour Government was not keeping its side of the agreement and they decided that they would try to get higher wage increases. To achieve this many unions took strike action in 1978/79. This period became known as the **winter of discontent**.

The action by the trade unions back-fired upon them as public support fell. The politicians decided that 'enough was enough' as graveyard workers, nurses, dustmen and others went on strike. The idea that the unions had become far too powerful became widespread.

Conservative Trade Union Legislation

Many union members voted for Mrs Thatcher's Conservative Party in 1979. Part of the manifesto promise of the Conservatives was to reduce the power of the trade unions and it appears that many union members agreed that should happen.

Soon after the election the Conservatives began to introduce a number of laws which reduced the power of the trade unions. Mr Lang (the President of the Board of Trade) threatened to introduce a ninth law which would allow the public to sue trade unions for damages if it could be proved that a strike had led to loss of profit. This was in response to the strike by post office workers.

Figure 3G is a short description of the eight laws introduced by the Conservative Party since 1980.

UNION TRAGEDY IN EIGHT ACTS

1980 The Employment Act started the latest Tory curbs on unions by outlawing some forms of secondary action and laying down legal restrictions for picketing.

1982 Norman (now Lord) Tebbit set about 'neutering' the trade unions with his Employment Act of 1982, or 'Tebbit's Law'. It reduced union legal immunities by making unions liable to be sued for the unlawful actions of their officials, exposing union funds to damages of up to £250,000. That Act also virtually outlawed sympathy or political strikes.

1984 Another Trade Union Act which, although it dealt mainly with internal union elections and ballots for political funds, also introduced new measures aimed again at curbing strikes. Unions were forced to ballot members before engaging in industrial action. Union immunity was lost and they could be taken to court for inducing breaches of contract.

1986 In came the Wages Act, under which manual workers had in future no right to be paid in cash. Workers under 21 removed from provisions of wages councils.

1988 Another Employment Act opened the way for dissident members to take their unions to court over the handling of strike ballots and made it unlawful for unions to discipline members for strike breaking.

1989 The abolition of the training commission.

1990 Another Employment Act abolished pre-entry closed shops. Union officials to take responsibility for unofficial strikes: legal immunity removed for actions supporting unofficial strikes. Remaining secondary actions made illegal.

1993 All industrial action ballots must be fully postal, complex procedures for notifying employers of a ballot were spelled out.

Figure 3G   Source: Herald, 31 July 1996

QUESTIONS

1 What was the Social Contract?
2 Why did the winter of discontent lead to trade unions becoming less popular?
3 Look at the list of laws against trade unions (Figure 3G). Which of the laws do you think hit trade unions the most?
4 What effect would Ian Lang's proposals have on public sector trade unions?

The Trades Union Congress

The Trades Union Congress (TUC) is a collection of 68 trade unions, representing almost 7 million members. It meets once a year to work out the **common policy** of all trade unions for the forthcoming year.

Union structure

TUC CONGRESS

Figure 3H   Source: Trade Unions, *SCIP*, *Cambridge Educational, 1983*

In Scotland the Scottish Trades Union (STUC) does a similar job to the TUC. Scottish trade unions belong to both the STUC and the TUC.

How Trade Unions are Organised

National Executive
Full-time officials run the union between National Conferences and are in charge of the daily business of the union. The General Secretary is the person who is in charge of the union.

National Conference (yearly)
Delegates of the union meet to work out the union's plans for the next year. They elect the National Executive.

District Committee
Shop stewards of different branches get together.

continued . . .

82

continued ...

The Branch
Lowest level of union activity. Shop steward and local committee.

Shop Steward in the Workplace
The shop steward represents the union at the place of work, dealing with pay, health and safety, overtime, victimisation and many other issues. The shop steward does not get paid for carrying out union duties.

Figure 3I   How trade unions are organised

The ordinary trade union members are called the **rank and file** or the **grassroots**. The grassroot members elect a **shop steward** who is their representative in their place of work. The ordinary members also participate in other elections in the workplace:
- secret ballots for industrial action;
- vote for **delegates** at the local and district level;
- vote for national executive representatives;
- vote for annual conference representatives.
Figure 3I gives an idea of how the unions are organised.

QUESTIONS
1 What is the TUC?
2 What is the STUC?
3 How do ordinary trade union members get involved?
4 What are the main duties of the shop steward?
5 In what ways can the structure of a trade union be described as being like a 'pyramid'?

Are Trade Unions in Decline?

The trade union membership in Britain is falling. Today there are only 8.3 million members of trade unions compared with 13.3 million in 1979.

What are the reasons for this decline?
- Attitudes towards trade unions have changed. The late 1970s brought chaos to many British industries and some people felt that the trade unions were responsible for this.
- More part-time and temporary workers have led to a reduction in trade union membership.
- Laws have been introduced to reduce the union influence in industry and its ability to take industrial action.
- The Labour Party has reduced the influence of trade unions on its actions and policies.

The biggest fall in union membership has been because of rising unemployment in the **traditional industries**, such as coal mining, shipbuilding and engineering. There has been an increase in the number of women members.

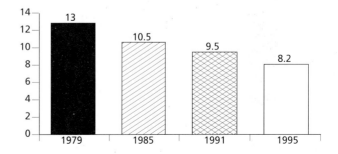

Figure 3J   TUC membership (in millions)

83

Conservatives, Trade Unions, and the Economy

Conservatives believe that trade unions are bad for British economy for the following reasons:

- they are a 'bad image' in British industry and they frighten off foreign companies;
- they stop the creation of jobs because they don't accept wage cuts when companies are in trouble;
- they affect customers if they go on strike;
- sometimes they act unlawfully.

Mrs Thatcher described the unions as the **'enemy within'** and introduced a number of laws to control the unions.

Figure 3K
Mrs Thatcher

The trade unions say that industrial action has fallen over the last 15 years because it might lead to the loss of jobs. Rising unemployment has 'frightened' union members from taking industrial action.

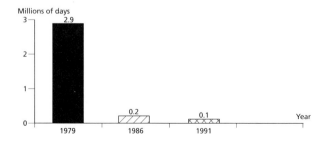

Figure 3L   Working days lost due to industrial action

Changes in employment

In the 1980s the British economy was hit by a large number of factories closing. This created the large levels of unemployment which were experienced at that time. Many factory closures were in the traditional industries which had high levels of trade union members.

Privatisation was also an important part of the Conservative Party policies and these industries, like coal, gas and British Airways, laid off large numbers of workers.

Some areas were worse hit by factory closures and unemployment than others. The areas with traditional industries like steel-making, coal-mining, engineering and shipbuilding were badly hit. These areas included Scotland, the north-east of England, the north-west of England and South Wales.

Trade union membership is still high in the above areas but is low in the south of England where **service industries** like banking and insurance are large employers.

QUESTIONS

1 Why has there been a decline in the number of trade unionists?
2 What are 'traditional industries'?
3 Why don't some Conservatives like trade unions?
4 Look at the number of days lost due to industrial action since 1979 (Figure 3L). Why might the Conservatives claim that their policies have been successful?
5 How might a trade unionist respond?
6 In what areas of the country is trade union membership low?

The Trade Union Movement and the Labour Party

The Labour Party has always had strong ties with the trade unions, as it was set up to be the representative of the workers at Parliament.

A lot of the money to support the Labour Party comes from trade union members in the form of a **political levy**. Another way that the trade unions provide finance to the Labour Party is through **sponsoring** of MPs. Tony Blair (Figure 3M) is sponsored by a trade union.

**Figure 3M
Tony Blair**

In return for their support the trade unions were given quite a big say on the policies of the Labour Party which has since tried to reduce the influence of trade unions on its plans. The poor public image of the unions brought attacks from the Conservatives on Labour.

Unions were seen as:

*   having an influence on Labour Party policies;
*   being undemocratic because of the **bloc voting system**. This allowed trade unions to count each member of the union as one vote.

New Labour and the Trade Unions

The influence of the trade unions on the Labour Party was seen by many as a reason why the Labour Party was not elected in the 1987 and 1992 general elections. The Miners' Strike of 1984–85 brought back the memory of the winter of discontent of the late 1970s. The Labour Party leadership felt that the influence of the unions would have to be reduced if they were to have a chance of winning a general election.

Reform of the Labour Party began in the 1980s as Figure 3N shows:

Year	Leader	Changes
1983	Neil Kinnock	Labour Party begins to reduce power of unions.
1992	John Smith	Continues Kinnock's reforms, 'One Man One Vote' (OMOV) passed. Union bloc-vote ends.
1994	Tony Blair	Rejection of Clause IV. Aim to increase Labour Party membership to reduce the need for trade union financial support. Plan to remove union sponsorship of MPs.

Figure 3N   The reform of the Labour Party

Changes in trade unions

85

There have been a number of changes in the trade unions since the 1970s. One important change has been the growth of **white-collar unions**, i.e. office staff, civil service, managers and professionals.

In the past white-collar workers had some security from unemployment as most job losses were in the manufacturing sector. In the 1980s many job losses affected these workers and the need to join trade unions became important.

'In the 1980s the **middle classes** are getting the same treatment as **working classes** as they face un-employment.'

Figure 3O   John Monks, General Secretary of TUC
Source: John Monks, abridged

QUESTIONS

1 Why was the Labour Party set up?
2 How do trade unions support the Labour Party financially?
3 In what ways did the Conservatives criticise the relationship between the trade unions and the Labour Party?
4 How have Labour leaders Kinnock, Smith and Blair changed the relationship with trade unions in recent years?
5 What are white-collar trade unions?
6 Why are more white-collar workers joining trade unions?

The World of Work in the 1990s

Low pay is another area of change. Trade unions want a **minimum wage** for the low-paid workers. The Conservative Government is against this, and this is the reason for not signing the Social Chapter of the European Union.

In the EU only Britain and Ireland don't have a minimum wage protection. The following extract from the *Herald* highlights the problem of low pay.

REPORT EXPOSES WORKERS' PLIGHT

The report by No Sweat on homeworkers shows that over 1 million workers in Britain today work up to 13 hours daily and receive an average hourly pay rate of £1.28.

Mr John Monks stated that the government has given Britain's sweatshop bosses a licence to exploit and pay poverty wages.

Figure 3P   *Source:* The Herald, *abridged*

Before 1986 there was a body which set a minimum wage for workers in poorly paid jobs. These **wages councils** for under-21s were disbanded and in 1993 all of them disappeared as a result of government policy. The Conservative Government feels that young people have a better chance of getting a job if there is no minimum wage.

Arguments for and against a national minimum wage

For:
- Higher wages will lead to higher Income Tax and National Insurance receipts.
- There will be savings on state benefits as people would come off Family Credit and Income Support.
- It is a fair way to distribute income and reduce the inequality gap.
- It is morally correct to pay a 'decent' wage and evidence shows where wages are low there is a high turnover of staff.
- Bad employers will not be subsidised by good employers.
- 'Every other country in Europe, bar Ireland, has minimum wage protection and the USA is now uprating its minimum wage.'
  Tony Blair, when Shadow Employment Secretary

Against
- It will cost employers more in wages and they might have to cut jobs, leading to higher unemployment.
- British employers will not be able to compete with low-wage firms in the Pacific Rim.
- Other workers will demand higher wages to 'maintain the differential' (the difference in pay between skilled and unskilled workers).
- Higher wage costs will pass to the customer, causing inflation.
- It goes against the spirit of the 'free market'. Workers are 'paid the rate for the job'.
- 'There can be no conceivable justification for a policy which on its own wrecks our economy and devastates job prospects.'
  Michael Howard, Employment Secretary

Figure 3Q

86

QUESTIONS

1 What criticisms are there of low pay?

2 What arguments are there against a minimum wage?

Trade Unions and Europe

In some European countries such as Germany, trade unions have a bigger influence on their government's policy than they have in Britain with a Conservative government.

British workers now co-operate closely with European trade unions. The European Union also appears to have taken the European workers seriously and brought in the Social Chapter of the Maastricht Treaty.

The Social Chapter

This piece of European Union Policy was not introduced into Britain because of opposition from the Conservative Government. The Conservatives believe the Social Chapter would give the unions back some of the power that they tried so hard to reduce.

The Social Chapter was introduced to protect workers' rights, for example working conditions, hours worked, paid leave and health and safety. There was also a plan to introduce European Works Councils (EWCS).

As there are about 15 million workers throughout Europe who are employed by multi-national companies, it was thought necessary to introduce a European system so that workers of the multi-nationals in different countries all had the same conditions.

Despite the Conservative Government's opposition to EWCS, many British firms had decided to set them up, as the *Herald* of 29 July 1996 reported.

A NEW CHAPTER AS FIRMS OPT IN

Scottish and Newcastle became the 17th UK-based company to ignore the government opt-out from the Social Chapter of the 1991 Maastricht Agreement and set up an EWC.

Another 25 companies are involved in negotiations with their unions to set up EWCs. Those who have already reached agreement include BT, ICI, Securicor, Pilkington Glass, Courtaulds and Zeneca.

Figure 3R   Source: Herald, *29 July 1996*

New Concerns for Trade Unions

British unions are more concerned now about saving jobs. There is also a move towards **single-union deals** where unions compete with each other to represent all workers in a factory. The new hi-tech industries prefer the single-union deals.

The 1990s has seen the introduction of the new **super union**. These are unions in certain industries which are the result of a number of unions **amalgamating** (joining together) to become a very large union. In 1993, three public sector unions – NUPE, COHSE and NALGO amalgamated to form UNISON, with 1.44 million members.

QUESTIONS

1 What rights does the Social Chapter give workers?

2 Why are the Conservatives against the Social Chapter?

3 What evidence is there that big companies see the benefit of trade unions?

4 What are super unions?

What are Trade Unions?

Modern day trade unions grew out of the formation of guilds and associations by workers in particular crafts. Early unions were usually associated with a particular craft, for example, barrel makers, blacksmiths, but as industry increasingly turned to factory production of goods, unskilled workers formed unions.

In their most basic aims, trade unions are about protecting workers' rights, conditions and pay. 150 years ago unions fought to protect people's jobs, to agree a guaranteed maximum working week and for the introduction of a national minimum wage. Little has changed today.

Trade unions after 1945

After the war ended in 1945 both major parties, Conservative and Labour, recognised that unions had a part to play in a modern, industrialised Britain.

However, both Labour and the Conservatives differed over what role and what power the unions should have in a modern industrialised society.

The setting up of the Welfare State and the maintenance of the **mixed economy**, an economic system in which government and private individuals run the economy, ensured that political and industrial activities became increasingly tied.

In the 1960s and the 1970s, governments tried to pursue income policies in order to secure wage restraint which they believed was necessary to reduce inflation and increase competitiveness. However, as a result of this, pay bargaining issues became wholly politicised and received the media attention they would not have attracted elsewhere in Europe.

QUESTIONS

1 Give two reasons why trade unions were first set up.
2 Why did Labour and the Conservatives differ over the role of unions?
3 What means did governments use in the 1960s and 1970s to secure wage restraint?

Why people join a trade union

People belong to trade unions for many different reasons, but these are considered to be the most important:

- to be able to negotiate the best possible working conditions such as paid holidays, health and safety, and higher rates of pay;
- to have job security, to consult over possible redundancies, thereby preventing unemployment;
- to prevent victimisation of workers through the idea 'unity is strength';
- to ensure benefits for workers who are not working through illness, sickness or old age;
- to provide legal backing and advice for members;
- to exert political power through sponsorship of MPs and the political levy.

Reasons for not joining a union

There are reasons also why people may not wish to join a trade union:

- many workers are well paid and do not see the need to join a union;
- some workers are in jobs where union activity is difficult to organise, e.g. shopworkers, homeworkers;
- many workers are employed in small family firms and can negotiate for themselves;
- many workers are self-employed;
- some employers refuse to recognise or deal with unions;
- people can get the benefits of union membership without actually joining.

88

Types of unions

There are four major types of trade union in Britain today. They cover all types of workers and employee disciplines.

Craft unions

These are the oldest and smallest unions. Many are skilled workers, e.g. musicians, cobblers and coopers. Membership is falling as many of these skills are dying out.

Industrial unions

Industrial unions had a very strong influence in the past and were mainly to be found in the manufacturing side of the economy, for example shipbuilding, heavy engineering. Their numbers have declined since the 1980s due to unemployment and a shift in the economy towards the tertiary sector.

General unions

These unions take in workers from a variety of jobs, which sometimes makes it difficult for workers to organise themselves, for example, Transport and General Workers' Union (TGWU).

White-collar unions

These unions represent office workers, professional people, government officials and clerical workers. They are the fastest-growing union sector, as these workers are currently threatened with redundancy, for example civil servants.

Look at Figure 3.1 and answer the questions which follow.

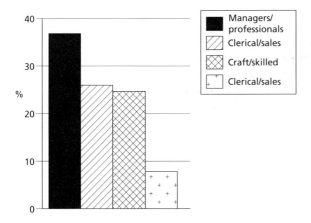

Figure 3.1   Union membership by job-type

Source: Labour Force Survey

QUESTIONS

1   What evidence is there that trade unions no longer represent the 'working class'?
2   What evidence is there that the structure of the British economy has changed?
3   In which area is union recruitment at its lowest? Why do you think this is the case?
4   Look at the reasons for and against joining a union. Overall, do you think the benefits of membership outweigh the disadvantages? Answer in detail.
5   Why might employers
    a Not want to deal with trade unions?
    b Want to negotiate with unions?
6   Which type of union is the fastest growing? Why is this the case?
7   Which type of union declined heavily in the 1980s? Why?
8   Why are general unions different from other types of unions?

Trade union activity

Trade unions negotiate pay and conditions for their members. This means that trade union representatives sit down with management and discuss changes to pay or conditions.

Usually the trade union representatives put forward one set of ideas and management puts forward another. Negotiations are most successful when both sides think they have won something for their side.

When negotiations between management and unions are unsuccessful and break down there are many actions a union can take to try to persuade employers to listen to them more seriously.

Strike action is only taken as a last resort.

The majority of pay settlements are arrived at as a result of what is known as **collective bargaining**. This involves unions negotiating with management on behalf of the union membership in an attempt to reach a settlement. Whenever a settlement cannot be reached, a union may wish to pursue the following types of action:

Restrictive practices

Overtime ban: workers refuse to work overtime and production is slowed down.

This costs the employers money. Employers use

overtime as it is cheaper than employing more full-time workers.

Workers also lose money through lost wages.

Go-slow: this is where workers slow down the production process which ultimately costs the employer money as less is produced in the normal day's work.

Work-to-rule: this is where workers adhere strictly to working at what they get paid for.

This might involve workers paying very close attention only to what they are paid for and not doing any 'extras' such as tidying up or taking jotters home to mark!

Token strike

These take place as a warning to employers and they also signal that the union is unhappy with the pay offer or conditions of employment. Token strikes usually last for a day.

Unofficial strike

This is where a strike takes place without union backing.

They were common in the past but are now very rare because government legislation means that unions can be sued in the courts if they fail to take adequate legal steps before calling a strike.

Unofficial strikes, it was argued, gave unions a bad image in the past.

Official strike

This is the most serious form of action and only takes place as a last resort.

A compulsory secret ballot must take place to comply with the law. Workers may receive strike pay.

Unions are reluctant to make strikes official as it costs them money through strike pay. Workers will also lose money when on strike.

An official strike is damaging to workers and employers, and, ultimately, the economy.

QUESTIONS

1 Explain the term **collective bargaining**.
2 What legal obligations must a union adhere to before an official strike is called?
3 How do strikes affect both employers and employees?
4 Why were unofficial strikes bad for unions in the past?
5 Explain what **restrictive practices** are, and how they might be damaging to both employers and employees.
6 How might industrial action affect the customers of private firms?
7 What might customers do if they cannot get the products from the firm affected by industrial action?
8 How might industrial action affect people who use public services, such as the NHS, social security or schools?
9 Suggest reasons why managements might want to prevent industrial action in:
   a **private firms**
   b **public services**.
10 Which group of union members do you think has more power:
   a **union members in private firms**
   b **union members in public services**.
   Give reasons for your answer.

Reductions in Trade Union Power

As far back as 1969 the Labour Government felt there was a need to curb the excessive power that many believed trade unions to have had.

In Place of Strife

A White Paper, *In Place of Strife*, was produced by the government. It was opposed by the trade unions, who provided the finance for the Labour Party, and by many Labour Party members. As a result, it failed to be implemented.

The Industrial Relations Act

The Conservative Government of 1970–74 introduced the Industrial Relations Act, which set up an Industrial Relations Court.

The Employment Secretary could apply to it if they felt that industrial action might be harmful to the economy.

The Trades Union Congress (TUC) threatened to call a General Strike of all British trade union members after five trade union members had been sentenced to jail for leading a strike in the London Docks.

They were hastily released on orders of the government and the General Strike was called off.

In 1974, the Conservative government called an election in the middle of a **Miners' Strike**. The government asked the voters, 'Who governs the country, the government or the miners?' The Conservatives lost the election.

The Labour Government 1974–79 repealed the Industrial Relations Act and introduced the Labour and Trade Disputes Act (1974) which strengthened the power of trade unions.

The Watershed

In 1976, the Labour Government agreed **The Social Contract** with the trade unions. In return for low wage increases (wage restraint), below the rate of inflation, the government promised to bring prices down. It also promised to invest more money in public services and cut unemployment.

By 1978, many trade union members felt that the government had not delivered on its promises.

Low-paid workers in the public services felt that they had suffered in particular from the Social Contract.

The winter of discontent was a popular description given to the widespread industrial action taken by various groups of public sector employees in the winter of 1978–79.

It proved to be a turning point in the post-war history of British trade unionism. Public hostility to the unions reached unprecedented levels as graveyard workers, nurses, firemen and refuse collectors all went on strike.

A popular view at the time was that unions were running the country and that they were destructive and too powerful.

The Conservatives won the election which followed the winter of discontent. They promised to reduce trade union power, and also to get rid of wage restraint.

They also promised a return to **free collective bargaining**, which meant that unions and employers would be able to negotiate wages and conditions free of government interference.

Many workers in more powerful trade unions deserted Labour and voted Conservative. These workers felt that free collective bargaining was better for them than wage restraint.

Many of these workers also benefited from Conservative policies in the 1980s. They were able to buy their council houses, get easier credit and buy shares in privatised companies.

Their own individual effort led to increases in their standards of living rather than the collective power of trade unions.

Other workers became unemployed. The government claimed that their firms had gone bankrupt because workers were getting too high wages and pricing themselves out of the market.

Changes in how many workers improved their standards of living, unemployment and the fear of unemployment reduced trade union membership and the power of trade unions.

Conservative Government legislation reduced it further.

91

QUESTIONS

1 How did governments seek to control trade union power between 1969 and 1979?
2 Why did many workers in more powerful trade unions desert Labour in 1979?
3 How did some of these workers benefit from Conservative policies in the 1980s?
4 How were other workers affected?
5 How did rising unemployment affect the power of trade unions?

Conservative Trade Union Legislation

The Conservatives, elected in 1979, sought to learn the lessons from previous failed attempts to introduce trade union laws.

Since 1979, six major pieces of legislation to regulate the affairs and activities of trade unions have been passed.

The Employment Act 1980

- New **closed shop** agreements (all workers must be members of a trade union) had to gain 80% support of the workforce in a secret ballot.
- Compensation would be made payable to employees who lost their jobs through refusing to join a union.
- Government funds to be given to unions to cover the cost of postal ballots for strike action and union elections.
- **Picketing** and **sympathy action** (industrial action in support of weaker groups of workers) was to be severely limited.

The Employment Act 1982

- Existing closed shop agreements had to be supported by at least 80% of the workforce in a secret ballot.
- Compensation was to be increased for those who lost jobs through refusal to join unions.
- Sympathy action, politically motivated strikes and industrial action against other non-unionised companies, were all made illegal.

The Trade Union Act 1984

- Strikes would only be lawful if a ballot of the workforce had been held, and had produced a majority in favour of industrial action.
- Trade unions were now obliged to conduct secret ballots at least once every 10 years to see if their members wished to maintain the **political levy** (financial support for political activities, including contributions to the Labour Party).
- Trade unions were further required to conduct a secret ballot for the election of senior officials, at least every five years.

The Employment Act 1988

- The closed shop was abolished.
- It was unlawful to dismiss an employee for refusal to join a trade union.
- It was unlawful for a trade union to take disciplinary action against any member who refused to participate in legal strike action.
- A Commission for the Rights of Trade Union Members (CROTUM) was set up to give legal support to individuals taking legal action against their unions.

The Employment Act 1990

- All **secondary** (industrial action against an employer not directly involved in the dispute) or sympathy action was made illegal.
- National unions became liable for damage caused by strikes, even if the strikes had not been called by them, unless they denounced the strikes.

The last piece of government legislation was introduced in 1992. The **Trade Union and Employment Rights Act 1992** (TURER) aims to extend the previous Acts or to reduce trade union power further in areas not already covered by the previous Acts.

The Trade Union and Employment Rights Act 1992 (TURER)

- This gave members of the public the right to sue unions if public services such as transport, education and refuse collection were affected by strike action.
- Money made available under the Act of 1984 for compulsory secret ballots was withdrawn.
- It became more difficult for unions to collect union dues directly from wages through the employer.
- It became legal to pay workers extra for not joining a union (i.e. it would be legal to pay trade unionists less than other workers).

Q UESTIONS

1 Under the following headings, explain how trade union power has been curtailed:
   a **Strikes**
   b **Sympathy action**
   c **Secondary picketing**
   d **Closed shop**
   e **Union discipline**
   f **Unions and the public**

continued . . .

92

QUESTIONS continued . . .

2 Which law sought to make unions more democratic? Explain in detail.

3 How might an employer's right to offer employment be affected by this trade union legislation?

4 How can trade unions be legally held accountable for their actions?

5 Find out as much as you can about the **closed shop**.

6 'Trade unions had too much power in the past. Now the balance has swung too far in the other direction.' Discuss in detail.

The Trades Union Congress

The Trades Union Congress (TUC) is a large umbrella organisation which co-ordinates the activities of 68 **affiliated unions** (unions which join the TUC and accept its rules).

It represents the interests of nearly 7 million members of trade unions in Britain.

The TUC has a structure which is outlined in Figure 3.2.

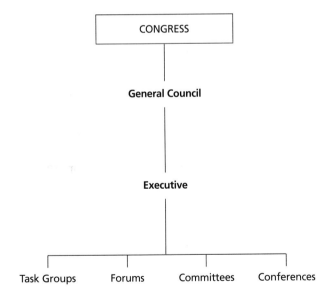

Figure 3.2 TUC structure

In Scotland, the Scottish Trades Union Congress (STUC) brings together all the Scottish trade unions in a similar way.

Most Scottish trade unions belong to the TUC and the STUC.

How Trade Unions are Organised

Trade union members

The ordinary trade union members are often referred to as the **rank and file**. They are the people who make up the membership. The **grass roots** is another term often used when talking about ordinary members.

Ordinary members play a very important role within the union. If a union decides to take industrial action then it is up to the grass roots to decide through a secret ballot whether or not industrial action might be taken.

The grass roots elect representatives who take decisions on their behalf. In the workplace these representatives are known as **shop stewards**.

Ordinary members also vote for a **national** or **executive committee** which is responsible for running the union.

Union members can also vote for delegates who can represent them at local/district level and at the annual conference.

The annual conference

This event is very important in the activities of a trade union.

It is held once a year and it decides the union's policies, which are usually voted on after motions from trade union **branches** have been debated and discussed.

The **delegates** (representatives) who attend the conference are elected by the ordinary union members.

The national executive

The executive or national committee is made up from full-time paid officials and elected union officials.

The head of the executive is known as the **General Secretary**. This person usually becomes the best-known union person as they represent the union to the media, e.g. Arthur Scargill of the National Union of Mineworkers (NUM).

The executive is responsible for the daily affairs of the union and they negotiate at national level over pay and conditions.

93

QUESTIONS

1 What two terms are used to describe ordinary union members?
2 Who represents the ordinary members on the factory floor?
3 What takes place at the annual conference?
4 Who is leader of the National Executive of a union? See if you can find the names of five famous union leaders and the unions they represent.

The shop steward

This is the person who ordinary members in the union identify with. They represent the union on the factory floor.

This person is elected by the rank and file. In large workplaces there may be a shop stewards' committee which brings together all the shop stewards representing large groups of workers. This is because representing the members would be too difficult for one person.

In certain workplaces there are several different unions, and sometimes a joint shop stewards' committee is formed.

The shop steward has four main functions as a union representative: representing, recruiting, communicating and informing.

The shop steward can keep the membership informed through regular meetings, and through handing out union literature.

There are many issues the shop steward will deal with: pay rises; health and safety; overtime allocation; victimisation; holiday and leave.

If a worker is disciplined by management, the shop steward will seek to defend them at a disciplinary hearing.

The shop steward is not a paid union official, and is allowed time off by the management to carry out union duties.

QUESTIONS

1 Who elects the shop steward?
2 Explain the terms shop steward committee and joint shop stewards' committee.
3 What type of issues does the shop steward deal with?
4 Explain why shop stewards need time off to do their duties.

Are Trade Unions in Decline?

Falling membership (see Figure 3.3), declining income and reduced power within the Labour Party have led some observers to suggest that Britain's trade unions are in terminal decline.

A number of reasons are generally held to be responsible for this trend:
- changing attitudes towards trade unions;
- changing employment structures;
- Conservative anti-union legislation since 1979;
- less influence within the Labour Party.

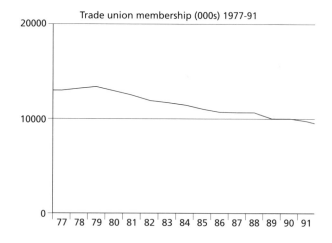

Figure 3.3   *Source:* Central Certification Office, *Department of Employment*

The biggest declines in trade union membership have been in the traditional industries such as engineering, shipbuilding, steel production and mining.

These industries have been declining and have been the major areas of job losses.

Figure 3.4

Source: Central Certification Office, *Department of Employment*

Q UESTIONS

1 What are the four main explanations for the decline in union power?
2 Study Figure 3.3 (Trade Union Membership 1977–91). In which years did trade unions lose most members?
3 In which types of industry did union membership suffer most?
4 What arguments could be put forward to suggest that British Conservative government legislation has not been the only cause of the decline in trade union power?

Conservatives, Trade Unions and the Economy

One of the Conservative policies in the 1980s was to reduce the number of regulations which employers had to obey, and reduce the amount of form filling.

The Conservatives argued that **red tape** and **bureaucracy** for employers stifled growth and cost jobs.

They also argued that trade unions gave Britain a bad image and frightened off foreign investment.

The Thatcher governments of the 1980s passed laws which took power out of the hands of the trade unions.

Margaret Thatcher had promised the British people that the 'days of beer and sandwiches at No 10 were over'. (Trade union leaders would no longer be able to influence the government.)

The Conservatives saw union power as a threat to the British economy and Mrs Thatcher even went so far as to refer to the unions as 'the enemy within'.

Conservatives argue that these laws have been successful in reducing trade union actions, especially strikes. However, trade union leaders also insist that rising unemployment and the fear that strike action could lead to unemployment has stopped workers taking industrial action.

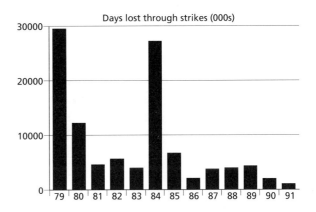

Figure 3.5   Annual days lost through strikes (thousands) 1977–1991

Source: Department of Employment

Changes in employment

An important feature of the British economy in the 1980s was an increase in the privatisation of nationalised industries, e.g. coal, gas and British Airways.

In order to make these industries profitable for shareholders, massive job cuts were made.

There was a corresponding decline in the manufacturing base which had traditionally been a trade union stronghold.

Certain parts of Britain were disproportionately affected by the loss of manufacturing jobs, for example Scotland, North-east England, North-west England and South Wales.

Figure 3.6 shows that union membership is still strongest in the North and weakest in the South, where the service industries, banking, insurance, finance, catering and so on, are mainly to be found. The service industries tend to be less unionised.

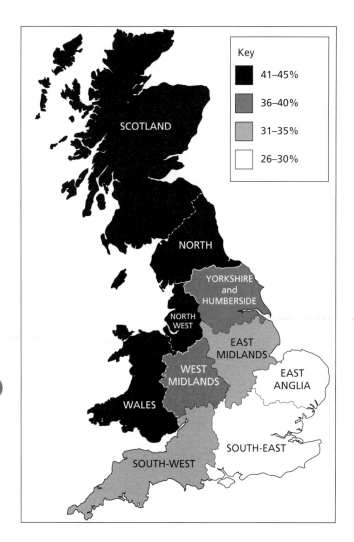

Key

■	41–45%
▨	36–40%
▨	31–35%
□	26–30%

SCOTLAND

NORTH

YORKSHIRE and HUMBERSIDE

NORTH WEST

EAST MIDLANDS

WEST MIDLANDS

EAST ANGLIA

WALES

SOUTH-EAST

SOUTH-WEST

Figure 3.6   Percentage of employees in trade union/staff associations, by region, 1992

Source: GMB study based on Labour Force Survey figures, 1992

Q UESTIONS

1 Why did the Conservatives want to weaken the power of the trade unions?
2 What evidence is there that Margaret Thatcher was personally hostile to trade unions?
3 What evidence is there in Figure 3.5 which would suggest the government had widespread public support for its actions?
4 What evidence is there in Figure 3.5 to suggest that trade union action was not totally subdued in the 1980s? Can you suggest a reason?
5 What is the **service sector**? Give examples.
6 What evidence in Figure 3.6 suggests union membership is weakest in the South-east and East Anglia?

The Trade Union Movement and the Labour Party

Unlike Socialist or Social Democratic parties in Europe, the Labour Party was originally formed by the trades unions to be the voice of, and represent, 'labour' (the workers) in Parliament.

Trade unions have also been the main source of finance for the Labour Party through the political levy and the sponsorship of Labour MPs in Parliament.

'He who pays the piper calls the tune'

Trade unions exercised a **bloc vote** at Labour Party Conferences, in elections for the Labour Party leader and in selecting candidates for local and national elections.

The bloc vote allowed trade unions to count each member of the union, who paid the political levy, as a vote. Trade unions with big memberships had more power.

The TGWU, for instance, had 1.75 million votes.

This relationship was attacked by Conservative governments who were anxious to portray Labour as undemocratic and under the control of the unions.

Neil Kinnock then began to reform the Labour Party to reduce the influence of the trade unions.

The Miners' Strike 1984–85 further strained the Labour/trade union relationship when the Labour leader, Neil Kinnock was accused of not giving support to the miners.

In 1992, John Smith became leader of the Labour Party, and continued the process of internal reform begun by Neil Kinnock.

In 1993, the Labour Party Conference passed the **OMOV** motion (One Member, One Vote), curtailing the unions' bloc vote and powers to select Labour candidates.

Tony Blair has continued this process, in distancing the Labour Party still further from the trade unions.

He has also gone on a massive individual membership recruitment drive to attract dues-paying members who will be an alternative source of finance for the Labour Party.

QUESTIONS

1 Why was the Labour Party set up?
2 Who provides most of its finance?
3 How could trade unions justify the bloc vote?
4 What criticisms did the Conservatives make of trade union power within the Labour Party?
5 How have Labour leaders distanced themselves, and the Labour Party sought to distance itself, from the trade unions?

New Labour and the Trade Unions

The September 1995 TUC annual conference was very important for the future of the Labour movement.

Tony Blair outlined his plans to distance the Labour Party further from the unions.

Tony Blair sees the unions in a very different light from Labour leaders in the past who saw them as Labour's natural allies.

He wants the unions to concentrate on trade union issues such as negotiating pay and working conditions in the workplace.

Trade-union-sponsored MPs

Trade unions still continue to sponsor MPs. This means that they contribute money to help in the Labour candidate's election campaign.

Once elected, trade unions support the MP's activities in Parliament by contributing to the cost of research assistants or publicity.

MPs are expected to support the policies of the trade union. If they do not they may lose the trade union's sponsorship.

One New Labour proposal is to remove the rights of trade unions to sponsor individual MPs. Instead, all trade union financial help to the Labour Party would come under the control of the Labour Party leadership.

This is resisted by trade unions who say that policies decided by the union's membership are not necessarily the policies of the Labour Party leadership.

Union	Number of sponsored MPs
TGWU	38
GMB	17
AEU	13
MSF	13
NUM	13
NUPE	12
RMT	12
USDAW	9
COHSE	6
GMPU	5
EEPTU	3
NCU	3
TSSA	2
UCW	2
ASLEF	1
NACODS	1
Total	150

Figure 3.7 Union-sponsored MPs elected at the 1992 general election. In July 1993, NUPE and COHSE combined with NALGO to form UNISON.

Source: Labour Research

QUESTIONS

1 What does Tony Blair see as the main role of trade unions?
2 Why do unions sponsor MPs?
3 What does this help MPs do?
4 What do unions expect in return?
5 What evidence is there in Figure 3.7 that unions still exercise influence on the Labour Party?
6 Why do trade unions oppose New Labour's proposals on sponsorship?

Changes in the trade union movement

Since the 1980s trade unions have been very active in recruiting members from the white collar sectors.

These workers have in the past felt safe from the threat of unemployment.

Many now feel they are as much at risk as those in the manufacturing sector who lost their jobs.

'The issue of the 1980s is that the middle classes are getting the treatment traditionally meted out to the working class . . . In that sense we are all working class now.'

Figure 3.8   John Monks, General Secretary of the TUC

Trade unions have also put much greater efforts into recruiting low-paid workers in **difficult to organise** sectors, such as shops and fast-food outlets.

Most trade unions support the introduction of a national minimum wage of £4.26 per hour.

Britain is the only country in Europe, apart from Ireland, that does not have some form of minimum wage protection.

QUESTIONS

1 Why are trade unions now being more successful in recruiting white-collar workers?
2 '. . . In that sense we are all working class now.' Explain what John Monks means in your own words.
3 Why might some workplaces be 'difficult to organise'?
4 Why is the campaign for a minimum wage important to:
   a **low-paid workers?**
   b **trade unions?**

The World of Work in the 1990s

Low pay, poor working conditions and the national minimum wage

Low pay is a misery for the millions of people who have to live without enough money.

£100 million a year is paid in Family Credit to low-paid workers to help them meet their financial needs.

Critics of low pay say this is a subsidy for the bad employers, a tax on good employers and the rest of the community.

Total annual expenditure on benefit paid to those in work is now nearly £2.4 billion. This figure has increased 100% since 1991.

Reasons for this increase are:
- employers are getting rid of full-time workers and sharing jobs between a larger pool of part-time staff;
- as a result staff have to subsidise their low pay through state benefits, e.g. Family Credit;
- many part-timers who earn less than £58 per week do not pay National Insurance, saving the employer from having to make contributions.

This type of employment practice is spreading to all forms of employment, in particular retail and catering.

Factfile on low pay and poor working conditions

Gateway Foodmarkets, with 25,000 staff, has embarked on an hour and pay-cutting exercise.

Some full-time workers on 39 hours per week have now been reduced to 16 hours. Some now have to work two shifts a day, without tea breaks.

Burtons has reduced the hours of the majority of its full-time workers from 39 to 15. In both cases staff were offered redundancy, but chose instead to work part-time.

Women particularly have been hit hardest. Between 1980–92 the number who did not pay National Insurance contributions (NIC) trebled. There are now 3 million women who earn below the NIC limit.

Zero hours is the new system which many workers now face. These workers are on constant standby, without any guarantee of work.

However, there has been the growth in the amount of workers who have part-time jobs.

It was the famous Conservative, Sir Winston Churchill, who first introduced minimum wage legislation, when he was a Liberal MP.

Wages councils were set up to agree guaranteed minimum wages for the workers in the poorest paid jobs.

The present Conservative government is firmly opposed to any plans to introduce a national minimum wage.

It believes the cost of setting a minimum hourly rate for workers will result in higher unemployment, because firms will pay fewer staff more, rather than add to their wage bill.

Arguments for and against a national minimum wage

For

- Higher wages will lead to higher Income Tax and National Insurance receipts to the government.
- There will be savings on state benefits as people would come off Family Credit and Income Support.
- It is a fair way to distribute income and reduce the inequality gap.
- It is morally correct to pay a 'decent' wage and evidence shows where wages are low there is a high turnover of staff.
- Bad employers will not be subsidised by good employers.
- 'Every other country in Europe, bar Ireland, has minimum wage protection, and the USA is now uprating its minimum wage.'

Tony Blair, when Shadow Employment Secretary

Against

- It will cost employers more in wages and they might have to cut jobs, leading to higher unemployment.
- British employers will not be able to compete with low-wage firms in the Pacific Rim.
- Other workers will demand higher wages to 'maintain the differential'.
- Higher wage costs will pass to the customer, causing inflation.
- It goes against the spirit of the 'free market'. Workers are 'paid the rate for the job'.
- 'There can be no conceivable justification for a policy which on its own wrecks our economy and devastates job prospects.'

Michael Howard, Employment Secretary

Figure 3.9 Arguments for and against a minimum wage

In 1986, the Conservative government abolished the wages councils for under-21s.

All wages councils were finally abolished in 1993. The government argued that young people would have a better chance of getting a job if employers were not forced to pay a set rate.

Q UESTIONS

1 What is the government's main argument against a minimum wage?
2 Look at the following statements. Write each one out and put **For** or **Against** the minimum wage.
  a **Inflation will increase**
  b **Higher taxes will more than offset a higher national wage bill**
  c **A minimum wage will help achieve a fairer distribution of income**
  d **A minimum will put an unnecessary burden on employers**
  e **Youth unemployment is already high and this will not help it**
  f **A national minimum wage would have little effect on those most in need – the unemployed.**
3 Overall, do you feel the advantages of a minimum wage are greater than the disadvantages? Give reasons for your answer.

Union action on low pay

Look at Figures 3.10, 3.11, 3.12 and answer the questions which follow.

Fast-food chain Burger King today contacted managers in its 350 restaurants to ensure there were no further cases of part-time staff being paid so-called 'slave' wages.

The move follows angry attacks from unions after a student revealed he was paid less than £1 for a five-hour shift at Bishopbriggs, Glasgow.

The row intensified yesterday, with the TUC denouncing the company's slave-labour practices.

TUC General Secretary John Monks said it was scandalous that anyone should have to work for such low wages.

No company should be allowed to get away with poverty pay, he said, but the government was happy to let employers treat workers as badly as they liked. He added that was the logical result of its hire-and-fire approach to the labour market.

Meanwhile, Asda supermarket workers will protest at the company's AGM today as part of their campaign for a minimum wage of at least £4 an hour.

At the Leeds meeting, employee shareholders, who are members of the GMB union, will be negotiating an increase for check-out staff who earn £3.67 an hour.

Figure 3.10 *Source: Herald, 20 September 1995*

The Transport and General Workers' Union set aside a £1m 'war chest' as part of a campaign to win a minimum wage of at least £4 an hour for its members.

The union estimates that 300,000 of its members – mainly in the catering, clothing, textile, agriculture and retail industries – earn below £4 an hour.

Over the weekend, the General Municipal and Boilermakers (GMB) launched its campaign which will involve demands for a minimum 'of over £4 an hour from all employers'.

Those high on the GMB target list include clothing companies such as Claremont Garments, Dewhursts and the Baird Group, all currently paying £2.86 an hour, the Asda supermarket group, which pays check-out staff £3.67 an hour, and those local authorities whose rates still fall below £4 an hour.

Figure 3.11   *Source: Herald, 5 September 1995*

The plight of low-paid workers in Scotland, most of whom are women, will form the central theme of the 1995 STUC women's conference in Perth next week.

The conference will hear motions that will reinforce demands for a national minimum wage.

Chairwoman Helen Stevens said: 'Women workers tend to feel the problem of poverty pay first because they are in the sort of areas in which employment is part-time or insecure, and companies take advantage.'

Figure 3.12   *Source: Herald, 11 November 1995*

Q UESTIONS

1 List the trade union actions on low pay.
2 Why might Burger King pay attention to bad publicity?
3 Why might low pay be 'the central theme of the 1995 STUC women's conference'?
4 Why is the campaign against low pay important to the Transport and General Workers' Union?
5 What indication is there that the TGWU regards that winning success will be a hard fight?
6 Who are the 'worst employers' targeted by the GMB?

Trade Unions and Europe

Trade unions have experienced a reduction in their influence on government decisions during the period of Conservative government.

In Germany, however, trade union views are taken seriously whichever political party is in power.

The relative strength of British trade unions in the past led them to adopt a superior attitude to their colleagues in Europe.

Conservative legislation not only weakened British trade unions, but led to British workers having fewer rights than most workers in the European Community (EC).

British trade unions now co-operate more closely with their Euro counterparts.

British trade unions were also suspicious of the European Union (EU).

All this changed, however, when Jacques Delors, the President of the European Commission, addressed the 1988 TUC Conference.

Under Delors, the European Commission had expressed fears that, when trade barriers came down in January 1993 (Single European Act), member states would seek to deprive their workers of basic entitlements.

Delors stated that the Euro-Commission would introduce the **European Social Chapter** to avoid this happening.

The Social Chapter of the Maastricht Treaty

This is also known as the Social Charter and is a guarantee of minimum working conditions such as hours worked, paid leave and health and safety.

The British government opposed the Social Chapter on the grounds that it would cost jobs and put unnecessary burdens on employers.

The government also believed that introducing the Social Chapter would 'undo all the good work they had done' reducing the power of trade unions.

Many trade unions supported the Social Chapter as a means of improving workers' rights in the face of a hostile Conservative government and with a Labour government nowhere in sight.

Transnational co-operation

It was initially feared that when trade barriers came down in January 1993, transnational corporations would shift their production to those member states where costs and wages were lower.

This would lead to **social dumping**.

An example of this is when Hoover closed its plant in France and moved production to Scotland. It was clear that workers in the same companies, but operating in different European countries, would have to co-operate closely to prevent workers in one country losing out to their counterparts in another country.

As a result, the TUC is in favour of introducing European Works Councils (EWCs) into the British subsidiaries of Euro multi-nationals as set out in the Social Chapter.

European Works Councils

There are about 15 million workers in Europe employed by multi-nationals which will be affected by the EU directive on EWCs.

By September 1996, major companies such as Ford, BP, Barclays Bank and Sony must set up a system so that workers can be consulted on issues which will affect them.

This will allow them to compare pay and conditions and campaign on issues which affect the whole European workforce.

The Conservative government opposes these EWCs and the opt-out clauses negotiated in the Maastricht Treaty mean multi-nationals do not have to allow EWCs in Britain. However, many companies have already signed EWC agreements with trade unions.

QUESTIONS

1 How does the British government's attitude to trade unions differ from that in Germany?
2 What fears did the Euro-Commission express about the Single European Act?
3 How do trade unions view the Social Chapter?
4 Why does the British government oppose it?

New Concerns for Trade Unions

British trade unions have copied the German example by widening their responsibilities and facilities for members. They have managed to shake off their old-fashioned strike-bound image in the interests of a better PR image.

The more media-conscious unions stress their role in improving health and safety conditions.

Trade union efforts now focus on the protection of jobs and benefits as well as traditional collective bargaining.

The growing trend for **single-union deals** since the 1980s has encouraged unions to compete with each other for employers and employees, especially in the new hi-tech industries.

Unions now compete in 'beauty contests' hoping that prospective employers will sign them up as their union will offer the best deal. Japanese investors have been particularly keen on this approach.

The modern working environment is increasingly **structured and privatised** operating in a **service**-dominated economy.

Thus unions need to target highly skilled and/or white-collar workers resistant to membership on one hand and casual low paid workers on the other.

Another trend in the late 1990s has been the creation of new **super unions**. The smaller unions may find themselves playing second fiddle to these super unions.

In 1993, three public sector unions, NUPE, COHSE and NALGO amalgamated to form **UNISON** with 1.44 million members. It is now the biggest union and has a two-thirds female membership.

QUESTIONS

1 What 'new issues' are trade unions tackling according to Figure 3.13. (See page 102.)
2 What type of workers do trade unions now try to recruit?
3 Explain what single-union deals are and why many employers would want them.
4 Give an example of a super union and explain why female workers are important to it.
5 Explain why modern trade unions have to compete with each other.

Figure 3.13   Trade Union promotional material

four

Employment/Unemployment

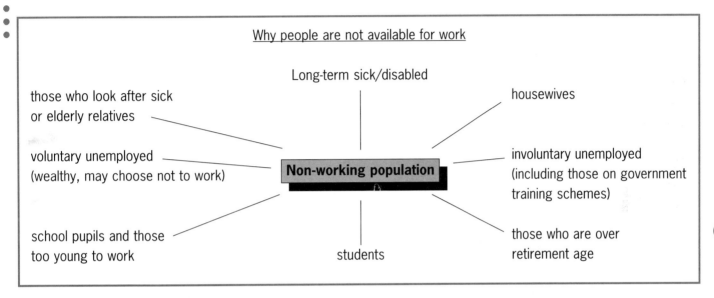

Why people are not available for work

Long-term sick/disabled

those who look after sick or elderly relatives

housewives

voluntary unemployed (wealthy, may choose not to work)

Non-working population

involuntary unemployed (including those on government training schemes)

school pupils and those too young to work

students

those who are over retirement age

Figure 4A   Reasons why people are unavailable for work

The UK's population is just over 58 million, and out of this, the working population us just over 28 million. So just over half the population is not available for work (see Figure 4A).

The Labour Force

It is useful to know the number of workers in the different age groups of the population, to see where there is a growth or fall in the recorded numbers. The number of workers in the under-24 age group fell by almost 2 million between 1986 and 1996, due to the fall in the UK's birth rate and the amount of youngsters going on to further education.

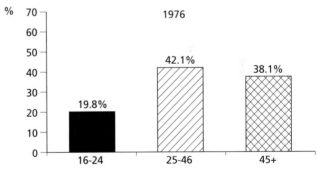

Figure 4B   The number of workers in the population in 1976

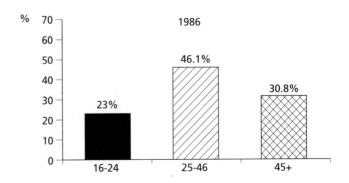

Figure 4C   The number of workers in the population in 1986

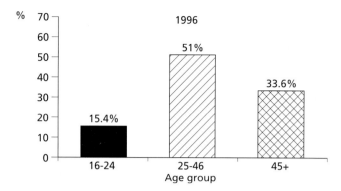

Figure 4D The number of workers in the population in 1996

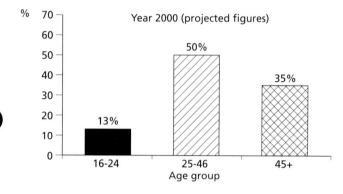

Figure 4E The projected number of workers in the year 2000

104

QUESTIONS

1 Give five reasons why people are not available for work.
2 Compare the age group tables (Figures 4B to 4D) and draw three new bar charts.
  a One bar chart should show 16–24-year-olds in 1976, 1986 and 1996.
  b One bar chart should show 26–46-year olds in 1976, 1986 and 1996.
  c One bar chart should show over-45-year-olds in 1976, 1986 and 1996.
3 Write a sentence for each bar chart saying what is happening to the percentage of each group.

Who are the unemployed?

The **unemployed** are those people who do not have a job. Most of the unemployed register for work, i.e. 'sign on the buroo', at the employment centres run by the government. They include those people:
• out of work and available to work;
• registered as unemployed;
• receiving unemployment benefit.
Unemployment has been a big problem in Britain since the 1970s. It leads to poverty and it is on the increase, especially long-term unemployment.

Measuring unemployment is not easy, and since 1980 there have been 30 changes to the method used to calculate it. The method used today is the **claimant count**, i.e. the number of people claiming unemployment benefit as a percentage of the working population. For example, at present the number of unemployed is under 3 million. If we use the figure of 3 million as being the figure used by the government then:

$$\frac{3\text{ million}}{28\text{ million}} \times 100 = 10.7\%$$

The unemployment rate is 10.7% (remember the figures are rounded to the nearest million, to make it easier to work out).

The UK's figures can be broken down to get an unemployment rate for Scotland. (Figure 4F.)

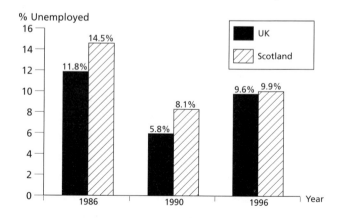

Figure 4F The unemployed in UK and Scotland (% of working population unemployed)

Groups of people not included in government unemployment figures include:
- part-time workers;
- people under 18 years old;
- people who gave up their jobs (banned from signing on for 26 weeks).

Different ways of calculating unemployment are used by other groups. The level of unemployment is higher than the government figures suggest. One such group is the Labour Force Survey which uses its own measurement of unemployment. It works out the number of people who haven't worked for pay in the previous week, who want to work, and who have looked for a job during the last month. Some people claim that this is a better way to work out the figures.

The difference between the government unemployment figures and those of the Labour Force Survey are shown in Figure 4G.

SCOTTISH UNEMPLOYMENT

Year	Labour Force Survey rate	Claimant rate
1993	10.8%	9.8%
1994	10.1%	9.3%

Figure 4G

QUESTIONS

1 How is the population likely to continue to change by 2000?
2 Why is unemployment a problem?
3 Look at the table of unemployment in the UK and Scotland (Figure 4F).
  a **What has happened to the number of unemployed in the UK between 1986 and 1996?**
  b **What has happened to the number of unemployed in Scotland between 1986 and 1996?**
4 Which people do not count as unemployed?
5 Give one reason why the government doesn't use the Labour Force Survey figures.

Changing patterns of employment

Since the 1980s, there have been some major changes in the employment situation in the UK, apart from the increase in unemployment. There has been:
- a large reduction in the number of people working in primary and secondary type jobs;
- a rise in the number of people working in tertiary industries;
- an increase in the number of people working part-time, temporary or on short-term contracts.

Primary industries are those which are involved in producing raw materials, for example, farming, mining, oil industries and the fishing industry.

105

Figure 4H   Empty dry docks for ship-building. Glasgow used to be famous for this

Secondary industries are those in which goods are made from the raw materials or from other goods, for example, car manufacturers, shoes, refrigeration, clothing and many others.

Tertiary industries do not produce goods, but are involved in providing a service, e.g. banking, insurance, civil servants, teachers, hotel workers and hairdressers.

Over the period 1971–1994 there have been some quite dramatic changes in British industry:

- an increase of 26% in the number of working women. Now women amount to almost 50% of all employees;
- a fall of 15% in the number of people working in manufacturing;
- a rise of 18.5% in the number of people working in providing services.

Growth in these industries in Scotland has meant a bigger increase in the number of jobs, 2% more than in the growth of jobs in the UK as a whole, and in 1.8% more over the last ten years or so.

It is in the tertiary or **service sector** where the biggest growth in jobs has been, however some secondary industries are growing, especially in micro-technology manufacturing, which includes computers, mobile phones, cable and satellite TV. These industries employ mostly women who are part-time, unskilled and low paid.

Types of unemployment

As unemployment means being out of work it would seem that everyone without a job faces the same problems. However, this is not the case. There are different types of unemployment and each of these has a different effect on the person concerned.

Structural unemployment

This happens when the country does not require that type of worker any more, for example, the closure of the British Steel factory at Ravenscraig in Motherwell, Lanarkshire. The UK does not want to make as much steel as it did in the past. The steel workers will find it hard to find another job which uses the skills learnt at British Steel. It is likely that this type of worker will not find another job in their area. They are also likely to become one of the **long-term** unemployed.

Technological unemployment

This occurs when machinery and new technology replace people in doing a job. This has happened in the newspaper industry with thousands of newspaper workers losing their jobs. It is likely that the people who lose these jobs will also become part of the long-term unemployed.

Cyclical, frictional and seasonal unemployment

These are other types of unemployment. Workers are usually unemployed for short lengths of time and have a good chance of finding another job quite quickly.

Effects of unemployment

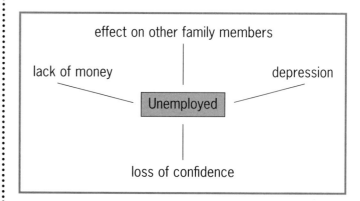

Figure 4I   The effects of unemployment on the unemployed

Figure 4J   Signing on

The effects of any type of unemployment can be quite difficult on the unemployed and their family. Long-term unemployment has a much greater effect on the person who is unemployed, their family and their chance of getting another job.

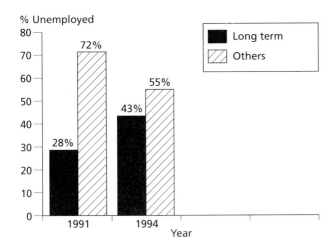

Figure 4K   Long-term unemployed as a proportion of total unemployed 1991 and 1994

QUESTIONS

1 What kind of jobs are there in primary industries?
2 What kind of jobs are there in secondary industries?
3 What kind of jobs are there in tertiary industries?
4 What has happened to the number of women working since 1971?
5 What has happened to the number of people working in manufacturing since 1971?
6 What has happened to the number of people working in services since 1971?
7 What type of jobs are lost because of structural unemployment?
8 What type of jobs are lost because of technological unemployment?
9 What type of jobs are lost because of cyclical unemployment?
10 What are some of the effects of unemployment on a person?

New Technology

New technology refers to the new machines and household appliances which make work easier and quicker to do, in the workplace and at home. People can now use a computer to buy goods from home, or use personal computers at home and at work.

Bar codes make life easier at cash desks. They are much quicker and tell the manager how much of a product is left in the shop.

Cash dispensers outside banks means that customers can use some bank facilities 24 hours a day and at the weekend.

Microwave ovens make cooking much easier.

Cable TV and telephone companies provide a large number of TV channels and cheap phone calls.

Most hospitals use new technology in the treatment of illness. Computers are used to link major hospitals to small ones on islands or in the highlands.

Figure 4L highlights the advantages and disadvantages of new technology.

Pros	Cons
More goods produced.	Unemployment as machines take over jobs.
Cheaper goods.	
Better quality.	Workers require training for new machines.
Helps in the home.	
Helpful in medical centres/hospitals.	Stress caused by working too fast on new machinery.
Boring/repetitive jobs done by robots.	Some jobs disappear altogether.
Days lost to strike/ ill health not a problem.	Trade unions affected by drop in members.
Will create some jobs.	
Easier for communicating with others.	

Figure 4L   Pros and cons of new technology

QUESTION

1 Write two short paragraphs, one about the good things about new technology, and one about the bad things.

New Technology Job Creation in Scotland

Scotland has benefited from the new technology because a lot of foreign companies are building factories there. For example:

- IBM at Greenock;
- Digital at Ayr;
- BSB Sky at Dunfermline;
- Hughes Unisys at Livingstone;
- Motorola at East Kilbride.

During 1995 **Locate in Scotland** managed to attract over 12000 jobs to Scotland by persuading Japanese and American companies to locate there. The biggest success was attracting Chunghwa Picture Tube Factory to Lanarkshire.

KOREAN JOBS BOOST

Today Scottish Secretary, Michael Forsyth, will announce the arrival of a Korean company to Scotland, bringing 200 jobs.

Locate in Scotland hope that more jobs will follow as Korean firms seek European bases and Scotland already has a workforce who are skilled and available.

Mr Forsyth has recently been on a sales drive to the Far East and has emphasised the flexibility of the Scottish workers in the countries he visited.

On his sales drive, Mr Forsyth has already made two successes in Japan which will lead to a £5 million expansion in Cumbernauld by Terma and a £6.5 million factory at Dunfermline by the Kohdensha Company.

Figure 4M   *Source: Herald, 29 May 1996, abridged*

QUESTIONS

1 What type of firms have been set up in Scotland?
2 Look at the Korean jobs boost article in Figure 4M. What benefits might Korean firms bring to Scotland?

Case Study

The Office

New technology has completely changed office work. Even the smallest office has the ability to be very efficient and to communicate worldwide.

Word processors Typewriters have been replaced by word processors which can alter mistakes very easily. They can print hundreds of letters to different people simply by changing the names. A great deal of time and effort is saved.

Computers Files and information are now kept on computers or discs. Saves space and time. No need for filing cabinets or for staff to take up as much time filing and retrieving information.

Fax Allows copies of documents to be sent to other areas of the country/world instantly.

Call Connect Systems Modern phone network system which can 'queue' calls, divert calls and tell you when someone else is trying to get through to you.

Figure 4N   The modern office

Video Conferencing Businessmen wanting to have face-to-face meetings no longer have to travel. This allows them to see and speak to each other while seeing what their reactions and facial expressions are.

Internet/Teletext Instant access to large amounts of current information using the television and phone network. Can be used for passing information, advertising or specialised data.

The North–South Divide

The UK can be divided into separate areas when looking at unemployment:
- **The North:** Scotland, the North of England and Northern Ireland;
- **The South:** English Midlands and South-east England.

Scotland had a rate of unemployment of 9.9% in 1994. East Anglia, in the South-east of England, had a rate of 7.4%.

The low levels of unemployment in the South-east of England and the high levels in other parts of the country have led people to think that a North–South divide really does exist.

In Glasgow, for example, some areas have very large rates of unemployment, as Figure 4O highlights.

A JOB OASIS

In the great City of Glasgow there are areas of severe poverty, areas of very high unemployment, and no-go areas of scarred tenements where some people have given up hope. These areas exist everywhere, but in Glasgow they are concentrated in seven areas: Govan, Easterhouse, Castlemilk, Drumchapel, Glasgow North, Pollok and the Gorbals. This area covers 44% of Glasgow's total population.

Figure 4O The Herald Essay by Sir Graham Hills
Source: Herald, 27 July 1996

Recently, the North–South divide area has been questioned because of rising unemployment in the Midlands and the South-east which have been hit quite badly. Some other facts have to be looked at before it can be said that the North–South divide no longer exists.

Region	1990	1994	1996
North	8.6	11.7	10.3
Yorkshire & Humberside	6.8	9.8	8.6
East Midlands	5.8	8.3	7.4
East Anglia	3.8	7.4	6.3
South-east	3.9	9.6	7.8
South-west	4.5	7.5	7.1
West Midlands	5.9	9.9	8.1
North-west	7.5	10.2	8.4
Wales	6.6	9.4	8.3
Scotland	8.0	9.9	7.8
Northern Ireland	13.7	11.5	11.5

Figure 4P Regional unemployment 1990–96
Source: Social Trends and the Herald, June 1996

- All of the UK's regions had an increase in the level of unemployment from 1990 to 1994, although (as Figure 4P shows) the South-east and the Midlands increases were higher than others.
- The fall in unemployment from 1994 to 1996 was experienced by all regions, and the South-east had an above average fall.
- Part of the fall in unemployment is due to a fall in the population, rather than more jobs being available.
- Many of the new jobs are part-time, poorly paid and are aimed at women.

The newspaper articles in Figure 4Q and 4R give two views of the unemployment situation in June 1996.

In the same report the Labour Party also criticised the Conservatives.

JOBLESS TOTAL LOWEST FOR FIVE YEARS

Scottish Industry Minister George Kynoch described the fall in the number of jobless in Scotland by 500 as encouraging and said things look good for Scotland.

SNP spokeswoman, Mrs Anne McNair, responded by saying that the Scottish unemployment, which was above the UK average for 4½ years, is now below it. Scotland has been falling behind the rest of the UK for the last seven months.

Figure 4Q Source: Herald, 13 June 1996, abridged

John McFall, Labour's spokesman, said that a fall of 500 was miserable. The loss of 300 jobs at British Aerospace of Prestwick shows that job prospects in Scotland were not good.

Figure 4R Source: Herald, 13 June 1996

Figure 4S Source: Herald, 13 June 1996, abridged

Some MPs claim that Scotland will not have an increase in the number of jobs over the next 11 years, taking expected jobs and expected job losses into account. East Anglia expects an increase in jobs of 13%, the South-west will have an increase of 10%, East Midlands 9% and South-east 7%.

QUESTIONS

1 What areas are in the 'north' and what areas are in the 'south'?
2 What areas of Glasgow have very high areas of unemployment?
3 According to the author of the article in Figure 4O, how does unemployment affect people living in these areas?
4 Why have some people said that some areas of the 'south' are as bad as the 'north'?
5 Why might some of the new jobs being created not help men who are out of work?
6 What criticisms does Anne McNair make of George Kynoch's statement?
7 How does John McFall criticise George Kynoch's statement?
8 Look at Figure 4S. Say if you think the 'north–south divide' is still true.

Women and Work

The law of the UK now makes it illegal to **discriminate** against women in employment.

Two of the laws have been introduced since 1970. They have been very important in making sure that employers treat women equally at work:
- **Equal Pay Act 1970**
- **Sex Discrimination Act 1975**

Women, however, are still not treated equally at work. This happens because women are likely to have jobs in industries where part-time working is normal, pay is low and conditions are poor.

110

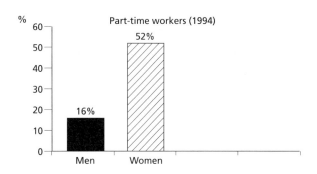

Figure 4W   Part-time workers (1994)

Figures 4U, 4V and 4W show the percentage of men and women in employment, in the population and in part-time work in 1994.

One reason why so many women work in part-time jobs is because their husbands are unemployed. The woman then becomes the **breadwinner**.

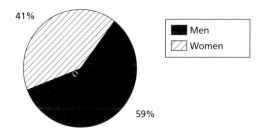

Figure 4X   Unemployment rates (% of total unemployed)

Figure 4X shows that 59% of the total unemployed are men, i.e. 11.4% of the 1994 national unemployment figure.

REASONS FOR NOT SEEKING WORK

	Men	Women
Waiting for result of job application	1%	1%
Student	16%	7%
Looking after family/home	6%	53%
Temporarily sick/disabled	5%	8%
Long-term sick/disabled	23%	3%
Believes no job available	22%	9%
Not yet started looking	7%	7%
Other reasons	20%	13%

Figure 4Y   *Source: Low Pay Unit*

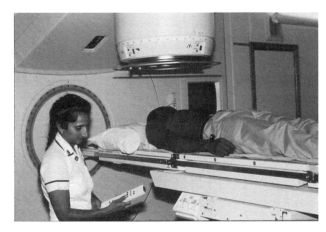

Figure 4T   Women at work

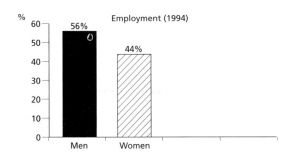

Figure 4U   Employment (1994)

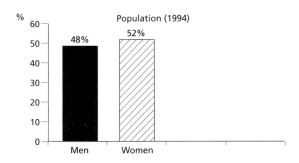

Figure 4V   Population (1994)

111

For women the national unemployment rate was 7.2%, or as it shows in Figure 4FF, 41% of the total unemployed. The figures are a little misleading because many women do not want to work as they have young children, so they are not included in the unemployment figures.

Other reasons for not seeking work are set out in Figure 4Y.

Different problems facing women at work are the **types of job** that they are working in and their **promotion prospects** in these. As women make up 52% of the UK's population it could be expected that they can be found in all jobs and at all levels of responsibility in these jobs. This is not the case; research found the following facts about women at work:

- men still earn more than women in terms of average wage;
- more women than men are in poorly paid and **low status** jobs;
- girls do better than boys in school exams, but fewer girls go to university;
- women make up 69% of school teachers but only 38.5% of headteachers;
- only 10% of women are MPs;
- 54% of solicitors qualifying in Scotland in 1994 were women, but Scotland only has one female judge.

In some jobs there are a lot more women than men. Figure 4Z gives examples.

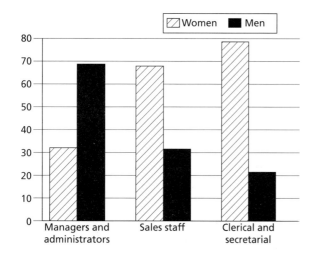

Figure 4Z   Occupational status by gender

QUESTIONS

1 Which two laws have been passed making it illegal to discriminate against women?
2 Look at Figures 4U, 4V and 4W. Give one reason why women might not have equality with men.
3 List the main reasons why women don't work.
4 Look at Figure 4Z. What does it tell you about the types of jobs women do?

Race and Employment

The UK is now a **multi-racial society**. Laws have been introduced over a period of time to try to make sure that all races are treated equally in employment, as well as in British society as a whole. But a close look at the levels of unemployment shows that equality does not really exist.

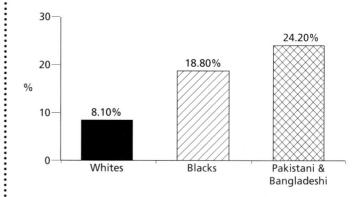

Figure 4AA   Unemployment rates by race (1995)

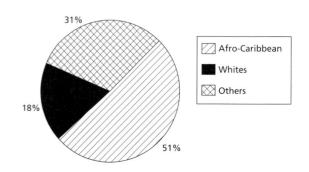

Figure 4BB   Youth unemployment (1995)

- Unemployment for white workers in 1995 was 8.1%, for black workers it was 18.8%, and for Pakistani and Bangladeshi workers it was 24.2%.
- Young blacks suffer the highest unemployment rates. Afro-Caribbean men aged 16–24 had an unemployment rate of 51%. For young whites it was 18%.

Long-term Unemployment

People who are middle-aged and older have more difficulty in finding work than younger people. Most of the long-term unemployed are older people. For many there is little chance of finding another job, even though they are more experienced and are found to be more reliable workers, on average, than young persons.

Figure 4CC shows the long-term unemployed as a percentage of the total unemployed in each age group in 1995.

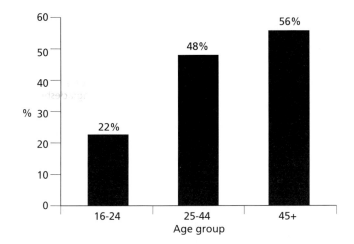

Figure 4CC   Long-term unemployment as percentage of total unemployed in each group
Source: Low Pay Unit, Labour Force Survey

Age and Employment

Some UK politicians have recognised the problem of age and employment and have tried to bring in a law to ban **age discrimination** in job adverts. David Winnick, MP, introduced a **Private Member's Bill** in February 1996 which was aimed at outlawing job adverts in the **media** which stated age limits for applicants.

Research into job adverts has found two important facts:
- Almost two-thirds of all job adverts put a limit on age to those who are under 40.
- 70% of job applicants failed to get the advertised job because of their age.

Many unemployed people feel that they are discriminated against because of their age. Many also feel that a law against **ageism**, if introduced, could easily be ignored and employers could find a way around it easily. Some companies prefer older workers because they:
- are more reliable;
- are less likely to take time off;
- are more likely to arrive at work on time;
- are more polite;
- can pass on their skills and experience to younger workers.

Firms like B&Q, Safeway, Marks and Spencer and the TSB take part in the **Campaign for Older Workers**.

QUESTIONS

1 Which racial groups suffer the worst unemployment?
2 Which age groups suffer most from long-term unemployment?
3 What have some MPs tried to do to deal with this?
4 In what way are older workers discriminated against in job adverts?
5 Why do some companies prefer to employ older workers?

113

Disability and Employment

Workers with disabilities often face discrimination from employers and 'workmates'. The government introduced a law to try to stop this, called the **Disability Discrimination Act**.

The Law tried to end this discrimination by making employers of more than 20 people responsible for making sure that such workers are treated fairly and equally in the following areas:

- dismissal;
- training;
- conditions of work;
- discrimination;
- recruitment.

Employers were also required to make some changes to the workplace to help people with disabilities at work, for example building ramps for wheelchair-bound workers.

QUESTION

1 How does the Disability Discrimination Act seek to help workers with disabilities?

The European Dimension

Figure 4DD   European Union flag

Unemployment is a problem that is affecting all European countries. There are 18 million Europeans out of work, which is 11% of Europe's working population.

Country	Unemployment rate
Spain	22%
Ireland	18%
Italy	11%
Denmark	11%
Germany	5%
Portugal	5%
UK	13%
Luxembourg	3%
France	11%
Holland	8%
Belgium	9%

Figure 4EE   Percentage of unemployment rates within the EU, May 1993

Source: Eurostat

The European Union (EU) gives support to member countries to help get the unemployed back to work. Since 1979, Scotland has received £1.4 billion from the EU.

However, the member countries of the EU have their own **domestic policies** for dealing with unemployment and this can lead to problems. For example, the UK decided to opt out of European Policy that would have gone against British ideas on how to deal with unemployment.

The **Social Chapter** of the **Maastricht Treaty** would have provided a number of new benefits to British workers, for example:

- the introduction of a minimum wage for workers in Britain;
- paternity leave for male workers when their wife has a child;
- the same pay rates for workers doing the same work in all EU countries.

The UK government felt that the Social Chapter would make Britain less attractive to foreign companies who wanted to build factories here.

European Comparisons

Studies carried out by the British **Trade Union Congress** (TUC) show that the unemployed in the UK receive less benefit than the unemployed in most EU member countries. They found that:

- Unemployment benefit in Britain was only £49.50 a week. In other member countries it could be as much as 80% of their earning while in work.
- All other EU member countries apart from the UK link unemployment benefit to previous earnings.
- National Insurance rates have risen by 50% in the UK since 1979, but unemployment benefit which is related to this has been reduced 12 times over the same period.

The TUC uses the information from these studies to show that the unemployed in the UK are worse off than most other EU member countries.

From October 1996, the UK government will introduce the **Jobseekers' Allowance**. This will mean that the unemployed will receive unemployment benefit for six months, instead of one year which they do at present. Also, unemployed people with savings of more than £8000, or a partner who has savings of this amount, will receive no social security after the six-month period.

Unemployment and Poverty

Since 1979 poverty in Britain has been on the increase. Today nearly 14 million people, almost one-quarter of the British population, are poor, according to the EU definition of poverty.

Poverty is linked to a number of causes, the main ones being:
- unemployment;
- changes in the economy;
- inequality;
- low social benefits.

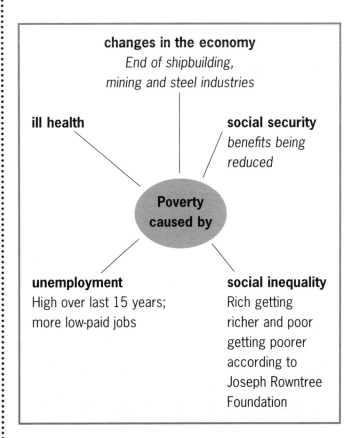

Figure 4FF   The main causes of poverty

115

Fact – the richest 10% in Britain have had an increase in income, whereas the poorest 10% in Britain have had a reduction in income.

Unemployment is lower in the 1990s than it was in 1980, but the **level of poverty is rising**. Figure 4GG shows the unemployment levels in two poor areas of the UK compared to the UK average and the Scottish average.

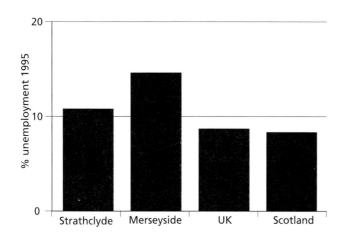

Figure 4GG   Local unemployment (1995/96)
Source: Strathclyde Economic Trends

QUESTIONS

1 How have changes in the economy led to more people becoming poor?

2 How do Strathclyde and Merseyside compare with the UK average?

Low Pay

Even if a person has a job they can still be poor if the pay is not enough to cover their family budget each week. There has been an increase in the number of jobs with low pay over the last 20 years.

Women workers are more likely to have low-paid jobs than male workers. In many families the woman is now the major wage earner, or the only wage earner, as jobs in the **traditional industries**, mainly male, are lost.

The Scottish Low Pay Unit states that poverty in 1990 would have been much higher if women were not earning a wage.

Figure 4HH   Percentage of female workers on low pay in Scotland in 1994

43% of all Scottish workers are low paid

Figure 4II   Percentage of male workers on low pay in Scotland in 1994   *Source: Low Pay Unit*

Effects of poverty

Life on the dole is very hard, especially if a person is long-term unemployed. The money is not available to meet their needs or those of their family. The poverty that often results from unemployment affects families in many different ways:

- health, e.g. depression;
- education – children leave school earlier;
- housing – can only afford to pay low rent;
- poor life chances.

Some information from the Benefits Agency and the Census provide an insight to the **cycle of poverty**:

- unemployment over the last 15 years has soared;
- the amount of low-paid work has led to poverty in many cases;
- changes in the economy have led to a decline in the traditional industries;
- people are having to pay more for their groceries, as VAT has been increased by government;
- one in three children in Scotland are living in poverty;
- death rates in deprived areas were 62% above those in other areas.

Social problems

HOUSEHOLDS WITH BELOW AVERAGE INCOME

Type of household	Numbers (thousands)	Percentage
Self-employed	1344000	9.5
Single or couple in full-time work	252000	1.8
One working full time, one part-time	395000	2.8
One working full time, one unemployed	1411000	10.1
One or more in part-time work	1152000	8.3
Aged over 60	3600000	25.9
Unemployed	2812000	20.2
Others	2974600	21.4
Total	13900000	100

Figure 4JJ Households with below average income
Source: Joseph Rowntree Report 1995

Social problems like crime, drug and solvent abuse, school problems and even suicide are more likely to occur in areas of **depression**.

- Between 1981 and 1991 total reported **crime**, including juvenile crime, increased by almost 80%.
- The number of **drug offenders** between the ages of 17 and 29 doubled between 1979 and 1989.

- There were big increases in **school expulsions** for all age groups between 1986 and 1991.
- Death by **solvent abuse** increased dramatically between 1980 and 1990.
- The **suicide rate** among young men aged 15 to 24 increased by 75% from 1983 to reach a peak in 1990.
- The rates of **children receiving serious injuries** increased by 50% between 1979 and 1989.

QUESTIONS

1 How does the percentage of women on low pay compare with the number of men on low pay?
2 What kind of problems arise from poverty?
3 Look at Figure 4II from the Joseph Rowntree Report. Which types of people are most likely to be poor?

117

What the Politicians Say

Figure 4KK features four excerpts which give different opinions on the effects of unemployment on society.

'If we are no better off, why do I see so many satellite dishes?'
Kenneth Clarke, Chancellor of the Exchequer, 1995

'The government is to blame for the rise in inequality (poverty) in Britain.'
Gordon Brown, Shadow Chancellor of the Exchequer, 1995

'No one wants to grow vegetables. They sit in front of the TV for hours on end, complaining about their poverty, and not growing vegetables when they could do so easily and cheaply.'
Toby Jessel, MP, 1995

'Despite a full year of growth in the Scottish economy as much as 8.3% of the workforce is still out of work.'
Campbell Christie, General Secretary, STUC, 1995

Figure 4KK

Meeting the Unemployed's Needs

The **Welfare State** was set up in Britain in 1948 to make sure that everyone in the country would be looked after by the government. The government at that time recognised that it had a responsibility for the British population.

The unemployed are also the responsibility of the government and it should introduce measures to help them.

The government has brought in measures to give the unemployed financial support and to get them back to work.

Financial support for the unemployed

Unemployment benefit

- It is paid if an unemployed person has paid national insurance contributions when in work.
- It is a cash payment for one year after losing one's job.
- A person's savings, or those of their partner, do not affect it.
- The partner's earnings do not affect unemployment benefit.

Jobseeker's allowance

In October 1996 a new benefit was introduced called **The Jobseeker's Allowance** (JSA). The JSA replaced both unemployment benefit and income support.

- It is paid for six months based on national insurance contributions.
- After six months the JSA will be **means-tested**, which means that people with £8000 savings or a working wife/husband will get no JSA.
- JSA claimants will have to go on work or training schemes. Refusal will result in JSA withdrawal from claimant.

Income support

- This doesn't depend on national insurance contributions (i.e. it is non-contributory).
- It is a means-tested benefit.
- It is available to over 18s only.
- It is paid if income is below a certain amount.
- The claimant will be working less than 16 hours per week.
- The claimant must be available for work and *must prove it* if asked to do so.

Other benefits

People on a means-tested JSA (which most unemployed people will go on to after the six-month period) can claim:

- housing benefit;
- council tax benefit;
- back to work credit.

Type of benefit	What it means
Housing benefit	Reduction in rent/cost of paying accommodation.
Council tax benefit	Reduction in amount paid for council tax.
Back to work credits	People on low pay, working less than 16 hours a week, get wages 'topped-up'.

Figure 4LL

A major criticism of back to work credits is that some employers know that the government will 'top up' their employees' pay, so they keep their wages low.

QUESTIONS

1. How would you answer Toby Jessel (Figure 4KK)?
2. What financial support does unemployment benefit give?
3. What difference will the Jobseeker's Allowance make?
4. What kind of people can get Income Support?
5. What other benefits can people claim?

Back to Work Programmes

The unemployed often have to have help to find jobs. Sometimes they will have to improve their qualifications to get work. The government offers help to do this.

Jobcentres display job vacancies and provide information on where to find work in their offices throughout the country. If a person is keen to find a job they can go and see a **client advisor**, who will draw up a **Back to Work Plan**. The cost of travel to an interview can also be paid by the local Jobcentre.

The long-term unemployed are offered other services by the Jobcentres:

- **Restart interviews** – to find out what the person needs to get back to work;
- **Job Club** – helps to prepare application forms, gives access to phone, letter writing equipment and materials;
- **Work Trials** – up to three weeks' training with an employer to see how a type of job suits;
- **Training for Work programmes** – training and education to help the unemployed person prepare for work. Benefit + £10 per week extra;
- **Community Action** – environment and conservation work. Benefit + £10 per week extra.

All of the above are aimed at preparing a person to get back into work by providing interview experiences and work training.

Scottish Enterprise

Set up in 1991, **Scottish Enterprise**'s aim was to improve the Scottish economy so that jobs could be created. Its operation covers 94% of the Scottish population. Highlands and Islands Enterprise deals with the Highlands and the Islands.

Figure 4MM   Scottish Enterprise Logo

Scottish Enterprise aims to:

- develop and enlarge existing businesses;
- promote more and better new businesses;
- attract foreign investment into Scotland;
- improve Scottish exports;
- improve the environment;
- promote skills and knowledge;
- promote access to opportunity.

Scottish Enterprise has been successful in supporting the Scottish economy by helping the firms already in Scotland to expand and create new jobs. The **Small Business Loan Scheme** was set up to provide loans to small companies.

Young people and women are focused on, for instance, to be given help starting up a business. **Locate in Scotland**, a part of Scottish Enterprise, has been successful in bringing new firms to Scotland. Recently, a third Taiwanese firm has announced it intends to build a new factory at Bellshill in Lanarkshire, bringing 200 jobs to the area.

QUESTIONS

1 What help can Jobcentres give the unemployed?
2 How does Scottish Enterprise seek to help create jobs?
3 Why are foreign firms important in creating jobs?

119

Other Government Assistance

Assisted areas

These are areas of the country with the highest levels of unemployment. They receive two main forms of help from the government.

- **Regional Selective Assistance** which gives grants to employers who create jobs;
- **Regional Enterprise Grants**. There are two types of grant. One for companies with less than 25 people and one for companies who employ up to 50 people. The grants are intended to help to set up new projects.

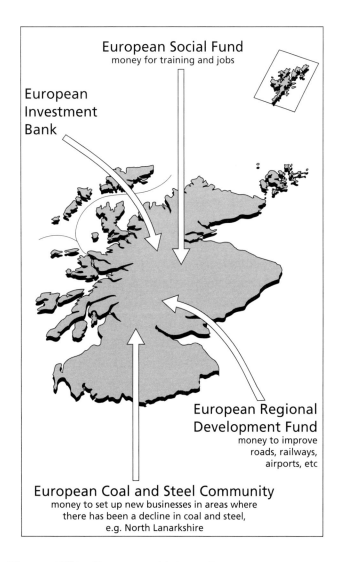

Figure 4NN Types of aid from Europe

European Social Fund
money for training and jobs

European Investment Bank

European Regional Development Fund
money to improve roads, railways, airports, etc

European Coal and Steel Community
money to set up new businesses in areas where there has been a decline in coal and steel, e.g. North Lanarkshire

Enterprise zones

There are four areas in Scotland:
- North Lanarkshire;
- Invergordon;
- Inverclyde;
- Tayside.

These special areas receive many benefits including tax reductions, grants to companies to 'open companies there', grants to purchase machinery and tax reductions.

European assistance to deprived areas

This is in the form of money to create jobs and clean up the environment to help attract new companies. Large amounts of money have come to Scotland for this. (See Figure 4NN.)

QUESTION

1 How does the government help areas where there is high unemployment?

Young People and Training

Many young people leaving school find it hard to get a job. In 1995 the government started the **Skillseekers Scheme** to help youngsters find work. Similar schemes in the past were criticised for offering poor training and many did not provide jobs at the end of the training, for example the **Youth Opportunities Scheme** (YOP) or the **Youth Training Scheme** (YTS). Skillseekers is run by **Local Enterprise Councils** (LECs) and involves colleges, training firms or voluntary agencies which provide training in many skills to young school-leavers and unemployed. Now most young Skillseekers (90%) are working towards vocational qualifications and 63% are working with firms

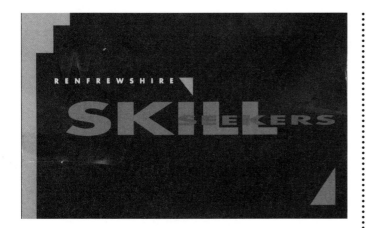

Figure 400

which provide prospects of a job at the end of their training.

The **guaranteed place** scheme tries to place every summer school-leaver in training by September, so that youngsters would either be in training, in a job or at school.

It is still too early to get a good idea of the Skillseekers programme, but some criticisms have been made of the YTS and the YOP schemes that could apply to this one as well:

- 16–18-year-olds can't claim Income Support or other benefit as they are forced to live at home on a low income;
- some employers used it as a cheap labour scheme;
- it sometimes involved little or no training;
- no guarantee of a job at the end.

Project Work

Project Work, set up in April 1996, is a work experience programme open to all people aged between 18 and 50 who have been unemployed for two years or more. It is a **compulsory** programme and anyone who refuses to enter, or drops out of the work experience programme without good reason, will have their benefit stopped.

Projects will be set up in different parts of the country and the people who live in these areas are expected to take part. The programme will last for 13 weeks.

Project Work has been introduced to show that the government believes in making people do something for their benefit. The government's argument is: Why should people work and pay taxes, which are then paid to the unemployed for doing nothing?

Critics argue that this is not a solution to reducing unemployment. No new skills will be learned from the projects and full-time employment will not result for those taking part in the schemes.

QUESTIONS

1 What criticisms were there of Youth Training Schemes?
2 List the reasons for **and** against Project Work.

121

> 'Everyone had the right to work, to free choice of employment, to just and free favourable conditions of work, and to protection against unemployment.'

Figure 4.1 *Source: Article 23 of the* UN Declaration of Human Rights

The population of the UK is 58.2 million people. The labour force is 28.1 million.

This means that almost half the population of the UK is not available for employment.

There are many reasons why people are not available for work.

Mainly the non-working part of the population are too old or too young to work. This would include children under 16 years of age, students who are in full-time education, men over 65 years of age and women over 60 years.

It also includes people who are disabled or are unable to work because of illness.

Many women are not counted as part of the working population because they work at home as housewives. Some have to stay at home to look after their children and others may be caring for a sick or elderly relative.

Not all of the available working population is in employment. Many are unemployed, while others are participating in some form of government training scheme.

The Labour Force

Figure 4.2 shows the age structure of the British labour force. When you look at it you can see how the structure has changed in the last 20 years.

You can see that the numbers of people in the working population aged under 24 fell by 1.8 million between 1986 and 1996.

This is mainly due to the increased numbers of young people continuing in some form of

education after they leave school, as well as a general decrease in the birth rate in the country.

	AGES			
	16–24	**25–44**	**45+**	**Total**
Estimates (numbers in thousands)				
1976	5095	10824	9782	25700
1981	5832	11358	9052	26242
1986	6173	12455	8310	26938
1991	5536	13879	8714	28129
1996	4339	14346	9477	28162
Projections				
2001	4206	14678	9951	28835
2006	4434	14389	10587	29409

Figure 4.2   British labour force by age

Source: Department of Employment

Who are the unemployed?

Quite simply the unemployed are those members of the population who would be part of the workforce if they had a job. To be counted by the government as an unemployed person you must be:
- out of work and available for employment;
- signing on the unemployment register;
- receiving some form of unemployment-related state benefit.

Unemployment has become a more serious problem in the UK during the 1980s and 1990s. It is a major cause of poverty and long-term unemployment, and is increasing among workers aged 25–49.

Calculating the real level of unemployment has become increasingly controversial and difficult. Since 1980 the government has made some 30 changes to the way unemployment statistics are calculated.

The current method used is called **the claimant count** and is reached by calculating those signing on, claiming and receiving unemployment benefit as a percentage of the workforce.

	UK	Scotland
1986	11.8	14.5
1987	10.6	14.1
1988	8.4	11.8
1989	6.4	9.4
1990	5.8	8.1
1991	8.8	9.2
1992	9.5	9.5
1993	10.3	10.1
1994	9.6	9.9

Figure 4.3 Percentage unemployment in the UK and Scotland

Source: Department of Employment

Unemployed people who don't count

Many critics of the government, however, argue that this method hides the real level of unemployment in the country.

Women

Women, in particular, are often not counted in the unemployment figures.

This is because many unemployed women are unable to claim benefit as they have not paid enough national insurance contributions. Many other women are part-time workers whose earnings are too low to pay national insurance.

Other groups

Other groups who do not count in the government's unemployment figures are:
- unemployed people who are under 18 years old. They do not qualify for income support and are therefore not claimants;
- people on government training schemes. They are not unemployed, but neither are they in full-time paid employment.
- people who have left a job through their own choice. They are banned from 'signing on' for 26 weeks. They are not claimants, so do not count.

Other ways of counting the unemployed

Alternatives to the government's methods include the **Labour Force Survey's** count using the International Labour Organisation's (ILO) definition of unemployment.

The ILO definition counts as unemployed those people who have not done any work for pay or profit in the week that the count was taken.

To be eligible for the count, the people must also want to work, be available to start work and have looked for work in the last four weeks.

Many think that this is a much more realistic way to measure unemployment.

Figure 4.4 shows information using both the claimant count and the labour force survey methods.

Although both measures show a slight decline in unemployment between 1993 and 1994 there is a difference between the government's level of unemployment figures and those of the labour force survey.

Year	Labour force survey rate %	Claimant rate %
1993	10.8	9.8
1994	10.1	9.3

Figure 4.4 Unemployment in Scotland 1993/1994

Source: Labour Force Survey

QUESTIONS

1 List the reasons why people are not available for work.
2 In what way has the age structure of the British labour force changed in the last 20 years?
3 Examine Figure 4.3. Draw two bar graphs showing the unemployment rates for the UK and Scotland between 1986 and 1994.
4 Compare the two ways of counting the unemployed. Which do you think is more reliable. Give reasons for your answer.

Changing Patterns of Employment

During the 1980s the UK experienced a decline in its industrial and manufacturing jobs and a rise in employment in the **service sector**.

The greatest job losses have been in what are called the **traditional industries** of shipbuilding, mining, steel, car production and textiles.

	Males				Females		
	1971	**1994**	**% change**		**1971**	**1994**	**% change**
Agriculture	2	2	0	Agriculture	1	1	0
Energy and water supply	5	2	−3	Energy and water supply	1	1	0
Manufacturing	41	28	−13	Manufacturing	29	12	−17
Construction	8	6	−2	Construction	1	1	0
Distribution, hotels and catering	13	20	+7	Distribution, hotels and catering	23	24	+1
Transport and communications	10	9	−1	Transport and communications	3	3	0
Financial and business services	5	13	+8	Financial and business services	7	13	+6
Other services	15	21	+6	Other services	35	45	+10
Total numbers of all employees (thousands)	13425	10539		Total numbers of all employees (thousands)	8224	10363	

Figure 4.5 Employees by industry (UK) in percentages

Source: Social Trends 1995

However, many thousands of new jobs have been created in the service sector. This sector includes banking, insurance and finance as well as hotels, catering, transport and communications.

As a result of this there has actually been a rise in the numbers in employment.

Employment in Scotland actually grew by around 2% over the decade, and by 1.5% in Great Britain as a whole.

Figure 4.5 shows how employment in the different industries has changed since 1971. There has been a switch away from the **manufacturing industries** towards the service sector. The proportion of people employed in the financial and business sector has also increased.

Overall, women accounted for 38% of employees in 1971 compared with almost 50% in 1994.

Since 1994, the communications sector has been growing with many new jobs being created because of advances in cable, satellite and mobile phone networks. Jobs have also been created manufacturing these products. These new jobs also employ mostly women.

One problem of traditional sector jobs being replaced by jobs in the service sector is that many are part-time, lower paid and less secure.

Look at Figure 4.5 and answer the questions which follow.

QUESTIONS

1 In what ways has employment in the UK changed in the last 20 years?
2 What is the difference between the type of work in traditional industries and in the service sector?
3 Study Figure 4.5. Which jobs have experienced the biggest changes in the period 1971–94?
4 Which jobs saw the biggest rise in female employees?
5 What are the problems with some of the newer types of employment?

	1981	**1991**	**Percentage change**
Agriculture	44100	27500	−37.6
Energy and water supply	73700	59300	−19.5
Manufacturing	495200	380900	−28
Construction	137900	130100	−5.7
Distribution, hotels and catering	374800	410500	+9.5
Transport and communications	125400	116100	−7.4
Financial and business services	128000	198400	+55
Other services	586000	680000	+16
Total number of employees	1965500	2002900	+1.9

Figure 4.6 Employees by industry. Changes in Scotland

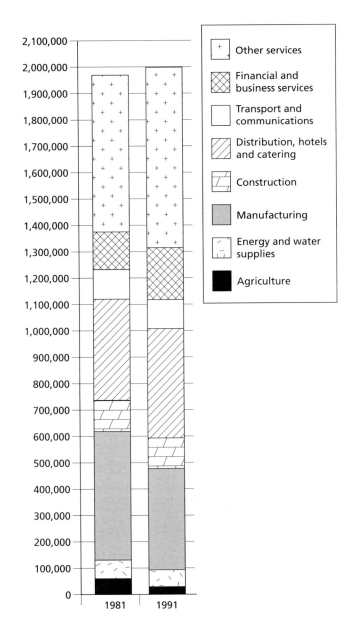

Figure 4.7 Employees by industry. Changes in Scotland
Source: Department of Employment

Legend:
- Other services (+)
- Financial and business services
- Transport and communications
- Distribution, hotels and catering
- Construction
- Manufacturing
- Energy and water supplies
- Agriculture

New Technology

New technology is found increasingly in our everyday lives. It is all around us. In our homes there are many household appliances as well as computer games and electronic toys which are the result of new technology.

In shops the introduction of bar codes and scanners helps lessen the queues at the checkout and also tells the shop when items have to be reordered.

In factories the use of robots and other machines is now commonplace.

Banks, also, are very highly computerised. Cash dispensers allow customers to have a range of services other than just withdrawing cash, and the use of 'switch' cards could eventually lead the way to cashless shopping.

Figure 4.8 Cash dispensers allow customers to have a range of services

In hospitals and doctors' surgeries new technology can help doctors diagnose and treat illness. Doctors in cities can even use technology to treat people in rural or island communities.

The use of computers and wordprocessors in offices have made them more efficient and easier to run.

However, one result of the introduction of new technology is that many workers' jobs have been lost. The development of the technology itself has meant that other types of new jobs have been created to replace some of those lost.

Figure 4.9 shows the arguments for and against new technology.

125

Q UESTIONS

1 Study Figures 4.6 and 4.7. Which industries have grown in Scotland between 1981 and 1991?
2 Which industries have declined in Scotland between 1981 and 1991?
3 Suggest reasons for these changes.
4 Compare the changes in the UK and Scotland. Using the percentage figures say how the growth and decline of Scottish industries compares with UK industries.

For	Against
New technology will lead to increased production of cheaper, better quality goods. Far less goods will be sub-standard, more will be sold. This will increase the firm's profits and eventually the entire country will benefit.	Unemployment will increase as machines and robots take over the jobs of working people.
Workers will be needed to produce much of the new technology: from household electrical appliances to home and office computers; from robots to personal mobile phones and the miniaturised computer chips that they use.	Many jobs using new technology lead to the **de-skilling** of formerly skilled jobs. De-skilling means that many of the old skilled jobs will disappear. Skilled workers may become machine minders.
New technology will take over the jobs which are repetitive, boring or dangerous to human life. This may mean that many worker-related problems such as days lost due to ill health or strikes are likely to be reduced.	New technology will change jobs so much that a great amount of retraining will be needed. This may not be a problem for younger workers, but the fast pace of working with new technology may cause stress among older workers.
Employee costs could be reduced. Fewer workers will be needed. This means that firms will make savings on their wages bill.	It will be harder for trade unions to recruit members and protect their interests. This could lead to a worsening of pay and conditions of employment.
Jobs which cannot be done due to a shortage of skilled labour will be carried out by machines or robots. This could lead to a shorter working week or even an earlier retirement age.	It is well known that new technology can cause job losses. British employers prefer to lose workers rather than cut the working week.
An increasing number of people are able to work from home as a result of advances in computer and telephone technology.	Home workers are amongst the lowest paid workers in Britain and are very difficult to organise into trade unions.

Figure 4.9   For and against new technology

QUESTIONS

1 Explain some of the ways in which new technology affects everyday life?

2 Give two other examples of new technology.

3 Look at the cases for new technology in Figure 4.9. Choose three points you consider to make the strongest case for increased new technology. Copy them out and explain why you consider them to be good points.

4 Which points against new technology do you consider to be the strongest? Give reasons for your answer.

5 From the information in Figure 4.9 say:
 a **which groups you think will be most in favour of new technology**
 b **which groups you think will be most against?**

6 Suggest ways in which those for and against new technology might come to agreement.

New Technology Job Creation in Scotland

The place mainly associated with micro chip technology is 'Silicon' Valley in Northern California, USA. It is the largest centre for new technology in the world.

Central Scotland has been successful in attracting leading overseas electronics firms to come and open factories. The result of this success is that this area of Scotland is now known as **Silicon Glen**.

The companies have set up in towns such as:
• Greenock (IBM) (US);
• Ayr (NEC) (Japanese);
• Erskine (Compaq) (US);
• East Kilbride (Motorola) (US);
• Livingston (Hughes Unisys) (US);
• Glenrothes (Shin Ho Tech) (South Korean);
• Cumbernauld (Tenma) (Japanese).

These companies have created over 50000 new jobs by deciding to set up factories in Scotland. Most of the companies – over 80% – are foreign owned.

126

They come mainly from the USA and Japan, with an increasing number from Korea.

In 1994 Motorola announced a multi-million pound investment in new facilities in East Kilbride. This project created 200 new jobs.

In the same year British Sky Broadcasting (BSkyB) announced a new £10m project in Dunfermline, creating up to 1000 full-time jobs by the year 2000.

During 1995 **Locate in Scotland**, a part of Scottish Enterprise, brought 97 projects to Scotland, with a planned investment of £1110 million. They were expected to create and safeguard 12,300 jobs.

Among the largest of them was the massive £260 million Chunghwa Picture tube factory lured to Lanarkshire in 1995.

Look at Figures 4.10 and 4.11 and answer the questions which follow.

Scottish Secretary Michael Forsyth will today give details of one of the largest investments yet by a Korean company in Scotland, bringing with it up to 200 jobs.

Officials from the government's inward investment agency, Locate in Scotland, has highlighted the ready supply of educated and available labour.

The Secretary of State will have been emphasising to the Koreans during his present sales mission to the Far East that employment in Scotland is very flexible through Britain not signing up to the EU's Social Chapter.

His sales mission took him to Japan last week where he was able to give details of two new Japanese investments in Scotland: a £5 million expansion by Tenma in Cumbernauld and a £6.5 million location by the Kohdensha Company in Dunfermline.

Figure 4.10   *Source: Herald, 29 May 1996*

Scottish Secretary Michael Forsyth crowned his two-day visit to South Korea yesterday with the announcement that Shin Ho Tech plans to build a new £8.6m factory to assemble computer monitors in Glenrothes. It should bring another 280 jobs to Fife.

Figure 4.11   *Source: Herald, 30 May 1996*

QUESTIONS

1 What are the main advantages of Scotland having a Silicon Glen?
2 What reasons does the newspaper article in Figure 4.10 give for Scotland being able to attract foreign investment?
3 How has new technology created jobs?
4 Read the case study which follows. Write a short report describing the ways in which new technology has affected office work.

Case Study

The Office

New technology has completely changed office work. Even the smallest office has the ability to be very efficient and to communicate worldwide.

Word processors Typewriters have been replaced by word processors which can alter mistakes very easily. They can print hundreds of letters to different people simply by changing the names. A great deal of time and effort is saved.

Computers Files and information are now kept on computers or discs. Saves space and time. No need for filing cabinets or for staff to take up as much time filing and retrieving information.

Fax Allows copies of documents to be sent to other areas of the country/world instantly.

Call Connect Systems Modern phone network system which can 'queue' calls, divert calls and tell you when someone else is trying to get through to you.

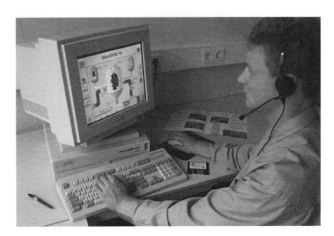

Figure 4.12

127

Video Conferencing Businessmen wanting to have face-to-face meetings no longer have to travel. This allows them to see and speak to each other while seeing their reactions and facial expressions. *Internet/Teletext* Instant access to large amounts of current information using the television and phone network. Can be used for passing information, advertising or specialised data.

The North–South Divide

During the 1980s there were large differences in unemployment levels in different parts of the UK. It became very obvious that it was easier to find jobs in some areas of the country than in others.

Unemployment was higher in areas such as Scotland, the north of England and Northern Ireland than it was in the Midlands and the south of England.

In 1994 Scotland had an unemployment rate of 9.9%, while in East Anglia, in the south-east, it was 7.4%. In some Scottish cities unemployment can be as high as 30%.

This stark situation led many people to believe that in terms of employment a north–south divide existed in the UK.

Others disagreed with this point of view. They point to the fact that recent large increases in unemployment in the Midlands and the south of England have disproved the argument. The unemployment figures for different regions would seem to back them up.

Figure 4.13 shows that in 1990 it was very easy to see a north–south divide. The regions in the Midlands and the south of England had low unemployment figures. By 1994 the situation was less clear.

Unemployment had increased in all regions, however, the increases in the south were much greater than in the north of the country.

Scotland's unemployment rate will soon be at its lowest level since the late 1970s, according to Strathclyde University's Fraser of Allender Institute. The institute is predicting an unemployment rate of 7.7% in 1997.

The fall in unemployment does not tell the whole story. Employment is expected to increase by 21900 jobs a year. This is less than a 1% growth despite annual GDP growth of around 3.5%. In other words the recovery in the economy is not matched by a similar increase in the number of jobs (firms are producing 3.5% more, but only employing 1% more workers).

It is more likely that the decrease in unemployment will be due to population falls rather than better economic prospects.

The reality behind Scottish employment statistics looks like a move away from male employment and a shift towards female part-time, low grade jobs, rather than an increase in the number of jobs available.

Indeed, Scotland alone will see no growth in its labour force over the next 11 years, according to latest estimates of labour market trends.

The Scottish labour force is forecast to fall by 0.2% by the year 2006 in contrast to a projected 5.9% increase for the UK.

East Anglia will see a rise of 12.7% in its labour force.

Other fast-growing areas identified in a survey by the Department of Employment in its official *Employment Gazette* include the south-west with a 10% increase, East Midlands, 9% increase and the south-east with a 7% increase.

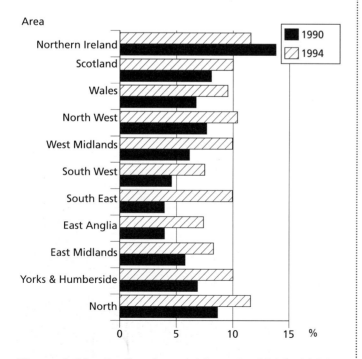

Figure 4.13   Regional unemployment 1990–1994
Source: Social Trends 1995

Read the article in Figure 4.14 and answer the questions which follow.

The number of Scots claiming unemployment benefit fell again last month, and the rate in Scotland is now below that of the south-east of England.

The June figures show a decrease of 2700 to 197600, or 7.9% of the Scottish workforce. The overall UK figure fell 4200 to 8.3% of the workforce.

Scottish Secretary Michael Forsyth said: 'It is testimony to the transformation of the Scottish economy that, in the unemployment figures announced today, Scotland's rate is 0.4 percentage points below the UK. It has now been below the UK rate for over three years and is even below the (8%) rate in the south-east of England.

'Scotland led the UK out of recession and unemployment has now been on a downward trend since December, 1992. Today's fall below 200000 is excellent news.'

For the Scottish Labour Party, assistant general secretary Tommy Sheppard said: 'Unemployment remains at an unacceptably high level. It is a cause of misery for 200000 families in Scotland.'

SNP employment spokesperson Anne McNair said 'About the only thing that can be read into these figures is that Scotland is still a land of mass unemployment. By crowing that unemployment is greater in other parts of the UK, Michael Forsyth betrays an extraordinarily complacent and London-centric attitude, which does nothing to address the misery of joblessness in Scotland.'

Figure 4.14   *Source:* Herald, *20 July 1995*

Women and Work

During the last 26 years laws have been passed which make it illegal for employers to discriminate against women in relation to jobs.

The **Sex Discrimination Act of 1975** and the **1970 Equal Pay Act** mean that women can expect to be treated equally with men when they are looking for a job or in employment.

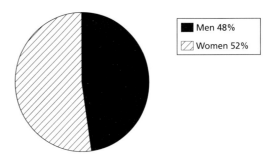

Men 48%
Women 52%

Figure 4.15   UK population by gender
Source: Social Trends 1995

Despite these laws and the fact that women account for almost 50% of the entire workforce, women are much more likely to be employed in part-time jobs, where pay is low and the working conditions are not as good as those for full-time employees.

According to the Employment Department's figures there were 998000 men and 5257000 women in part-time employment in 1994.

There are several reasons why so many women are in part-time employment.

Figure 4.16

129

One major reason is male unemployment. Many women have gone out to work to make up for the loss of their partner's earnings. In today's world many women need to work in order for families to make ends meet.

Many new jobs created tend to be part-time, unskilled and low paid, employing women, while full-time skilled jobs, employing well-paid men, are lost.

In 1994, the national unemployment rates were 11.4% for men and 7.2% for women.

The fact that the unemployment rate for women is lower does not mean that they find it easier to get employment. As Figure 4.17 shows, many women and men do not seek work and are not included in the unemployment figures.

	Men	Women
Waiting for result of job application	1%	1%
Student	16%	7%
Looking after family/home	6%	53%
Temporarily sick/disabled	5%	8%
Long-term sick/disabled	23%	3%
Believes no job available	22%	9%
Not yet started looking	7%	7%
Other reasons	20%	13%

Figure 4.17   Reasons for not seeking work

Source: Low Pay Unit

QUESTIONS

1 Which types of jobs are women more likely to do?
2 What jobs have been created and which have been lost in recent years?
3 How has this affected families' incomes?
4 Why might it be said that many women are only 'temporarily out of the paid labour force' when they are 'looking after families'?

Gender inequality in the workplace

As you can see, the main reason given by women for not seeking work was family responsibilities.

However, when women do get jobs, they tend not only to be part-time but also have lower status and pay than men.

Another area of concern is the types of jobs that women occupy and their promotion prospects in these jobs.

While 52% of the population is female they still hold less than 10% of the most influential jobs in politics, the law, education and business.

The general assumption that there has been an improvement in the status of women since laws were introduced in the 1970s is not borne out by research carried out by the Scottish women's organisation **Engender**.

Its main finding is that despite far more women being in the workplace, and a lessening of the wage gap between men and women, female employees are still over-represented in the low-status jobs and under-represented in the high-status ones.

In education, girls do better than boys in examination results, but while 32% of girls go on to full-time education compared to 27% of boys, fewer girls go to university.

In teaching, fewer women reach the top jobs than would be expected.

Women make up 99% of nursery teachers, 91% of primary teachers but only 66% of primary headteachers.

Women account for 46% of secondary teachers, but only 3% of secondary headteachers.

Figures 4.18, 4.19 and 4.20 show percentages of staff in Scottish universities by gender.

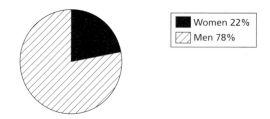

Women 22%
Men 78%

Figure 4.18   Academic staff by gender

Source: Engender

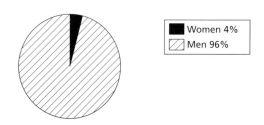

Women 4%
Men 96%

Figure 4.19   Professors by gender

Source: Engender

Figure 4.20 Lecturers by gender

Politics, business and the law

In politics women account for 9.7% of MPs and 24% of Scottish councillors.

In business only two of the top 150 company directors are women.

In law, Scotland has only one woman judge, but 54.2% of all solicitors qualifying in 1994 were women.

However, when these women seek to move up the legal profession they will find that the ratio of women to men changes rapidly. See Figures 4.21 and 4.22.

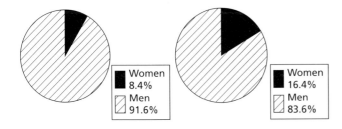

Figure 4.21
Sheriffs by gender

Figure 4.22
Advocates by gender

Figure 4.23 shows occupational status by gender, reinforcing the earlier statements that women are under-represented in high-status jobs, and over-represented in lower-status jobs.

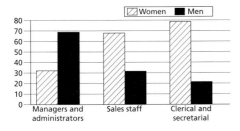

Figure 4.23 Occupational status by gender

QUESTIONS

1 Study Figures 4.24 and 4.25 and their captions. Which opinion is most accurate? Justify your answer using the source material provided.

Figure 4.24 'With the introduction of laws against discrimination and the acceptance of feminist attitudes, women have more and better career opportunities than they have ever had.'

131

Figure 4.25 'Despite the passing of laws and the fact that girls do better than boys at school, women still fail to get appointed to the top jobs in our society.'

2 Find out more about the Sex Discrimination Act and the Equal Pay Act. You can usually find resources in the Modern Studies Department or the school library. Remember good information is held not just in books but also on newspaper CDs.

Race and Employment

Race Relations Acts make it illegal to discriminate on the grounds of colour, race or religion. Nevertheless, members of **ethnic minority groups** still continue to encounter different treatment in employment.

Ethnic minority unemployment is, on average, twice the level of white unemployment.

Figure 4.26

Ethnic minorities and unemployment

Unemployment rates vary a great deal between ethnic groups in Great Britain.

'Black and betrayed', a recent report from the Trades Union Congress (TUC) reveals that the unemployment rates for black workers is double that of white workers.

Using employment department figures, the report shows that in spring 1995 the unemployment rate for white workers was 8.1% whilst for black workers it was 18.8%. Pakistani and Bangladeshi workers had the highest unemployment rate at 24.2%.

It also highlights the fact that young black workers suffer the highest unemployment rates.

African-Caribbean men aged 16–24 had an unemployment rate of 51% compared with 18% for young white men of the same age group.

Case Study

Government legislation obliging employers to make immigration checks is already making its mark.

Under the Asylum and Immigration Bill employers need to ask potential employees for a national insurance number or other proof of their right to work in the UK.

An employer who takes on an illegal immigrant could face fines of up to £5000.

In April 1996, 300 domestic staff at the University College London Hospital Trust received letters from the Trust telling them to ensure their work permits were up to date. It said, 'If it is discovered through spot checks that you do not have an up-to-date permit it will not be possible to continue your employment.'

The letters were sent only to domestics and porters, the two groups with the largest number of black and Asian staff.

However, following a campaign by the trade union, UNISON, the spot check plans were withdrawn. Staff were sent letters which apologised for the first one.

A trade union official said, 'Black workers will constantly have to worry about the tap on the shoulder which will lead to them being investigated.'

New guidelines, designed to ensure that employers avoid discrimination in recruitment are being drawn up by the Commission for Racial Equality.

Figure 4.27   *Source:* Labour Research

QUESTIONS

1 What evidence is there that members of ethnic minorities are more likely to be unemployed?
2 Which ethnic minority group is worst affected by unemployment?
3 Why might the Asylum and Immigration Bill make employers reluctant to employ black and Asian workers?
4 How might it affect existing workers?

Long-term Unemployment

Not all unemployed people are equal.

There is a big difference between those people who are changing jobs or those who are only unemployed for a short time, and those people who are classified as **long-term unemployed**.

In 1994 the long-term unemployed accounted for 45% of all unemployed people. This had increased from 28% in 1991.

Between 1991 and 1994 the long-term unemployed figure increased by 84% compared with a rise of 13% in total unemployment.

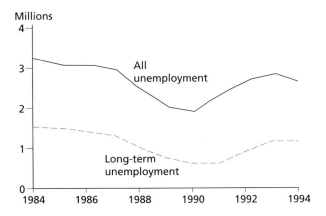

Figure 4.28 Unemployment and long-term unemployment

Source: Employment Department

Read the article in Figure 4.29 and answer the questions which follow.

I had been employed for 27 years. Now I was on the dole at the age of 44 in the middle of a recession.

Stunned but unbowed, I launched an intensive job search . . . 15 months and 500 job applications later I was still unemployed and feeling very ill.

During my long term of unemployment, I had become disillusioned with employers and very ill with depression and anxiety. I was diagnosed as suffering from severe reactive depression.

I am still unemployed and ill – and may never work again.

My wife Eileen and 15-year-old son Steven have suffered greatly. Eileen has been very ill with anxiety and Steven has been left with major psychological and physical problems. He played truant from school and ran away from home because he fell so far behind due to illness. His life has been permanently scarred.

Any employee over the age of 50 is now regarded as fair game for early retirement or redundancy. If you lose your job after 50 you have little chance of gaining permanent full-time employment. Even if you are under 50, it is becoming very difficult to find an interested employer.

Figure 4.29   *Source:* Herald, *20 April 1995*

Age and Employment

Many unemployed middle-aged and older people have severe problems in finding employment regardless of the skills they have or how well qualified they are.

Long-term unemployment is more heavily concentrated among older people. Employers also appear to provide less job-related training to those aged over 50.

Age	Long-term unemployed	All unemployed	Long-term unemployed as percentage of age group
16–24	189300	844000	22%
25–34	297300	664800	45%
35–44	237600	465600	51%
45–54	181900	358600	51%
55–64	131900	212400	62%

Figure 4.30 Labour force survey, Summer 1995

Source: Low Pay Unit

A **Private Member's Bill** seeking to outlaw age discrimination in job advertisements was introduced in the House of Commons on 9 February 1996 by David Winnick, MP.

The Bill would make it illegal for job advertisements to specify certain ages. Its supporters argued that up to 40% of job advertisements excluded applicants aged 40 or over.

They pointed to a survey by Gallup for the Brook Street employment agency which found that 70% of employees believed that they had failed to get a job because of their age.

Many people feel that age discrimination should be treated the same as race or sex discrimination, both of which are illegal.

133

The government argues that passing laws would have no effect. They claim that in countries which do have laws against **ageism**, the laws are unenforced and ignored.

However, an increasing amount of employees are realising that many older workers have a lot to offer.

Many companies like Marks & Spencer, B&Q, Safeways and the TSB take part in initiatives like the **Campaign for Older Workers**. They think that older people are often more reliable, better timekeepers, have better manners and can pass on their experience to younger workers.

Read Figure 4.31 and answer the questions which follow.

The Campaign Against Age Discrimination in Employment is a UK-wide campaign and is growing quickly. It lobbies MPs and has presented petitions to the Prime Minister. The aim is to get legislation passed in the UK to outlaw all forms of age discrimination in employment.

America, Canada, and various European countries have effective legislation. However, the Conservative Party is interested only in a voluntary code. Such codes are virtually worthless – toothless tigers.

Labour has recently announced that it favours legislation and will pass anti-discrimination laws if elected next time.

Paddy Ashdown, Lib-Dem leader, promised a full statement soon. I am confident he will support legislation.

More than 2 million people currently suffer from age discrimination in employment. In the near future, half of the working population will be more than 45 years old and will be potential candidates for age discrimination.

Figure 4.31 *Source: Herald, 20 April 1995*

QUESTIONS

1 In what ways do older workers feel discriminated against?
2 How do different employers respond differently to older workers?
3 What evidence do we have that 'ageism' is becoming a 'political issue'?

Disability and Employment

Another group of people who often face employment problems are those with disabilities.

75% of such people in the UK rely on benefits to meet their needs.

However, this is not solely as a result of their disability making them 'unfit for work'.

Workers with disabilities face prejudice from employers **and** fellow workers.

To try and combat this the government introduced the **Disability Discrimination Act**. UK employers of 20 or more people are legally liable, from Autumn 1996, for discrimination against disabled people in recruitment, promotion, training, working conditions and dismissal.

The same employers must make 'reasonable adjustment' to assist people with disabilities in their workplace.

Read Figure 4.32 and answer the questions which follow.

The Act replaces the existing 50-year-old law that places on employers an obligation to take on a quota of registered disabled people, usually 3 per cent of the workforce.

Michael Ryley, an employment law specialist, describes the old law as toothless and a nonsense. He says: 'A lot of people were not aware of the quota system and many employers who did know about it did not put it into operation'.

Employers also will need to start thinking about making alterations to premises.

On the government's own figures, the direct cost to employers of taking on disabled people will be about £8 million.

Adapting buildings and improving access for the disabled could cost from £380 million to £1.13 billion.

In addition to clauses dealing with employment, there is a section in the new legislation on the provision of services. Companies such as hotels and bus operators will pick up a bill.

Figure 4.32 *Source: The Times, 15 November 1995*

Q U E S T I O N S

1 How many disabled people are unemployed?
2 What did the government introduce to combat discrimination in the workplace?
3 What was wrong with the 'quota system'?
4 What will the costs to employers be to improve access?

Improving employment opportunities for people with disabilities

Figure 4.33

Case Studies

New technology has given Barbara Pestell independence. After an accident 18 years ago she is paralysed from the neck down and became totally dependent on other people.

When she worked for her Master's degree all her notes had to be dictated to a carer.

Recently Mrs Pestell acquired a voice-activated computer which has transformed her work as a counsellor.

She can now ensure complete confidentiality for her clients because she is able to write her own case studies.

Figure 4.34   *Source:* The Times, *1 May 1995*

The prime purpose in setting up Seaborn Industries, a training workshop of the Strathclyde Branch of EAS (Epilepsy Association of Scotland) in 1957, was to help people with varying mild disabilities to work towards securing employment in an integrated workplace.

It operates a Training for Work workshop with qualified trainers and the appropriate equipment to train in upholstery, joinery, spray polishing, picture framing, and office practice, offering training at the present time to SCOTVEC Level 2.

This is Richard Winters' second year on the programme.

'For the first year I worked on smaller types of chairs, and modern upholstery, but now I have moved on. This is my second year and I am still finding it quite difficult. The variety is unbelievable and it takes years to learn, but it is great to feel you are actually doing something. We see the finished product and it is very satisfying,' said Richard.

He has already achieved City & Guilds Level 1 and is now working towards SCOTVEC Level 2, and hopes that the standard qualification will give him a better chance of a job.

Trainee John McDermott, also working towards SCOTVEC Level 2, has been building traditional wood-carved fireplaces to order. Completed in two days, these are commercially viable products, and this ability to meet individual customer specifications is an obvious strength.

A recently completed chest of drawers was also built to a customer's specific requirements. 'The customer ordered a "two over four" drawers set which was made out of medium-density fibre and then taken into the paint shop and coloured. After it was finished he decided that he wanted a mirror to match on the top. We had all the measurements, so we built that on.'

Through in the picture-framing section, trainees Hugh McMillan and Robert Buchanan are putting the finishing touches on a framed set of mementos celebrating the Centenary of Cathcart Castle Golf Club. The skills here also owe a lot to the hands-on approach at Seaborn.

Seaborn Industries, 48 Govan Road, Glasgow. Telephone 0141 427 5225.

Figure 4.35   *Source:* Herald, *23 May 1995*

Access to work

The **Access to Work Scheme** was introduced in 1994. It helped 9000 disabled people get work. The government paid employers the full cost of employing a person with a disability.

In August 1995, the government announced proposals to shift half of the cost on to employers.

Ms Liz Lynne, Liberal Democrat spokesperson on Social Security and Disability, said: 'Cutting the amount it gives to employers to take on a disabled person will inevitably lead to more disabled people claiming benefit, with an added cost to the taxpayer.

'I urge the government to think again and rule out any further attacks on disabled people's access to employment.'

Figure 4.36   Source: Herald, *11 August 1995*

Q UESTIONS

1 What problems did Mrs Pestell have in doing her job?
2 How did new technology help her to solve these problems?
3 What is the aim of Seaborn Industries?
4 What types of jobs do the trainees do?
5 'It's great to feel that you are actually doing something.' What problems do you think people suffering from epilepsy might have in finding manual jobs?
6 How did the Access to Work scheme help disabled people get work?
7 How might the government's proposals change this?
8 How might this lead to 'an added cost to the taxpayer'?

The European Dimension

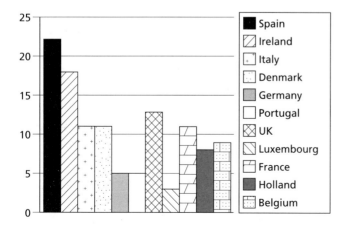

Figure 4.37   EU percentage unemployment rates, May 1993
Source: Eurostat

Unemployment is not only a problem for Britain, it is also a European problem. In 1995 there were 18 million people unemployed throughout Europe. That is 11% of all Europeans out of work.

Figure 4.37 shows the percentage of recorded unemployed workers in Europe.

European action on unemployment

The European Union (EU) has specific policies for those in and out of work. It is estimated that Scotland has received some £1.4 billion in grants from the EU since 1979. This comes mostly in the form of **European Structural Funds**.

The most important are:

- the **European Social Fund** (ESF) which supports projects for the unemployed;
- **European Regional Development Fund** (ERDF) which supports projects, such as roads, aimed at linking Scotland better with other areas in Europe and environmental works;
- **RECHAR Funds** which help areas affected by the closure of coal mines;
- and **RENAVAL Funds** which help areas affected by the decline of the shipbuilding industry.

Unfortunately, not all the funds available to Scotland are taken up. The rules say that these funds must be additional to what the government would spend anyway, and must be 'matched' by money from central or local government.

Bruce Millan, the European Commissioner in charge of Regional policy, criticised the government for not using all the money available because they would not match the funds with governmental cash.

The European Union announced that £84m will be spent in Britain in areas hit by the run-down in the defence industries.

Nearly £10m is coming to Scotland. The money, which is in a spending programme called Konver, is being used in Glasgow, Fife, Edinburgh, Cunninghame, and Argyll and Bute, where it has to be matched by local authority money.

Welcoming the money, Councillor Iain Macdonald of Strathclyde said there was still insufficient help from the government for local authorities. The EU also announced £5.5m for Scotland to help alternative economic activity in areas hit by textile closures.

Figure 4.38   Source: Herald, *23 December 1995*

Mrs Ewing, Euro MP for Highlands and Islands, said Scotland's fishermen had lost out because the London government had refused to match EU funding of various aid schemes.

Figure 4.39 *Source:* Herald, *12 July 1995*

The Scottish Secretary, Mr Michael Forsyth, has been urged to make sure that Scottish councils get their share of EU grants to revitalise former mining areas.

Lothian's Euro MP David Martin said yesterday that central and local government was required to match the £8.3m of European funding which was on offer with £8.9m of their own.

But the UK had all but abandoned regional policy, and local communities in Scotland depended on European Regional Funding to revive their economies and create jobs, he said. Areas which could benefit are Bathgate, Midlothian and Kirkcaldy.

Figure 4.40 *Source:* Herald, *3 August 1995*

European Comparisons

Britain negotiated an **opt-out** of the Social Chapter of Maastricht. This meant that Britain did not have to adopt European legislation on certain social and employment issues such as a minimum wage, paternity leave and paying rates for workers crossing EU borders.

The British government argued that this would provide more flexibility in working conditions and would make the UK a more attractive place to industrial investors.

Studies by the British TUC and the European Commission (EC) have claimed that social security support for unemployed Britons is almost the worst in the European Union.

UK unemployment benefit of £49.50 a week compares poorly with that paid out in other EU member countries, where it can be as much as 80% of previous earnings (see Figure 4.41).

Britain's unemployed are the only group in Europe without unemployment benefit linked to previous earnings. Only the Greeks and the Irish give less support to unemployed people than the British.

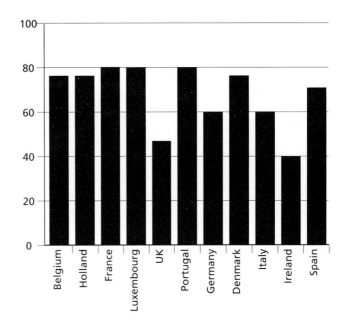

Figure 4.41 Unemployed benefit as a percentage of previous wage

Source: Eurostat

Britain had an earnings-related supplement until it was abolished in 1980, leaving just a flat-rate benefit. That is now to be changed.

From October 1996 unemployment benefit is to be replaced by the Jobseeker's Allowance which will be paid for six months, half the life of unemployment benefit, after which it will be **means-tested** and not available to anyone with savings of more than £8000 or a partner in full-time employment.

QUESTIONS

1 In what ways is unemployment a 'European problem'?
2 What are the main European Structural Funds?
3 How are they aimed to help Scotland's unemployment?
4 Why are not all available funds used?
5 'The government gives an unemployed person almost half of their previous wage in the form of unemployment benefit. Our policy is the same as our European partners.

'We wish to help unemployed people maintain a decent standard of living, while encouraging them to seek employment.' *Government spokesperson*

In what ways could the government spokesperson be accused of being selective with the facts?

Unemployment and Poverty

Britain is facing an increase in poverty and deprivation. According to government figures the number of poor has almost trebled from 5 million in 1979 to nearly 14 million today.

A quarter of the British population is now living in poverty as defined by the European Council (EC) definition. This figure includes 4 million children.

The UK has no official definition of poverty or a minimum standard of living. It is the only member of the EU not to have one.

There are many factors which can contribute to a rise in poverty in a country. Among the most common are:

- increasing unemployment;
- economic change;
- social inequality;
- reductions in benefits.

The gap between rich and poor

The 1995 Joseph Rowntree Foundation report stated that the gap between rich and poor in Britain is at its widest for 50 years.

The richest 10% of the income scale have seen their incomes increase considerably, while the poorest 10% have actually suffered a loss in income.

The pay of top directors increased by 551% in a decade.

The sales of Rolls-Royce cars increased by 24% in one year alone. More of these cars are in the UK than anywhere else in the world.

Britain is now eating more caviar – a 43% increase since 1991.

Unemployment

Unemployment is one of the most important factors in the increase in poverty.

Throughout the 1980s and 1990s the level of unemployment in the UK has been very high.

Figure 4.42 shows some of the changes in unemployment in Scotland since 1990. It shows both the official numbers of unemployed and the Labour Force Survey (LFS) measurements in percentages of the workforce.

Year	Official	LFS
1990	8.7%	12.1%
1991	9.0%	13.0%
1992	9.1%	13.1%
1993	9.3%	13.5%
1994	9.1%	13.1%
1995	8.5%	11.7%

Figure 4.42   Unemployment in Scotland, 1990–1995

Source: Working Brief & Employment Gazette

In May 1995 the LFS count was 294000 – over 95000 more than the government's count of the unemployed.

In addition, the government's figures show that in certain areas unemployment figures are unacceptably high. For example, in the Cumnock area of Ayrshire, male unemployment was 28.3%.

In the Belvedere area of Glasgow male unemployment was at 39.3% during the same period, and in Castlemilk it was as high as 50%.

Who are the poor?

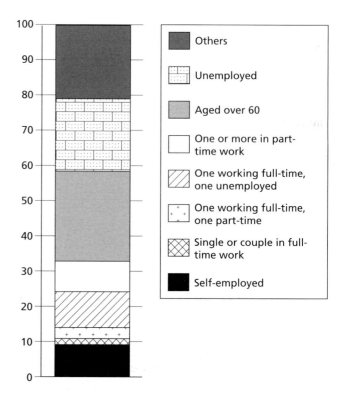

Figure 4.43   *Source:* Joseph Rowntree Report 1995

Type of household	Numbers (thousands)	%
Self-employed	1344	9.5
Single or couple in full-time work	252000	1.8
One working full-time, one part-time	395000	2.8
One working full-time, one unemployed	1411000	10.1
One or more in part-time work	1152000	8.3
Aged over 60	3600000	25.9
Unemployed	2812000	20.2
Others	2974600	21.4
Total	13900000	100

Figure 4.44   *Source:* Joseph Rowntree Report 1995

Cheered on by his backbenchers, Mr Major said: 'Average income has risen by over a third since 1979, the average income of all economic groups and family types has risen, vulnerable groups have been protected, average incomes are up by over 10% for poorer pensioners, up for the unemployed, and up for those in full-time work.'

Mr Dewar, Labour Social Security spokesman, told the House that, between 1981 and 1991, male mortality between the ages of 18 and 46 rose in Drumchapel by 9%, while in Bearsden it fell by 14%. Young men in Drumchapel were twice as likely to die and 75% more at risk from major surgery than in Bearsden. Life expectancy was 10 years shorter for men, seven years shorter for women.

Mr Lilley, Social Security Secretary, said the income support safety net was 15% higher than the supplementary benefit level the Tories had inherited in 1979, benefits for an unemployed couple with two children were 24% higher in real terms, and pensioners as a whole had higher incomes now than in 1979 – up 50%.

Figure 4.45   *Source:* Herald, *21 February 1995*

Q UESTIONS

1 What does the Joseph Rowntree Foundation Report say about the gap between rich and poor?

2 Which groups are the worst affected by poverty?

3 Which groups are the least affected by poverty?

4 How does John Major suggest that the people's income has risen?

5 How does Donald Dewar compare the effects of poverty in Drumchapel with the increases in wealth in Bearsden?

6 How does Peter Lilley's statement compare with the findings of the Joseph Rowntree Foundation?

Low Pay

Being in employment is no guarantee of escaping poverty. Low pay is a fact of life for hundreds of thousands of Scottish workers. Much of this is due to the decline of traditional industries and the increase in poorly paid, part-time working.

In 1993, 43% of both male and female workers were on low pay, but women workers, both full- and part-time were more likely to be low paid.

This is especially significant for low income families, due to the increasing importance of women's earnings to the household budget.

Since the early 1980s the average male contribution to the household budget has declined from 75% to around 60% today.

Women's earnings are therefore becoming crucial in preventing many families from falling below the poverty line.

Research from the Scottish Low Pay Unit estimates that the number of people living in poverty in 1990 would have been 50% higher had it not been for the contribution of women's earnings to the family budget.

139

The report by the Scottish Low Pay Unit shows that women are losing the battle to close the pay gap. In a detailed analysis of earnings figures from the government's New Earnings Survey, the report says 850000 workers in Scotland fell below the unit's low pay threshold.

However, there also are wide regional variations within Scotland.

The highest proportion of men on low pay were in Highland (30%), Borders (26.3%), and Dumfries and Galloway (25.7%). More than 60% of women in the same regions earned less than the low pay threshold of £208.53 per week.

The report also states that 445000 workers in Scotland would benefit from the introduction of a minimum wage set at half-median male earnings (£156.40 per week).

Overall, women would account for 78.6% (350000) of beneficiaries from a minimum wage.

The New Earnings Survey shows that full-time female employees in Scotland currently earn 72.7% of male earnings, while in non-professional classes it is nearer 65%.

Figure 4.46   *Source:* Herald, *30 August 1995*

The parents of one in three Scottish children are living on the breadline, according to a survey by Glasgow Caledonian University researchers.

The survey reveals that the growth of real poverty among Scottish families is linked to an alarming increase in the number of people in low-paid jobs.

In Scotland, 34% of children are living in households where their parents are either in receipt of Family Credit (a government benefit to help people living on low wages) or Income Support in 1993, according to the survey.

Almost half of Scotland's workforce, 43%, are low paid, the study found. More than 300000 Scottish women, in part-time jobs, are in the low-paid category, compared with 60000 men.

Figure 4.47   *Source:* Herald, 8 May 1995

	Manual		Non-manual	
	Men	**Women**	**Men**	**Women**
Borders	37.7	76.0	13.2	61.7
Central	26.1	85.1	9.5	45.2
Dumfries & Galloway	34.7	87.0	13.0	56.6
Fife	24.3	77.0	10.3	48.9
Grampian	28.3	79.0	9.7	40.3
Highland	36.8	86.4	22.0	58.6
Islands	25.7	62.5	3.4	51.5
Lothian	32.7	74.6	13.8	35.6
Strathclyde	26.5	72.6	13.9	39.2
Tayside	33.3	78.7	15.6	48.1
Scotland	28.9	75.7	13.2	41.4
Britain	26.0	73.4	11.5	34.7

Figure 4.48   Percentage of workers on low pay by region, 1994

Source: Low Pay Unit

Q UESTIONS

1 Why have female earnings become so important to family budgets?
2 What do the Family Benefit and income support figures tell us about the amount of people living in poverty?
3 How many Scottish workers are on low wages?
4 Write a paragraph describing the low wages by gender and region.

Factfile on unemployment, low pay and poverty

Information from the Benefits Agency and the 1991 Census highlighted the following connections between unemployment, low pay and poverty.

Economic change

Unemployment has increased in the last 15 years, particularly long-term unemployment amongst people aged 24–59.

Economic change with the decline of traditional industries and the rise in low-paid, part-time working has pushed many families into poverty. 43% of all Scotland's workers are low paid.

Government policy

Government policies are making some people poorer, for example, the imposition of VAT on fuel.

Families and children

17% of the population of Scotland are dependent on income support.

One in three children in Scotland is living in poverty.

Children from poorer, unemployed backgrounds are more likely to be taken into care. Strathclyde figures showed that 78% of children taken into care between 1985–92 were from families relying on benefits.

In 1993 in the UK one in three children from professional backgrounds obtained a degree. Only one in 30 from unskilled manual backgrounds obtained a degree.

Housing

Poverty limits access to decent housing. Those who are unemployed are twice as likely to live in a damp house as those who are employed.

Death

In 1991 mortality rates were 162% higher in the most deprived areas in Scotland than in the affluent areas.

Social problems

Unemployment can also lead to wider social problems.

'Households Below Average Income', a report published by the Department of Social Security in July 1994, highlights many of these problems.

Total reported **crime**, including juvenile crime,

increased by almost 80% and violent crime by 90% between 1981 and 1991.

The number of **drug offenders** between the ages of 17 and 29 doubled between 1979 and 1989.

A study of **school expulsions** covering the period 1986–1991 reported dramatic increases in the use of expulsions for all age groups.

There was a four- to five-fold increase in the number of deaths from **solvent abuse** between 1980 and 1990.

The **suicide rate** among young men aged 15 to 24 increased by 75% from 1983 to reach a peak in 1990.

The proportion of children on Child Protection Registers almost quadrupled during the 1980s. The rates of **children receiving serious injuries** increased by 50% between 1979 and 1989.

Q UESTIONS

1 'Poverty is not only about money. It affects every aspect of a person's life.' What arguments could be put forward to support this point of view?

2 Describe the social and economic problems experienced by many unemployed families.

What the Politicians Say

Figure 4.49 'If we are no better off, why do I see so many satellite dishes?' Kenneth Clarke, Chancellor of the Exchequer, 1995

Figure 4.50 'No one wants to grow vegetables. They sit in front of the television for hours on end, complaining about their poverty and not growing vegetables when they could do so easily and cheaply.' Toby Jessel, MP, 1995

Figure 4.51 'We are starting 1995 with Britain's economy in very good shape. Output is at record levels, exports are rising faster than imports, and consumer confidence is returning.' Michael Portillo, Employment Secretary, 1995

Figure 4.52 'Jobless Scots are growing tired of the government's ceaseless doctoring of the unemployment figures. 75% of jobless 16- and 17-year-olds received no benefits and are not counted as unemployed.' Nicola Sturgeon, SNP Employment Spokesperson, 1995

Figure 4.53 'Long-term unemployment remains the fastest-growing category of the jobless and by turning a blind eye to them the Tories are adding to their misery.' John McFall, Labour Scottish Employment Spokesperson, 1995

141

Figure 4.54 'The responsibility for the rise in inequality lies squarely with the government, which has presided over a Britain now more divided than it has been for generations.' Gordon Brown, Shadow Chancellor of the Exchequer, 1995

QUESTIONS

1 'These statements show that politicians are only interested in their own points of view. None of them is really interested in the unemployed.' Using the sources what arguments could be put forward for and against this point of view?

Meeting the Unemployed's Needs

Britain is called a **Welfare State**. This means that the government provides help and support to the less fortunate people in our society. Being unemployed most definitely decreases the life chances of those who experience it, and the government provides different forms of help to try and meet the needs of unemployed people.

The government has a number of schemes to help people who are unemployed. These fall into two distinct categories:
- financial benefits to help people cope with a loss of income;
- programmes to help people find work and to retrain for new jobs.

Financial benefits

The most obvious of these was **unemployment benefit** (now replaced by contributory Jobseeker's

Allowance). People who lost their jobs were entitled to unemployment benefit in return for national insurance contributions which they paid while in work.

Unemployment benefit

Unemployment benefit provided a cash payment for up to a year for people who were normally in work but who had lost their jobs. Unemployment benefit was not affected by a person's savings, their partner's savings or their partner's earnings.

When a person's unemployment benefit ran out, or unemployment benefit was not enough to survive on, they could apply for **income support**. Most people who received unemployment benefit also received income support because unemployment benefit was not enough to survive on.

Income support

This is a non-contributory benefit. This means it does not depend on national insurance contributions.

It is also a **means-tested** benefit. You get it only if you do not have the 'means' (income or savings) to survive.

It is normally available only to people over 18 whose income falls below a certain level and who are not working more than 16 hours a week.

(In 1988, the government took away the automatic right of 16–18-year-olds to claim income support. It is now only available in very exceptional circumstances). To qualify for income support you must be available for work and show that you are attempting to find work.

There are certain exemptions to the need to look for work; for instance if you are a single parent, are sick or disabled or over 60 years of age.

Jobseeker's allowance (JSA)

This came into complete effect in October 1996 and replaced both unemployment benefit and most income support payments for the unemployed.

There is a contributory JSA element and a non-contributory element. Instead of getting unemployment benefit for one year, the unemployed will get JSA for six months only.

Once the six months is up, the JSA is means-tested. This will mean that people with a working partner or savings of more than £8000 will lose benefit.

Stricter rules will apply to eligibility and tougher sanctions for those who don't comply fully with the requirements.

Claimants will be compelled to go on work schemes or programmes they are offered. If they refuse their benefits will be cut for up to 26 weeks.

The government believes that the JSA will save it £270 million in 1997–98 and that it will only 'pay benefits to the jobseeker, not the job shy'.

Other benefits

Other benefits for those on means-tested JSA include housing benefit, council tax benefit and family credit. The last of these has also come in for criticism.

Family credit is a benefit under which parents working 16 or more hours a week can get their low pay topped up.

In July 1995, the number of families receiving family credit was 626300, of whom 276840 were one-parent families.

The main criticism of this benefit is that people in low-paid employment can have their pay topped up by the government, which encourages many employers to keep their wages down.

Working out what a person's benefit will be

How much each person receives depends on their individual circumstances, such as whether they have paid enough national insurance contributions, their age and family circumstances.

The amount each person receives is based on all the information relating to their personal circumstances and the amount the government thinks a person needs to survive in these circumstances.

This is called the **applicable amount** and is worked out by the Department of Social Security when a person becomes unemployed or their circumstances change, such as becoming ill, having an additional child or separating from their partner.

There are also other additions if a person is elderly, disabled, has a disabled child or needs care.

The applicable amount is expected to cover the costs of eating, clothing and heating. Housing costs are covered by housing benefit which a person can apply for if they are on income support. Those on income support are also entitled to other benefits

such as free prescriptions, clothing grants and free school meals. This is why it is called a **passport benefit**.

Look at the benefit levels for April 1996 in Figure 4.55.

Benefits payable per week	
Unemployment benefit	£48.25
(available for one year only if national insurance contributions have been paid)	
Income support (per person)	£
aged 18–24	37.90
aged 25 or over	47.90
Lone parent (over 18)	47.90
Couple (at least one over 18)	75.20
Added on to the above	
Dependent children aged 18 (at school or FE)	37.90
aged 16–17 (at school or FE)	28.85
aged 11–15	24.10
aged under 11	16.45
Family (at least one child)	10.55
Lone parent	5.20

Figure 4.55   *Source: Labour Research, April 1996*

Worked example

Anne is 43, unemployed and receives unemployment benefit of £48.25 per week. She is a single parent with three children, Nick who is 17 and still at school, Jean who is 14 and Mary who is ten. Her applicable amount is worked out in Figure 4.56.

aged 25 or over (for Anne)	£47.90
add for Nick	£28.85
add for Jean	£24.10
add for Mary	£16.45
add for Family	£10.55
add for Lone Parent	£5.20
Total needed	**£133.05**

Figure 4.56   Applicable amount worked example

Anne's unemployment benefit is not enough for her family to survive on. Therefore she is entitled to income support. It will be added to her unemployment benefit to bring her up to the applicable amount.

143

Therefore she will receive:
- unemployment benefit   £47.90
- income support   £85.15
- total   £133.05

QUESTIONS

1 Use Figure 4.56 to work out how much each of the following people will receive.

  a Jim is unemployed, aged 20 and single. He has not had a job since his YTS came to an end two years ago.

  b Hamish and Helen are partners. They are both unemployed and have two children, Margaret aged 11 and John aged 3.

2 Do you think that the applicable amounts are enough to survive on? Give reasons for your answer.

3 Why is income support called a 'passport benefit'?

144

Disability, Illness and Unemployment

In April 1995, the government introduced a new incapacity benefit. It replaces invalidity and sickness benefits.

The government claimed that there had been a large increase in unemployed people claiming these benefits, which are higher than income support levels. The government claimed that the increase was due to people wishing to increase their incomes, not because of genuine sickness or invalidity.

In August 1993, there were estimated to be 1.6 million people claiming these benefits.

Look at Figure 4.57 and answer the questions that follow.

From this Thursday people receiving sickness or invalidity benefit move on to the new incapacity benefit, as does anyone who applies on the grounds of disability in the future.

If they qualify on the higher rate of benefit they will, for the first time, be taxed on it. And new claimants qualifying for the first time will find the level of benefit available greatly reduced from the previous rates.

continued ...

continued ...

Then there are the tests. Interestingly, for the first time, part of these involve the sick or the disabled assessing themselves. This entails answering several hundred questions about your ability to perform tasks such as climbing stairs unaided or walking independently. The object of the exercise is not any more to assess your ability to do the job you once did . . . but to find out if you can do any kind of work at all (called the **all work test**).

So, for the sake of argument, if you happen to be an ex-miner unable to work because your lungs have packed up, these tests can establish that there's absolutely nothing wrong with your hand-and-eye co-ordination.

There's not the slightest little thing preventing you from becoming an ace seamstress. The fact that you don't as yet know which end of the needle is up needn't count against you.

After all, are there not all these wonderful retraining programmes for people enterprising enough to understand that brave new worlders can't hang about at home while there are new employment fields to be explored?

This department confidently predicts that in the first three years of the new benefits £3.2 billion will be taken out of payments to the sick and disabled.

Almost a quarter of a million people currently on invalidity payments won't remain on the new incapacity benefit.

And some 85000 people on income support who have a disability premium will find the latter disappears.

Then there are the new claimants. Apparently some 160000 people who would have got invalidity benefit simply won't pass the new tests, and another 35000 won't be eligible for a disability premium.

Figure 4.57 *Source: Herald, 10 April 1995*

QUESTIONS

1 Why did the government introduce incapacity benefit?
2 What effect will this have on people?
3 What are the tests aimed to do?
4 How might the tests result in the ex-miner losing his right to benefit?
5 How much does the government expect to save?
6 How will the new benefit affect the number of claimants?

Back to Work Programmes

Figure 4.58

Unemployed people need different types of help in their search for work. They need to know:

- what types of jobs are available and where they are to be found;
- how to go about improving their skills and qualifications to compete better in the jobs market;
- how to apply for jobs properly.

The government provides a range of schemes to help in these areas.

Jobcentres

Jobcentres are a good place to start a search for work. They cater for all people, whether it is a young person looking for their first job or someone trying to find work after being made unemployed or redundant.

Job vacancies are displayed on cards for people to browse through. They also have information on other places a person can find work in their local area, such as local papers, local employers and private employment agencies.

They provide unemployed people with a **client adviser**, who provides advice on how to find a job.

They will also draw up a **Back to Work Plan** which details how the Jobcentre can help and how people can help themselves find a job.

An unemployed person is entitled to regular meetings with their adviser and they can have their plan reviewed and updated if necessary.

The Jobcentre can also provide help to try for jobs outside the local area. If you have been looking for work for more than four weeks and the job you are applying for is full-time and permanent, you can claim financial help from the **Travel to Interview** scheme.

Jobcentres and longer-term unemployed

Jobcentres provide different types of help related to the amount of time that a person has been unemployed.

Stage One – 3 months (13 week review)

If no job has been found after three months of looking an adviser gives extra help to:

- put the person in touch with local employers with vacancies;
- arrange a place on a **job search seminar**. These last for four days, spread over five weeks. They look at things such as the way a person comes over in job interviews and helps with the practical details of applying for work. This includes letter writing, preparing a CV, making telephone calls properly, typing and help with postage costs.

  Attending the seminar doesn't affect benefit and travel is paid to and from the seminars.
- arrange a place on a **job review workshop**. Workshops last two days and a computer programme is used to help match skills to areas of work. They are especially useful if the unemployed person has a professional or executive background.

  Again benefits are not affected and travel costs are paid.

Stage Two – 6 months

- **Restart interviews** This interview is designed to give a fresh start to the search for work. The client adviser reassesses the person's needs and decides upon a course of action to take.
- **Jobclubs** The club helps the unemployed person to prepare job applications. They provide access to stamps, telephones, newspapers and stationery free of charge.

  It is estimated that around 50% of people who take part in a jobclub find a job.

  Joining a jobclub does not affect benefit and travel expenses are given.

145

- **Job interview guarantee scheme** If a person has the right skills and qualifications they can be matched quickly against employers' vacancies and an interview for the job is guaranteed.

    Job preparation courses offer help and support to improve interview techniques to increase a person's chances at the guaranteed interview.

    Employers are also encouraged to recruit from these courses and specialised training can be given to prepare people for specific jobs.

- **Work trials** This gives people a chance to do real work with an employer who is looking to fill a vacancy.

    Work trials last up to three weeks and are useful to find out whether a person likes the job and to show the employer how suitable they may be.

    During a work trial the unemployed person continues to receive their benefit as well as travel expenses of up to £5 per day and meal expenses of £1.50 per day.

- **Training for Work Programmes** It is claimed that these are a very useful way to train or gain valuable work experience that is related to the type of work that a person may want to do.

    The programme could involve job-specific training, working towards a General Scottish Vocational Qualification (GSVQ) in Scotland and National Vocational Qualification (NVQ) in England and Wales, temporary work to keep skills up to date or actual work preparation. It could also be a mixture of all of these.

    While the training is being completed the person continues to get their usual benefit plus an extra £10 per week, and perhaps help with travel, accommodation or childcare.

Stage Three – 1 year plus

- **Job plan workshops** The workshops last four or five days and are designed to help people rethink their future. They enable people to discuss their situation on an individual basis and share experiences with others in a similar situation. Participants are helped to:
    - decide what their skills and strengths are;
    - look at new options;
    - make contact with people who can give extra help;
    - use computer programmes to help find possible jobs.

- **Community action** This involves a wide range of activities from voluntary caring projects to environmental and conservation work. While helping the community, the person still receives help in looking for work and the use of the same type of facilities that are given in jobclubs.

    People who take part in these schemes receive an allowance which is the equivalent to their benefit plus £10 per week.

- **Restart course** People who have been out of work for two years and have not taken up a place on an Employment Department programme are asked to attend a Restart Course. The course is part-time and lasts for two weeks. It tries to help people by:
    - informing them of the employment and training opportunities available;
    - developing techniques to get back to work;
    - developing a further plan of action to get back to work.

Attending does not affect a person's benefits and travel expenses to and from the course are paid.

Read the article in Figure 4.59 and answer the questions which follow.

One of the most successful and long-running of the government's initiatives is the Jobclub. Since they were set up in 1984 it is estimated that they have helped more than one million people to get back into some sort of employment and there are now 1400 Jobclubs throughout the country, 129 of them in Scotland. In the past financial year 22840 Scots passed through the Jobclubs in Scotland.

My own experience of two Jobclubs, one in Ayr and one in South St Andrews Street in Edinburgh, was that, although the jobclubs themselves were very helpful with free stationery, stamps, access to telephones and photocopiers etc, the general atmosphere was negative.

It can be very depressing to be surrounded by people who have a low self-esteem and to be in that environment day after day.

Lack of experience is still the biggest obstacle to getting a job. No job, no experience; no experience, no job. It is still the classic Catch-22 situation. A place on a government training scheme doesn't necessarily guarantee anything.

A good example of this is the Community Action Programme which started a few years ago. It provides an opportunity for people who have been unemployed for more

continued . . .

146

than a year to do part-time voluntary work in the community for an allowance which is equivalent to their benefit, plus £10 a week extra.

Having your hopes raised only to have them dashed affects people in different ways. A friend of mine who went on a Restart Programme was asked by the person who was running it what he expected to get out of it and he replied, 'Parole'. My friend didn't have to finish his sentence.

Figure 4.59 *Source: Herald, 2 September 1995*

Q UESTIONS

1 'The jobcentre told me lots of things I should be doing to try and find a job. In fact there was a lot that I didn't know that the jobcentre could do for me.'

  What types of things might the person making this statement be referring to?

2 'I was having no luck finding a job and had not worked for over four months. At this point the jobcentre recommended a job search seminar.'

  Why might the jobcentre have recommended this course of action?

3 'The jobcentre advised a jobclub, but it was a total waste of time. All I did was sit around and fill in forms all day.'

  In what ways would you argue against the opinion expressed above?

4 After six months on benefit an unemployed person might be offered a training for work programme. What points could be put for and against these programmes?

5 'People who have been out of work for over two years are unemployable. Restart courses are of no use to them.'

  How would you answer a person who expressed this opinion?

6 Find out the address and telephone number of your local jobcentre. Write or telephone to arrange a visit to find out more about the type of work that it does.

Scottish Enterprise

The **Scottish Enterprise** network is the main government body aiming to create jobs and improve skills and training. It was set up in 1991. Since then it has taken a leading role in economic developments in Scotland. The Scottish Enterprise network consists of Scottish Enterprise National (SE) and 13 Local Enterprise Companies (LECs).

The network covers southern and central Scotland, from the Borders to the Highlands. This is an area representing 94% of Scotland's population. The final 6% of the population is served by Highlands and Islands Enterprise (see Figure 4.60).

'The purpose of SE is to help generate jobs for the people of Scotland.'

Crawford Beveridge, Chief Executive of SE

Figure 4.60   Scottish Enterprise – towards jobs and prosperity for the people of Scotland

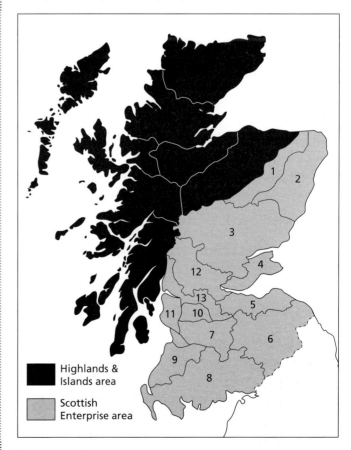

Highlands & Islands area

Scottish Enterprise area

Figure 4.61

147

In order to try and achieve this, SE has identified seven main aims which it tries to pursue. These are to:

- develop and enlarge existing businesses;
- promote more and better new businesses;
- attract foreign investment into Scotland;
- improve Scottish exports;
- improve the environment;
- promote skills and knowledge;
- promote access to opportunity.

Existing business

SE plays a very important role in developing and enlarging Scotland's existing businesses.

It does this in many ways, but providing finance is one of the most important. The **Small Business Loan Scheme** was launched in 1994. It offers loans from the four main Scottish banks. In 1995 alone £20m was advanced to 150 companies.

As well as companies in general, SE also targets and provides support for specific growth areas. The most important of these areas is electronics.

SE also provides specific support to tourism and other areas, such as textiles. Their biggest support for this area to date was to help bring the Clothes Show to the SECC, Glasgow, in June 1995.

New business

Starting up new businesses is an area in which SE is particularly keen. It provides help to start up a business and is particularly interested in giving help to women and all people under 35.

One success in this area is SE's sponsorship of the Business Game TV series, on Scottish Television and Grampian Television.

It has launched a **Women Starting Business** campaign and is planning another one aimed at young people.

QUESTIONS

1 What are the seven main aims of Scottish Enterprise?
2 Copy the map showing the areas covered by Scottish Enterprise and Highlands and Islands Enterprise.
3 How does Scottish Enterprise help existing and new businesses?

Inward investment – Locate in Scotland

Foreign investment is important for the growth of the Scottish economy. Foreign owners account for around 25% of manufacturing employment in Scotland.

These activities are run by **Locate in Scotland** whose main job is to encourage foreign investment and jobs to come to Scotland. It does this by:

- advising potential investors;
- marketing Scotland as an attractive area for firms to invest in;
- providing financial incentives for firms to come to Scotland.

Its main successes have been in the electronics industry and foreign firms are particularly dominant in this area. For example, **Silicon Glen** accounts for:

- 11% of Europe's electronic parts;
- 35% of Europe's personal computers;
- over 50% of Europe's automated banking machines;
- nearly 60% of Europe's workstations.

Lanarkshire's new industrial revolution is made in Taiwan.

On a 100-acre site between the M8 and Scotland's Channel Tunnel freight depot, and two miles from the closed British steel works at Ravenscraig, the two giant Tiapei-based electronics firms – Chungwa and Lite-On – are building factories that will create up to 8000 jobs by the year 2000.

They will make screens for a third of the computers and TV sets sold in Europe.

The new Taiwanese manufacturers are among the Monarchs of Scotland's 'Silicon Glen' – the hi-tech Ayr to Aberdeen corridor that has transformed Scotland's industrial base.

Seven of the world's leading electronics companies, backed by local firms, now employ more than 100,000 Scots, three times the number of steelmen working in the mills in the 1970s.

In this US and Asian-led renaissance, unions are out, wages are down and women are in.

Figure 4.62

Source: The Observer, 28 June 1996

QUESTIONS

1 What is Locate in Scotland's role?

2 In what ways can Silicon Glen be regarded as one of Europe's major producers of electronic goods?

3 How has the electronics industry made 'Lanarkshire's new industrial revolution'?

4 How has improved employment in Silicon Glen helped offset the closure of such plants as Ravenscraig?

5 Describe in your own words the positive and negative features of 'Lanarkshire's new industrial revolution'.

Exports

SE helps Scottish companies in markets outside the EU. It also helps the Scottish Tourist Board to improve the image of Scotland.

In the USA, it works closely with QVC Cable Television, which is the largest telemarketing sales company in the country.

In 1994, QVC (Quality, Value and Convenience) broadcast a three-hour show featuring only Scottish products. QVC have offices in Washington, USA and in Beijing, China.

Environment

A healthy and pleasant environment is important for people who live within it. It is also important for tourism and attracting foreign investment.

During 1995 SE renewed 805 hectares of derelict land, and also spent £19.6m buying land to create projects within the Lanarkshire Development Zone.

SE also helps with projects to improve the urban environment so that Scotland's towns and cities can compete as quality locations.

Skills and knowledge

SE runs a wide range of programmes to enable people to improve their skills. These activities include:

- Skillseekers;
- Training for Work;
- Training and Employment Grants Scheme;
- Investors in People;
- recruitment and training support for foreign investors.

One of their main aims is to train the workforce of the future. This aims to improve skill levels amongst young people in Scotland, and encourage employers to offer more jobs with training.

Access to opportunity

Within certain areas of Scotland, mainly inner cities and housing estates on the outskirts of cities, there are widescale problems of unemployment and disadvantage associated with poverty. SE runs several schemes to help combat these problems and help with urban regeneration.

The **Training and Employment Grant Scheme** (TEGS) provides financial support to employers to help with the costs of wages and training new employees.

Many people on TEGS gain extra qualifications which help their employment prospects as well as helping employers create jobs which would otherwise not have existed.

Lothian and Edinburgh Enterprise runs a **Steps into Work** scheme in partnership with business and the community.

It is a 12-week training programme which helps people improve their ability to compete for jobs. Companies such as Marks & Spencer, Kwik-Fit and the Royal Bank of Scotland guarantee participants a job interview.

In Glasgow, the **Glasgow Regeneration Alliance** includes the Glasgow Development Agency, Glasgow City Council and Scottish Homes. Its aim is to regenerate areas within the city which suffer from disadvantage.

Other Government Assistance

The government also offers other types of assistance to certain areas.

Assisted areas

These are parts of the country which have the highest levels of unemployment. They receive two main forms of help from the government.

Regional Selective Assistance

This grant is given to employers willing to set up and create jobs in employment black spots.

These grants can be between 10% and 30% of the total set-up costs.

Regional Enterprise Grants

These come in the form of Investment Grants and Innovation Grants. The first is available to small companies who employ fewer than 25 people; the second to companies who employ up to 50 people. They both provide help with the set-up costs of new projects.

Enterprise zones

There are currently over 30 Enterprise Zones in the UK. Scotland has four, at Invergordon, Inverclyde, Tayside and North Lanarkshire.

These are mainly areas which suffer high unemployment as a result of the decline of the **traditional industries**. Incentives are given for companies to set up within these zones and these include:
* planning regulations made easier;
* less government red tape;
* exemption from certain taxes and rates.

As well as these government schemes many City Development Agencies and New Towns provide extra offers for firms to set up within their areas.

150

Q UESTIONS

1 'The purpose of Scottish Enterprise is to generate jobs for the people of Scotland.' Crawford B. Beveridge, Chief Executive, SE.

Write a report describing the ways in which Scottish Enterprise meets the task set out by its Chief Executive.

2 Look back at the aims of Scottish Enterprise. List them in what you consider to be order of importance. Write a sentence about each aim saying why you consider it to be more or less important.

3 'Scottish Enterprise has had great success in attracting foreign investment to Scotland. Its achievements in attracting jobs for the new electronics industry have been outstanding.' How could this claim be justified?

4 'Scotland is a growing economy and a very attractive country in which to open our new factory.' What are the factors which would make Scotland so attractive to foreign business people?

5 Look back at pages 136 and 137. How does the EU help job creation and training in Scotland?

Young People and Training

In 1988, the government withdrew the right to income support for 16–18-year-olds. It introduced the **Guaranteed place scheme** which aimed to ensure that every June school-leaver who was not in work or college would receive a place on a Youth Training (YT) scheme by September.

The YT scheme came in for a great deal of criticism. The main ones were that:
* the training allowance was not a real wage. It was very low and resulted in many employers reducing wages of young workers to near the YT level because they knew that young people had no alternative;
* it was used by some employers as a cheap labour scheme;
* even good employers used it as a probationary scheme. Only the very good trainees had a chance of a job at the end of it;
* usually the quality of training was very low;
* often the 'guarantee' did not work in practice, with many young people not gaining a training place by September;
* trainees had very few of the rights that other workers take for granted. They could be dismissed very easily;
* removing the right to income support makes it more difficult to receive other benefits, especially housing benefit;
* young people are forced to live at home on low incomes and many become homeless because of family disputes over money.

Skillseekers

The main government scheme is **Skillseekers** which replaced Youth Training in 1995. This is run by LECs which are part of the Scottish Enterprise network.

Training is provided by either specialised training firms, colleges, local councils or voluntary bodies.

The options on offer to young people leaving school are limited, and many of the training schemes of the past offered poor quality training and failed to prepare young people for employment or lead to jobs.

Skillseekers has tried to correct some of these faults and it points to the fact that, through

Skillseekers, 90% of young people are working towards vocational qualifications compared to 82% through YT.

63% of Skillseekers are in training with real job status, a good deal more than YT's 42%.

A recent report by Youthaid and the Children's Society points out the need for a better national policy on the employment, training and education of young people.

Young people in further education should receive an allowance in the form of a grant or income support. The report also recommends an immediate increase in the Skillseekers allowance to a minimum of £50 per week, to improve the image of training, to help attract young people and to enable them to meet their basic needs.

The proportion who stayed in full-time education after 16 rose from 46% to 58%, an increase offset by a fall in full-time employment.

The fastest increase in participation in fifth and sixth years, and in further and higher education, occurred in the group with the lowest fourth-year attainment, and more girls than boys participated.

Professor David Raffe said: 'Staying-on rates have risen fastest among the least-qualified 16-year-olds.'

Figure 4.63 *Source:* Herald, *3 July 1995*

'Give our Kids a Job'

Many organisations consider the level of youth unemployment to be so dangerous for the future of the country that some private firms and local newspapers have begun to run their own initiatives and schemes.

The *Glasgow Evening Times* joined together with Glasgow's Education Business Partnership to launch a 'give our kids a job scheme'.

The main targets of the scheme were 16–19-year-olds and the idea was for firms to give them a job, take them on a Skillseekers course or to offer them short work 'tasters'.

Figure 4.64 *Source:* Glasgow Evening Times, *10 June 1996*

151

Many local and national companies joined the scheme. Among them were Safeway, McDonalds, Asda, Royal Mail, ScotRail and Whitbread brewery.

QUESTION

1 Using Figure 4.64 explain whether you think this type of campaign does any good. Give reasons for your answer.

Project Work

The government introduced a pilot compulsory programme, **Project Work**, in April 1996.

The compulsory approach is not completely new. There are already three compulsory programmes of a very similar nature in existence for the long-term unemployed; Restart Courses, Jobplan Workshops and Workwise.

It is similar to the United States 'work for benefits' scheme called **Workfare**.

'The new scheme would offer a programme of structured help in finding a job as well as practical work experience,' he said.

Mr Forth, the Employment Secretary added: 'The long-term unemployed can be at a disadvantage in the job market because they lack motivation or confidence after being away from work.'

Everyone taking part in the new scheme would receive help and advice appropriate to their needs, and would have their job-finding skills sharpened.

'But we will expect something in return. Most long-term unemployed want to get back to work and will value the help this scheme gives,' he went on.

'Some, however, may have no intention of finding work. Anyone who refuses to enter, or drops off the work experience programme for no good reason, will normally have their benefits stopped.'

The Education and Employment Department said the type of work experience offered could include painting and decorating, construction and gardening work.

Figure 4.65   *Source:* Herald, *30 November 1995*

Look at Figures 4.65 and 4.66 then answer the questions which follow.

A Workfare-style 'Project Work' scheme for up to 6000 long-term unemployed people was launched by the government yesterday.

Under it, people between 18 and 50 who have been jobless for more than two years will have to attend a work experience programme or lose benefit.

Mrs Shephard, the Employment Minister, said the government would now be setting up two pilot schemes in April to deal with the recalcitrant few who did not want to go back to work.

The Prime Minister, John Major, said: 'The majority genuinely seeking work will find this a lifeline. But those who refuse to take the offer of work experience will lose some or all of their benefit.'

Mrs Shephard said, 'It's called paying for what you get – making some effort in return for help given.'

Placement would last up to six months, comprising three months of training and three months' work experience.

People who refused or dropped out would lose two weeks benefit at first. The second time it happened the person could lose a month's benefit and a third drop out could lead to total loss of benefit. Hardship cases, where dependent children were involved, probably would retain about 60% of benefit.

Figure 4.66   *Source:* Herald, *2 December 1995*

QUESTIONS

1 What schemes for unemployed people are already compulsory?
2 What is the US 'work for benefits' scheme called?
3 Which age group is Project Work aimed at?
4 What sanctions will the unemployed suffer if they refuse to take part, or drop out?
5 According to Mr Forth, what benefits will the unemployed get from the scheme?
6 'It's called paying for what you get – making some effort in return for help given.'

Do you think that government training schemes for the unemployed should be compulsory. Give reasons for your answer.

Some sections of the UK population are more likely to suffer from poverty than others. One such section has been that of **lone parents**. This includes lone males, but usually it refers to lone females and their children.

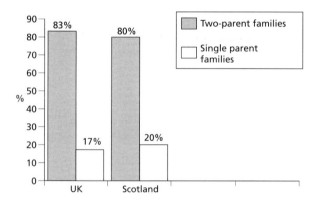

Figure 5A   Lone parent families in UK and Scotland

Single parent families are the result of people being divorced, separated, widowed or unmarried. The number in each of these categories is increasing each year.

The number of births outside marriage is also increasing as a percentage of all births.

Year	Per cent
1970	7.7
1980	11.3
1990	27.1
1992	30.3

Figure 5B   Births outside marriage as a percentage of all births in Scotland

Source: Registrar General, Scotland

Recently single parents have been singled out for special criticism from the government and the media as the headline from the *Sunday Times* in Figure 5C shows.

> **Public enemy or backbone of Britain?**
> **THE TRUTH ABOUT SINGLE MOTHERS**

Figure 5C

Lone parents: the facts and figures

153

How many?
1.5 million lone parents care for 2 million children; 57% are divorced, widowed or separated women, 33% are women who have never been married; 9% are men.

Maintenance
43% of lone parents have an agreement on maintenance. Only 30% receive it. The average payment is £20 per week, which is forfeited from income support.

Work
42% of lone parents are working, most part-time. The average full-time wage for fathers is £200 a week; for mothers, £130.

Cost
Single parents receive £9 billion in benefits a year, one-tenth of the benefits budget.

Support
Whether in or out of work, 80% rely on **means-tested** benefits; 20% earn enough to be independent and/or receive maintenance. Lone parents are not compelled to sign on for work.

Income

45% of one-parent families have an income of less than £100 a week, compared with 4% of those with two parents.

Added benefits

Lone Parent Premium for those on income support (£5.20) and One Parent Benefit for those in work (£6.30), now frozen, will be phased out. Family credit compensates over 16% of lone parents for low pay (hours worked, number of children and child care costs are taken into account). A lone parent receiving maintenance who returns to work will also get £1000 in back payments in April.

The investigation by the *Sunday Times* into lone parents discovered information which destroys the idea that this group is mainly made up of young teenage girls. Instead they discovered the following:

> The average lone parent in Britain is a woman of about 34 who has been married or stayed with a partner for a long period of time. Lone parenthood means one child by one partner. Single parents don't remain that way and usually return to a two-parent situation after about four years.

Figure 5D   *Source: Sunday Times, 28 July 1996, abridged*

Income

> The abolition of the lone parent premium would increase poverty of some of the poorest families. Scotland has 132,000 lone parents, and 40% of these live on less than £100 per week. At the end of the day, the cuts are an attack on the welfare of children.

Figure 5E   *Source: Herald, 9 November 1995, abridged*

In November 1993 the Labour Party criticised government plans to cut or freeze benefit to one-parent families. At present benefits are £77.90 per week, but to cut this would throw many families into even deeper poverty, as the *Herald* article in Figure 5E shows.

Case Study

> Margaret Proudfoot is 23. She shares her two-apartment council flat in the Millerston area of Glasgow with two-year-old Declan.
>
> Her weekly income is £77.90 out of which she has to pay nearly £10 towards housing costs plus fuel, and a small debt to a catalogue company for children's clothes. She also receives housing benefit. She's currently undertaking a course in budgeting organised by the charity One Plus but it's hard to see how she could make her meagre income go any further.
>
> 'I'm already at rock bottom. I've nothing left to cut. I don't drink, smoke, or go out. I buy food from the cheapest shops and we eat loads of pasta. If they cut my money I can't think what I'd do. I'd have to get Declan's clothes in charity shops.
>
> 'I'd love to get back to my job as a telephonist but can't afford the child care. If one-parent benefit is frozen, it would make it even harder for people like me to get back to work. I don't understand this government.'

Figure 5F   *Source: Adapted from the Herald, 9 November 1995*

Changes to the Benefits System

The Child Poverty Action Group claims that a freezing of lone parent benefit would affect over 2 million children living in single-parent families.

The Social Security Secretary, Peter Lilley, also wants to introduce a scheme to help lone parents to get back to work. This scheme involves training and help with looking for a job, and would affect about 25000 lone parents.

Mr Lilley intends to increase **family credit** to £60.00 from £40.00 by raising the child care allowance within this benefit.

QUESTIONS

1 What is the main reason for lone parent families?
2 What effect would phasing out the lone parent premium have on families?
3 How might raising the child care allowance help Margaret Proudfoot?

Child Support Agency (CSA)

Set up in 1993, the CSA tries to sort out who is responsible for the **maintenance** of a family that has split up.

The CSA has been heavily criticised for the way it goes about its investigations into who is responsible to pay for the family's costs. For example, lone parents who are receiving government benefits must give the CSA permission to investigate the absent parent. Also, some lone parents are worse off after receiving maintenance from their absent partner because they lose out on other government benefits, like free school meals or housing benefit.

Other problems can be:
- parents paying maintenance complain that they are not left enough money to live on, especially if they have another family;
- absent parents who are unemployed have money deducted from their benefits;
- many lone parents suffer hardship because the maintenance set by the CSA is not paid regularly. Government benefits are paid regularly;

- most of the money collected by the CSA doesn't go to the lone parent, but is used to pay running costs.

A spokesman for the CSA in defending its methods said,

'The CSA has traced over 66,000 absent parents. More than 26,000 earnings orders were made, where absent parents failed to pay maintenance.'

Figure 5G   *Source: Herald, 6 April 1995, abridged*

QUESTIONS

1 What are the criticisms of the Child Support Agency?
2 How might the government defend the Child Support Agency?

Housing

In 1993, almost one-third of all homeless in Scotland were lone parents. Many others live in very poor housing, in the worst areas. Some other facts on housing and lone parents are:
- 85.7% stay in rented accommodation, i.e. council owned, Scottish Homes, housing associations or privately rented;
- many are to be found in the most deprived areas of towns and cities;
- 69% of households receiving housing benefit in Strathclyde in 1991 were lone parent families. In Glasgow it is 89.5%, but in Bearsden and Milngavie it is 47.6%.

Children in Care

Strathclyde Region, before the new councils were set up in April 1996, covered an area with 50% of the Scottish population.

The Social Work Department, who organised child care in the Strathclyde Region, found that in the period 1983–92 almost half of the children taken into care were from lone-parent families.

Family type	Per cent
Natural parents	31
Lone parents	49
Families with step-parents	17
Others	3

Figure 5H   Children taken into care 1985–92
Source: Strathclyde Social Work Department

It was also discovered children from lone parent families do less well at school than children from other family types, and are likely to be less well behaved.

Pressure Groups and Support Groups

The rise in the number of lone-parent families has resulted in an increase in the amount of groups who put forward the case for them, including:

- Lone Parent Forums;
- One Plus;
- women's groups;
- anti-poverty groups;
- self-help groups.

Facilities for these lone parents, such as crèches and nurseries, are important to allow the parent to work or be trained. Without such facilities the lone parent cannot improve their prospects for work through training/education.

One support group, **One Plus**, has tried to provide some of the facilities needed for lone parent families, as Figure 5I shows.

CHILD CARE PROJECT

One Plus received a local council grant to organise and run a play scheme for the Easter, Summer and October holiday periods. The play scheme was staffed by One Plus workers and ran for two sessions per day, with a maximum of 50 children per session. The scheme catered for children aged 5–12 years.

The programme for the play scheme was very varied and planned in advance. It offered a wide range of play opportunities for all the children which included: T-shirt printing, American Independence Day, Barbecue, Baking and Planting Seeds.

The response from children and parents was very good. A few quotes were: 'I have four kids and it gives me a break during the day', 'It gives the kids an interest and keeps them off the street'.

Figure 5I   One Plus Child Care Project
Adapted from One Plus News, November 1995

QUESTIONS

1 In what ways do lone parents suffer from worse housing than others?
2 How are children from lone parent families worse off?
3 How do lone parent groups help?

Families with Dependent Children

5

Changes to the patterns of family life in the last decade mean that some sections of the population are much more vulnerable to poverty and all the problems that it brings than others.

Divorce, separation and births outside marriage have been increasing at a very high rate.

According to the 1991 UK census, 74% of children live in married couple families with both their natural parents. 3% live with unmarried parents and 6% were step-children in a married couple family. This meant that 17% of children live in lone parent families.

Lone Parents

The census shows that in Scotland 20% of families were headed by lone parents and 92% of these parents were women. The proportion of lone mothers has increased so much that by 1992 one in five mothers with dependent children was a lone mother. This figure increases to one in three in Glasgow. Teenage mothers make up only 3–4% of the total.

LONE MOTHERS

Year	Single	Divorced	Separated	Widowed	All
1971	1	2	2	2	7
1981	2	4	2	2	11
1992	7	6	5	1	19

Figure 5.1   Percentage of families in each family type

Source: 1991 Census Great Britain

Marriage and divorce

Until the 1980s, the gradual increase in the proportion of lone mothers was mainly the result of the increasing rate of divorce in the country.

Since then, the number of divorces has not increased significantly, but the number of single, never married, mothers has more than doubled.

Despite this increase in the number of single mothers, marriage breakdown is still the most common reason for lone parent families.

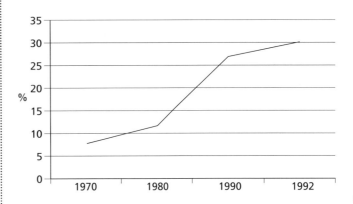

Figure 5.2   Births outside marriage as percentage of all births: Scotland

Source: Registrar General, Scotland

In 1973, 6604 marriages ended in divorce. By 1993, this had risen to 12788. Today, in Scotland, this amounts to one in four marriages ending in divorce. For England and Wales the figure is one in three.

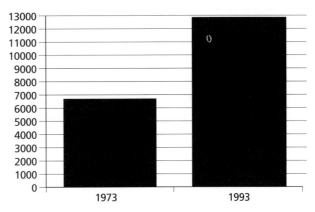

Figure 5.3   Divorces in Scotland 1973 and 1993

Source: Registrar General, Scotland

QUESTION

1 Using statistics outline the main causes of the changes in family life in the UK.

Income

Some 75% of Scottish lone parent families are dependent on **income support**, according to the **Benefits Agency**.

There is increasing evidence to show that income support is not enough to meet the basic needs of many parents.

Children from lone parent households are increasingly vulnerable to poverty.

These children currently make up 16% of all Scottish children. A higher number of children from lone parent families are also dependent on family credit than children from two-parent families. (Family credit is paid to working parents whose income is too low to meet the basic needs of the family.)

The **Child Poverty Action Group** (CPAG) has calculated that many lone parents have to survive on a very low-cost budget.

Parents often go without essentials to provide for their children. For those who operate on a low-cost budget, the CPAG claims that income support meets only 79% of their budget needs.

Not all lone parents have to rely on income support. Many are divorced or separated people who are well provided for by affluent partners.

The vast majority do, however, rely on income support and family credit and their children experience a wide range of disadvantage.

> The number of children in poverty in Scotland has trebled in the last 15 years. Poverty is not simply about lack of income: it adversely affects health, education, and housing choice, and damages children's chances for the future.

Figure 5.4 *Source: The Child Poverty Resource Unit*

There are also psychological effects on such children, for example of not being able to go on certain school trips, or even applying for free school meals.

There is also a disproportionate number of children from lone parent families taken into care each year.

Case Study

> Margaret Proudfoot is 23. She shares her two-apartment council flat in the Millerston area of Glasgow with two-year-old Declan.
>
> Her weekly income is £77.90 out of which she has to pay nearly £10 towards housing costs such as electricity and fuel, and a small debt to a catalogue company for children's clothes. She also receives housing benefit.
>
> She's currently undertaking a course in budgeting organised by the charity One Plus but it's hard to see how she could make her meagre income go any further.
>
> 'I'm already at rock bottom. I've nothing left to cut. I don't drink, smoke, or go out. I buy food from the cheapest shops and we eat loads of pasta.
>
> 'If they cut my money I can't think what I'd do. I'd have to get Declan's clothes in charity shops.
>
> 'I'd love to get back to my job as a telephonist but can't afford the child care. If one-parent benefit is frozen, it would make it even harder for people like me to get back to work. I don't understand this government.'

Figure 5.5 *Source: Adapted from the* Herald, *9 November 1995*

QUESTIONS

1 What evidence is there that most lone parents are on a low income?
2 How does this affect the children?
3 How much has Margaret got to survive on?
4 What problems does Margaret have feeding and clothing Declan?
5 Look at Figure 5.6. Using the figures for April 1996, work out how much Margaret will be receiving after April 1996.
6 How does One Plus seek to help families like Margaret's?
7 What difficulties would Margaret have if she tried to get back into employment?

Changes to the Benefits System

Peter Lilley, the Social Security Secretary, announced far-reaching changes to welfare benefits for lone parents in the November 1995 Budget.

Income Support (per person)	
Personal Allowance	**£**
aged 18–24	37.90
aged 25 or over	47.90
Lone parent (over 18)	47.90
Added on to the above	
Dependent children	
aged 18 (at school or FE)	37.90
aged 16–17 (at school or FE)	28.85
aged 11–15	24.10
aged under 11	16.45
Premiums	
Family (at least one child)	10.55
Lone parent	5.20

Figure 5.6   Benefit rates from April 1996

Source: Labour Research, April 1996

The changes included the freezing of lone parent premium at £5.20 per week.

Social Security Secretary Peter Lilley said the changes would end the system's discrimination in favour of lone parents.

Announcing details of the proposals following the Budget, Mr Lilley disclosed long-term plans to phase out special benefit help for 1.5m lone parents.

'While I cannot prejudge what I will do in future years, my intention over time is to narrow the gap between lone parent benefits and those which go to couples.'

Figure 5.7   *Source: Herald, 29 November 1995*

Other changes announced included:
- introducing a pilot scheme from April 1997 to provide help with job search and skills training for up to 25000 lone parents;
- increasing the child care allowance in family credit from £40 to £60.

Campaigners CPAG warned that the end to special lone parent benefits would hit the 2.3 million youngsters living in such families in the UK.

'The right approach is to neither penalise nor to promote lone parenthood,' Mr Lilley told the Commons yesterday.

In political terms this is clearly a move designed to pander to the Tory right who have caricatured lone mothers as unmarried teenagers, happy to live off the state and even deliberately becoming pregnant in order to maximise their benefits, despite ample evidence to the contrary.

The phasing out of lone parent premium is likely to increase the hardship of some of the most vulnerable families.

Around 40% of Scotland's 132,000 lone parents live on less than £100 a week, compared with just 2% of two-parent families, according to One Plus, which helps and lobbies for one-parent families in Strathclyde.

'There can be no excuse for taking away benefits which so many families need simply to survive,' said One Plus director, John Findlay.

Figure 5.8   *Source: Herald, 30 November 1995*

Q UESTIONS

1   Look at Figure 5.6. What would the effect of the abolition of the lone parent premium have on Margaret?
2   How would the abolition of the lone parent personal allowance for 18–25-year-olds affect younger lone parents?
3   How might the other changes help people like Margaret get back into work?
4   According to the article above, how do the Tory right 'view lone parents'?
5   'The right approach is to neither penalise nor to promote lone parenthood.'

    In what ways can Peter Lilley be accused of being selective with the facts?

Child Support Agency

The **Child Support Agency** (CSA) was set up in April 1993 as part of the **Child Support Act**.

One of the aims of the Child Support Act was to save £500 million per year by removing income support from lone parent families.

How the Child Support Act works

Stage 1

Lone parents receiving or applying for income support would be required to inform the Department of Social Security (DSS) of the name(s) of the absent parent of their children.

If the lone parent does not supply the name of the absent parent, their income support entitlement is reduced.

Stage 2

The CSA assesses the needs of the lone parent family (income support levels and housing costs).

Stage 3

The CSA also assesses the needs of the absent parent (income support levels and housing costs).

Stage 4

If the absent parent had any income over and above their basic needs, this would be liable for payment as a contribution towards the needs of the lone parent family.

Stage 5

The lone parent's needs are met (income support levels and housing costs).

Q UESTIONS

1 What is the aim of the Child Support Act?
2 What would be the overall effect on the amount of money the lone parent received?
3 What would be the overall effect on the finances of the absent parent?
4 What benefits might the lone parent lose if they stopped receiving income support?

Criticisms of the Child Support Act

The Child Support Act has been very controversial and has attracted criticism from parents, women's groups and children's organisations.

These include:

- many lone parents feel forced to give the name(s) of absent parents with whom they have had no contact, nor the wish to have contact;
- good relationships between both parents are put under strain because of increased financial demands on the absent parent;

- some lone parents may find themselves a little better or even worse off when they count the loss of other benefits which come with income support, such as free school meals or housing benefit. This can be the case even when maintenance payments are as much as doubled;
- the loss of income support makes it more difficult for the lone parent to budget properly, especially when maintenance payments are not met regularly;
- absent parents who are unemployed and receive income support have a minimum of £4.80 per week deducted from their benefit;
- others who are in employment have seen a large rise in the amount they have to pay since the CSA came into existence;
- absent fathers complain that the income they are allowed to keep after paying the maintenance decided by the CSA is not enough to live on (income support levels and housing costs);
- if the absent parent has a second family the income of the absent parent's new partner is taken into consideration. This could mean the new partner 'paying for the needs' of the absent parent's first family;
- the Child Support Act has affected 'the easy targets' – absent parents who keep contact with their children and whose addresses are known. It has not targeted those who wish to pay nothing and do not want to keep contact with their children;
- the CSA has made mistakes, sending maintenance demands to the wrong people, leading to more family break ups and some suicides.

Q UESTIONS

1 Look at the list of criticisms of the Child Support Act. Say which you think are the most important. Give reasons for your choices.
2 In what ways can it be said that the Child Support Act makes absent parents face up to their responsibilities?

Look at Figures 5.9 to 5.12 and answer the questions which follow.

Before (on income support)	
Maintenance	£30.00
Child benefit and one parent benefit	£16.05
Housing benefit	£21.80
Council tax benefit	£8.84
Income support	£27.55
Free school meals and health benefits	£7.10
Total income	**£111.34**
After (on maintenance and benefits)	
Maintenance	£65.26
Child benefit and one parent benefit	£16.05
Housing benefit	£20.68
Council tax benefit	£8.41
Total income	**£110.40**
When the parent is no longer receiving income support, however, they have other new expenditures	
Rent	£1.12
Council tax	£0.43
School meals	£4.50
School milk	£1.60
Health benefits	£1.00
Total losses	**£8.65**
Total income	**£101.75**

Figure 5.9   Weekly budget of a lone parent before and after the introduction of the Child Support Act

Source: Child Poverty Action Group 1994

More than half the maintenance assessments carried out by the Child Support Agency (CSA) last year were wrong, the National Audit Office disclosed yesterday.

Errors – which in the worst case led to a father paying out £55 a week too much – were found in 37% of cases and doubt was cast on a further 17% where there was insufficient evidence to tell if the demands were accurate or not.

The CSA had been reformed after a disastrous beginning, dominated by complaints of harassment and unfairness and accusations that it had forced men to attempt suicide.

Mr Donald Dewar, Labour spokesman for Social Security, said, 'In its second year, it has directly collected only £76m and claims a further £111m has been transferred between parents . . . these look desperately inadequate figures when measured against operating costs of £200m.'

Figure 5.10   *Source: Herald, 19 September 1995*

'The CSA is hated by absent parents and feared by lone mothers.'

Figure 5.11   John Findlay, Director of One Plus

A spokesman for the CSA said, 'The agency has traced over 66,000 absent parents, a success rate of 73%. More than 26,000 deductions from earnings orders have been made where the absent parent has failed to make payments.'

Figure 5.12   *Source: Herald, 6 April 1995*

Q U E S T I O N S

1   'The CSA is hated by absent fathers and feared by lone mothers.'
    Why would John Findlay make this statement?
2   Explain how many lone parents are worse off since the setting up of the Child Support Agency.
3   Write a report outlining the criticisms and successes of the Child Support Act.

Housing

'We live in the poorest houses in the worst areas. On top of everything, we have to put up with people looking down on us all the time. Did you know that in 1993 32% of all homeless people were lone parents.'

Figure 5.13   A single parent

Only 14.3% of lone parents live in owner occupation compared with 57% of the population as a whole.

85.7% live in rented accommodation.

Since 1979, council house sales in better off areas have reduced the number of good quality council housing.

Lone parents have not benefited from council house sales because of their low income, reliance on income support and housing benefit.

161

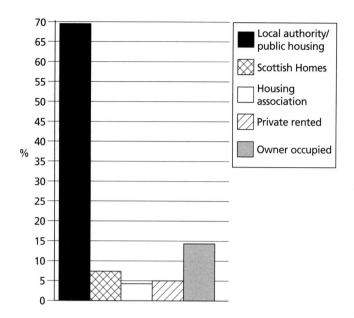

Figure 5.14 Lone parents household type in Scotland, 1991

Source: Scottish Homes

162

Instead, lone parents tend to be more concentrated in poorer areas, with lower quality council houses.

Look at Figure 5.15 and answer the questions which follow.

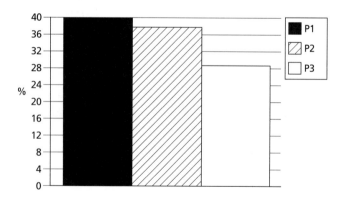

Figure 5.15 Percentage of lone parents living in Strathclyde priority areas (areas of poverty). (P1 is the poorest followed by P2 and P3)

Source: Strathclyde Social Trends 1995

Q UESTIONS

1 What housing and social problems do lone parents have according to the statement by the lone parent (Figure 5.13).

continued ...

3 How has the sale of council houses affected lone parents?

4 What evidence is there that lone parents are concentrated in the worst off areas?

Children in Care

Children in families who are separating or have separated are more likely to be at risk of ending up in **care** than children from other families.

Until it was disbanded in April 1996, Strathclyde Regional Council covered an area with half of Scotland's population. The council's social work department found that at one time almost half of all children being taken into care were from lone parent families.

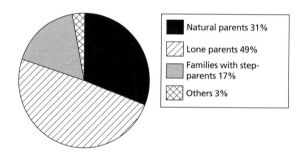

Figure 5.16 Children received into care 1985–92

Source: Strathclyde Social Work Department

Health and Education

There is a great deal of research which shows that people living on low incomes experience greater health problems.

This has been shown to be the result of a combination of factors such as stress, diet, housing and environment.

There is also increasing evidence which shows that many children from lone parent families do less well and display more behavioural problems in school.

Q UESTION

1 How can being part of lone parent family affect children?

Pressure Groups and Support Groups

Pressure groups have developed to provide support and champion the cause of lone parents. These groups include Lone Parent Forums, women's groups and One Plus.

Many lone parents need child care support such as nurseries and creche facilities to allow them to look for work or take part in opportunities for training and education.

Read Figure 5.17 and then answer the question.

The One Plus AGM will take place on the 10th of October this year. It will be held in the Council Chambers of Glasgow City Council in George Square, Glasgow. Starting at 9 a.m. and finishing at 1 p.m. with a Civic Reception lunch.

The theme this year is Family Policy. Britain does not have one and One Plus are determined to pressurise the government into developing a policy on family life. An adequate family policy would give parents opportunities and choices which they do not have at present.

We will be having a party night this year. Details will follow shortly. Put the dates in your diary and start discussing the campaign ahead.

One Plus ran a play scheme for the Easter, Summer and October holiday periods. The play scheme ran for two sessions per day, with a maximum of 50 children per session. The scheme catered for children aged 5–12 years.

It offered a wide range of play opportunities for all the children which included: T-shirt printing, American Independence Day, Barbecue, Baking and Planting Seeds.

The response from children and parents was very good. A few quotes were: 'I have four kids and it gives me a break during the day', 'It gives the kids an interest and keeps them off the street.'

Figure 5.17 Adapted from *One Plus News*, November 1995

QUESTION

1 Describe some of the work of lone parent groups.

Europe

The number of people getting married is decreasing and divorce rates are rising throughout the European Union.

Divorce rates, however, are low in Spain, Italy and Greece. The UK had the highest divorce rate in 1992, at almost twice the EU average.

RATES PER 1000 POPULATION

	Marriages		Divorces	
	1981	1992	1981	1992
UK	7.1	5.4	2.8	3.0
Belgium	6.5	5.8	1.6	2.2
Denmark	5.0	6.2	2.8	2.5
France	5.8	4.7	1.6	1.9
Germany	5.8	5.6	2.0	1.7
Eire	6.0	4.5	–	–
Italy	5.6	5.3	0.2	0.5
Luxembourg	5.5	6.4	1.4	1.8
Holland	6.0	6.2	2.0	2.0
Portugal	7.7	7.1	0.7	1.3
Spain	5.4	5.5	0.3	0.7
EU average	6.0	5.4	1.5	1.6

Figure 5.18 Marriage and divorce in EU 1981–92
Source: Eurostat

163

The Future

Lone parent households increased by 74% between 1981 and 1991. A further 54% increase is expected by the year 2001 when around 25% of all households with children will be lone parent households.

QUESTIONS

1 How are divorce rates changing in Europe?
2 In what ways will the number of lone parents in the UK change in the future?
3 'Lone parenthood is something which is forced on individuals. Nobody would willingly choose it as a way of life.' Sue Robertson, Director of One Parent Families.

Write a report on lone parent families, outlining the difficulties they face and suggest ways to improve the quality of their lives.

The Elderly

6

UK Population Growth

The number of people living in the UK today is about 58 million. This figure is expected to rise to around 60 million by the year 2000. One of the main reasons is people are living longer.

As well as the number of births and deaths being important to the UK's population, the number of people coming to stay or leaving to stay in another country is important.

RISING LIFE EXPECTANCY IN BRITAIN

	Male	Female		Male	Female
1841*	41.2	43.3	**1951**	65.6	70.4
1911	50.4	53.9	**1961**	67.8	73.6
1921	55.8	59.6	**1971**	69.1	75.3
1931	57.7	61.6	**1981**	70.9	76.9
1941	59.0	64.0	**1991**	73.2	78.7

* England and Wales only

STRETCHING THE AGE BARRIER

The oldest officially authenticated person in this country so far was **Charlotte Hughes**, who was 115 years and 229 days old when she died in March 1993.

In 1917, when the practice began of the monarch sending telegrams to those people reaching 100, there were 110 centenarians in Britain. According to the latest figures, Buckingham Palace sent out 3,089 such telegrams last year.

Figure 6A   *Source:* Sunday Times, *14 January 1996*

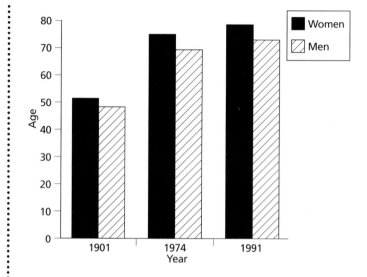

Figure 6B   Life expectancy

Ageing Britain

The rise in the number of elderly, now about 9 million, is partly due to the success of the National Health Service (NHS), which has provided free medical care for everyone.

Many diseases have been wiped out completely and others are controllable.

New medical developments have helped the elderly to have a better quality of life.

However, old age for many of the elderly is not pleasant. Many old people live close to the **poverty line** because they do not have enough money to live on. State benefits do not provide for a quality of life and there are many ailments that affect the elderly which reduce their movements, for example, hip and joint ailments. So for many of the elderly, old age brings a different set of problems (see Figure 6C).

Physical
- Poor eyesight
- Weak muscles
- Warmth (possibility of climatic changes – hypothermia

Emotional
- Loneliness
- Isolation
- Fear
- Worry
- Too proud to accept help

Housing
- Cold/damp
- Too big
- Too many stairs
- Poor facilities

Social
- Lack of contact with family
- Friends dwindling
- Independent

Financial
- Pension inadequate (since 1980 rise based only on rate of inflation)
- Cost of living
- Bus fares to hospital etc.

Medical
- Spectacles (90% of people who have poor eyesight are over 60)
- Hospital (over 65s occupy 50% of NHS beds)
- Dementia (50,000 people in Scotland have Dementia)
- Hearing (43% of 75+)

Figure 6C   Problems facing the elderly

The Scottish Dimension

Scotland has a population of just over 5 million. The elderly make up almost 1 million (17.8%) of these. This figure is slightly higher than the UK average of about 9 million (15.8%

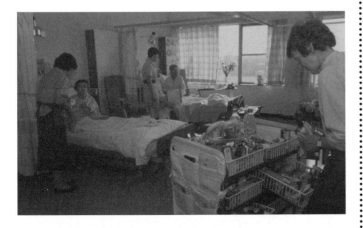

Figure 6D   Older people in the population

in 1993). This group makes large demands upon the **Welfare State**.

The Welfare State was set up in 1948 to help the population of the UK become healthier, wealthier, better educated and sheltered. To do this the government took responsibility for medical treatment, schooling, public housing and other **social services**.

As a result the UK population enjoys quite a safe way of life compared to some other countries, although some critics say it could be much better.

This is not to say that most of the people in the UK are well off because that is not the case, as we saw from the problems faced by many of the elderly. What we can say is that the growth in the number of elderly in the population has created a bigger problem for the government because the costs to meet their needs will also grow.

Meeting the Elderly's Needs

A growing elderly population will mean the following:

- more spending by the social services, e.g. **income support**, optician, dentist, and medical services (40% of the NHS medical bill and 80% of hospital beds are allocated to the elderly. Spending on GPs and nurses will also increase);
- pensions will have to be paid for a longer period of time to a larger group;
- meals on wheels and other services like **home helps** will have to increase;
- family carers will have to pay out more;
- **sheltered housing** and **geriatric** medical wards will have to be provided for more people;
- homes for the elderly will have to be increased in number;
- Social Workers, housing officials, doctors, nurses and other necessary staff will have to increase.

All the above must increase if there is to be proper care provided for our growing elderly population. The money to do this will probably come from increased taxes on the **working population** and from the savings of the elderly themselves.

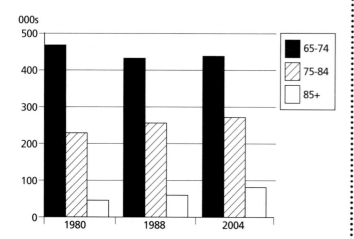

Figure 6E   Older people in the population

Figure 6F is an extract from the Social Work Department which gives an idea of the social services available from that department for the elderly.

Services for Older People

Our worker can give information on the kinds of services available for older people in your area. These may include:

- **home helps** – to assist with washing, dressing and meals as well as shopping, laundry and housework;
- **community alarms** – if you need to summon help quickly in an emergency;
- **hot meals** – at home or in lunch clubs;
- **day centres** – for social activities or personal care;
- **occupational therapy** – equipment or adaptations for your home;
- **help for your carer** – including extra help at home so your carer can have a break or go on holiday;
- **short-term care** – in a residential nursing home;
- **long-term care** – in a residential or nursing home;
- **assistance** – when you have sight loss, or hearing loss, physical or learning disabilities or dementia;
- **advice** – on welfare benefits.

Figure 6F   Some services available from the Social Services

Care in the Community

Before 1993 many elderly and other groups who were in need of close supervision and care were looked after in geriatric and psychiatric hospitals, and other institutions like **old folks homes**. All the needs of the elderly patients and others would be provided for them in these hospitals.

Since 1993, when the government introduced a new law (the Care in the

Community Act), many of the patients from geriatric and psychiatric hospitals have been placed back into the community, i.e. in housing and centres within the local area. The needs of the elderly would be provided by local authority social services. Many of the elderly receiving the services would have to pay a fee for them, based on the **income** that they had.

Community Care is the responsibility of a number of agencies – the government, local authorities and the health boards – and with each of these the comment is the same, 'lack of money brings about cuts in services and provision'. A lot of the provision therefore falls upon the **voluntary agencies** to provide support. You may have already heard of Alzheimer Scotland but there is a large number of other voluntary agencies, for example Help the Aged, Age Concern and Shelter. All of these offer assistance and advice to the old, but because of all the agencies concerned, it just adds to the confusion facing our elderly population.

Problems with Care in the Community

Alzheimer Scotland – Action on Dementia published research which shows that people with dementia manage better in small, local units attached to the local community. But the research also states that there is a need for improvement in the quality of long-stay accommodation. Also, many elderly are placed in the wrong sort of accommodation because they have not been properly assessed.

Mr Jim Jackson, the executive director of Alzheimer Scotland, thinks that 40% of the 61000 dementia victims in Scotland live in institutions where the quality of care is very low and their needs are not being recognised.

Figure 6G is an abridged version of a report in the *Herald* of June 1996.

The growing elderly population is a result of the 'baby boom' that followed the First World War. The same situation happened again after the last World War which ended in 1945 and this will ensure that the elderly in our population will continue to grow in numbers over the next 20 to 30 years. Estimates state that one in six of them will need long-term care before they die. The Care in the Community system which provides for the elderly is already beginning to show cracks. The main users of the social work services, those aged over 85, have increased by 60% between 1980 and 1994 and the figure is expected to reach 90,000 by the year 2001.

A senior social work director states that they do not have enough money and **cutbacks** in the service will have to be made. The number of home helps has already been cut, yet their workload has increased over the last 15 years from an average 6.9 clients to 8.3 each. Health board services are also being reduced as savings have to be made to pay for the costs of Care in the Community.

Figure 6G *Source: Herald, June 1996, abridged*

Figure 6G highlights some of the problems facing the elderly being transferred into care in the community but there are others which affect many of the elderly, not just those suffering from long-term illness.

- Budgeting problems as they try to feed and clothe themselves and pay other bills, all of which they did not have to do before.
- Having to cope with vandalism and other community problems such as 'mugging'.
- Loss of friends and other social activities.
- Organisation of their time.
- Possibility of injury while on their own.

There are day-care centres provided by the **local authorities** but these do not supply the full range of services that are provided in full-time care.

Who pays for community care?

Since the Community Care Act the local authority where an old person lives has to pay about 50% of the cost of community care. The local authorities say that they cannot afford to finance community care adequately and that the elderly must suffer as a result.

In May 1996, local government re-organisation took place and the new local authorities stated that they did not have enough money to pay for all the services they are expected to provide.

There is still residential care for those old people 'who need specialist and nursing supervision' and this group is looked after by the NHS. Other elderly people who are in residential care, who do not qualify for free NHS care, must pay towards their care.

The Social Work Department would make an **assessment** of how much they should pay out of their income and savings.

For example, if an elderly person has savings of over £8000, they would have to pay towards the cost of their care until their savings are reduced to this amount. Some others with less than £8000 in savings may receive income support towards the cost of their care.

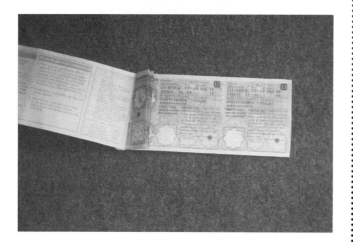

Figure 6H   Pension book

Private care for the elderly!

Over the last 15 years there has been an increase in the number of private nursing homes for the elderly. Some residents pay the full cost of their care, while others, with savings of less than £8000, pay only part of it. The Department of Social Security would make up the difference.

Equality and Inequality

To help ease the problem of paying pensions to women over 60 for a longer period of time the government has suggested bringing women into equality with men by raising the retirement age for women to 65. However, because of the problem of young people finding jobs, the critics of the government plan want to reduce the retirement age for men to 60. The cost to do this could be as high as £5000 million.

Women often have **career breaks** when they have children. This means they stop working and do not make any contributions to pension funds. Many women also work in low-paid jobs and therefore cannot afford to put extra money into private pension funds to help with their living costs after they retire.

The result is by the time women reach 60 (65 later on) they do not get a lot of money from **private pension schemes** or **occupational pension schemes** and have to depend on the state pension, which was £58.85 per week in 1996. At present 79% of all women over 60 depend upon state pensions.

The future does not look good for women as far as pensions are concerned because of the housekeeping/child-rearing role that they carry out in most societies including the UK. So, even in the foreseeable future, many women will be faced with **poverty** unless the government can find a way to make more money available to them when they reach retirement age.

Fact In 1992 Social Security benefits made up 55% of pensioner's income.

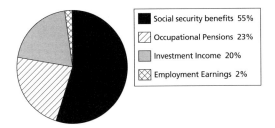

Social security benefits 55%
Occupational Pensions 23%
Investment Income 20%
Employment Earnings 2%

Figure 6I

Housing Inequalities

Not all pensioners are poor. Some have savings or receive an occupational pension weekly with their state pension. This group of pensioners can afford to have a quite good **standard of living** and have been given nicknames which reflect this, i.e. whoopies and glams. (**Whoopies** means well off older people and **glams** means greying, leisurely, affluent and married.)

The well-off elderly can afford to have holidays abroad and buy expensive retirement homes in select areas. For example, part of the Ayrshire coast has so many retired persons staying there that it has been nicknamed 'Costa Geriatric' by local people.

The remainder of the elderly who are not well-off cannot afford to stay in housing of their own choice. There is a lack of suitable housing for the elderly and this can have a negative effect on their quality of life.

High-rise flats and houses with a lot of stairs are inconvenient for the elderly, especially those with physical problems. On the other hand **sheltered housing** for the elderly is ideal but there is not enough for everyone who needs it.

There are different types of housing for the elderly which are provided by private and public agencies, for example:
- retirement homes;
- care housing;
- nursing homes;
- sheltered housing.

The cost of staying in some of these is too expensive for some elderly people, so they are forced into poor housing.

Pressure Groups

To assist the elderly in getting some of their problems solved there are a number of different agencies called **pressure groups**, e.g. Age Concern. These groups bring the problems facing the elderly to the public's attention.

169

Figure 6J

Figure 6K   Help the Aged is also a pressure group

A recent issue where the pressure groups have raised public awareness is the addition of VAT on domestic fuel (heating).

A major cause of concern for the elderly are cutbacks in local authority services which affect them.

Ageing Europe

Most member countries of the European Community (EC) face a problem similar to that of the UK with regard to an **ageing population**. For example, Greece, Belgium and Italy have larger ageing populations than the UK but the other EC members have less.

In all EU countries the proportion of the population aged over 60 is very high and set to rise in the foreseeable future.

Country	% of population over 60 (1993)
Italy	21
Belgium	20
Greece	20
UK	19
Spain	17.5
France	17
Eire	16

Figure 6L

British pensioners have the lowest pensions in the European Union. The government defends this by saying that pensioners can claim income support. Unfortunately, many pensioners are too proud to claim, or do not know what they are entitled to.

The Elderly

UK Population Growth

In 1971 the population of the UK was 55.9 million. This figure rose to 58.2 million in 1993 and is expected to rise to around 59.8 million by the end of the century.

By global standards this is a very slow rate of increase. Indeed some of the latest projections suggest additions to the population will soon reach **replacement level** only. This would mean that the UK would have 'zero population growth'.

Causes of population change

A country's population changes as a result of deaths, births, emigration and immigration.

In the first half of the twentieth century there were declining death rates and increasing birth rates, so the population grew.

Immediately after World War Two there was also an increase in birth rates known as the **baby boom**. Since the 1960s, however, birth rates have fallen.

Consequences of population change

As a result of these changes the UK has an **ageing population**.

In 1971 13.2% of the population was 65 years of age or over; this proportion rose to 15.8% in 1993 and is expected to rise to 24.1% by the year 2051.

This means that, by 2051, almost a quarter of the entire UK population will be pensioners.

This, however, is not the full story.

For within this group the proportion of people aged 80 or over is expected to more than double between 1993 and 2051, from 3.9% to 9.2%.

This is mainly due to those born in the 1960s baby boom reaching their 80s, and to people living longer in general.

Look at Figures 6.1 to 6.4, which show actual and estimated population figures by age.

1971 Total population 55.9 million

Age	%
under-16s	25.5
16–39	31.4
40–64	29.9
65–79	10.9
over-80s	2.3

Figure 6.1   *Source:* Social Trends 1995

1993 Total population 58.2 million

Males 28.5 m	Females 29.7 m
Age	**%**
under-16s	20.6
16–39	34.9
40–64	28.8
65–79	11.9
over-80s	3.9

Figure 6.2   *Source:* Social Trends 1995

2021 (estimate) Total population 62.1 million

Age	%
under-16s	18.3
16–39	29.7
40–64	32.7
65–79	14.3
over-80s	5.0

Figure 6.3   *Source:* Social Trends 1995

2051 (estimate) Total population 59.6 million

Age	%
under-16s	17.6
16–39	28.0
40–64	30.3
65–79	14.9
over-80s	9.2

Figure 6.4   *Source:* Social Trends 1995

Ageing Britain

Now study Figures 6.5 to 6.7.

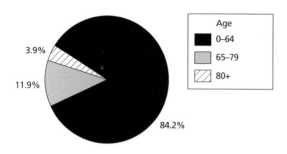

Figure 6.5   Structure of the population 1993

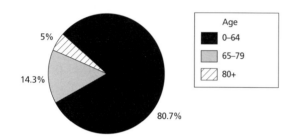

Figure 6.6   Structure of the population 2021 (estimate)

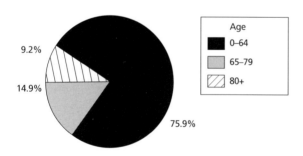

Figure 6.7   Structure of the population 2051 (estimate)

Q UESTIONS

1 What are the causes of population change in a country?

2 Examine the information shown in Figures 6.2 and 6.4. They show the breakdown of different age groups in the UK in 1993 and the projections for 2051.

   Draw two bar graphs showing the information for these two years.

3 Study the pie charts in Figures 6.5 to 6.7. What do they show about changes in the number of elderly population in the UK?

Figure 6.8

Living longer

Today in Britain we have over 9 million pensioners.

One of the main reasons people are living longer is through better health care from the National Health Service (NHS). This provides free medical care for everyone.

Medical discoveries and research have also managed to wipe out many diseases. There have also been other medical advances which prolong the length of people's lives and help improve the quality of that life.

The improved quality of housing and welfare state benefits systems have also contributed to people living longer.

However, this rapid increase in the number of elderly people in the UK brings extra problems for the government in trying to meet the needs of these people.

Consequences

As a result of this increase in the numbers of old people there is expected to be a greater strain on the social services in the future.

• Social security spending on the elderly will increase as more people live longer.

   More state pensions will have to be paid out, and paid for a longer period of time. Spending on other social security benefits such as income support will also increase.

• Currently 40% of the NHS medical bill and 50% of NHS beds are allocated to elderly patients.

   This will increase, as will the demand for GP services and district nurses.

- Services such as **meals on wheels** and **home helps** will be in demand, and an increased burden will be placed on family carers.
- Because of the increase in the number of elderly people, the demand for sheltered housing and geriatric medical wards will also increase.

There will also be a severe strain on state-funded elderly care homes.

Figure 6.9   An increased burden will be placed on family carers

Q UESTIONS

1 Why does Britain have an increasing number of elderly people?
2 What are the implications of this trend for social security spending in Britain?
3 Why will the increases in the numbers of elderly people have implications for the country's housing policies?
4 What might the effect of this trend be on other areas such as leisure facilities or nursing homes?

The Scottish Dimension

Scottish factfile

- The population of Scotland is 5,120,200;
- 911,789 people are over pensionable age;
- This is 17.8% of the population. Only 15% of the population are schoolchildren;
- Life expectancy is 77.6 years for men and 81.2 years for women;
- 67% of people aged 75+ are women and 33% are men;
- 177,600 Scottish pensioners receive income support, which

is a social security benefit given to all those, 18 and above, whose income is below a certain level;

- 25% of pensioners entitled to income support do not claim it;
- 36% of all households include an elderly person;
- Over 50% of elderly people have no care needs;
- There are 401 sheltered houses compared with an estimated need for 1500;
- 25% of elderly people have no heating in their bedroom;
- 83% of all households have central heating, compared to 69% of pensioners;
- 90% of all households have a telephone, compared to 82% of pensioners;
- 89% of households have a washing machine compared to 59% of pensioners;
- 69% of all households have a car compared to 10% of pensioners.

Figure 6.10   *Source:* General Register Office for Scotland 1994

173

Q UESTIONS

1 How many Scottish pensioners are entitled to income support?
2 How many actually claim it?
3 Use the information in Figure 6.10 to say whether the elderly are worse off than others.

Needs and problems

Old people have many needs and problems. They may suffer emotional problems because of loneliness, physical and medical problems because of their age, or financial problems caused by being on a pension.

Their needs may be for warmer or more suitable clothing depending on the time of year, more money to help pay for the basic necessities of life, company, especially of people their own age, as well as general care and attention.

These are general problems which the elderly may suffer from. However, many old people may have specialised needs.

Emotional

Many elderly people have to cope with occasional or permanent loneliness. Their partner may have died, they may have no family, or their family may have moved away from the area in which they live. Women tend to suffer more from loneliness as they generally live longer than men.

Local government provides a range of services under **Care in the Community** which attempts to meet the emotional needs of the elderly.

Physical and medical

Certain illnesses affect the elderly more than other groups. The elderly are much more prone to diseases such as hypothermia (when body temperature drops due to the cold), arthritis, bad eyesight and hearing, and brittle bones or bronchitis.

Other special needs may be having to be bathed by a district nurse, or they may be incontinent (unable to control their toilet habits) and require a nurse to clean, wash and change them every day if they are unable to do so themselves or have no family carer to do it for them.

In 1993 more elderly people were chronically sick than ever before.

A survey shows that 50% of people aged over 75 years and 40% of those in the 65–74 years group were considered to be chronically sick. See Figure 6.11.

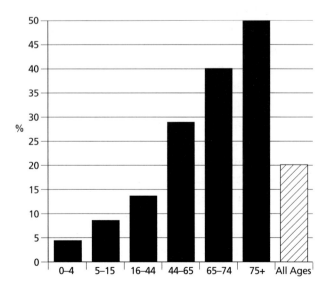

Figure 6.11   Chronic sickness by age 1993
Source: Office of Population Censuses and Surveys

This sickness can take many forms:
- 90% of people with visual impairment are aged 60+;
- an estimated 50,000 people in Scotland suffer dementia, 96% are aged 65+;
- 43% of those aged 75+ have hearing difficulties;
- 51% of people aged 75+ have an illness or disability which limits their movements.

Q UESTIONS

1 'Women are more likely to suffer from loneliness.' Why might this be the case?
2 What illness affects the elderly more than other groups?
3 What special health needs might an elderly person have at home?
4 Describe the findings in Figure 6.11 in a paragraph.
5 What other problems might many of the elderly have coping with everyday life?

Meeting the Elderly's Medical Needs

Many of the health problems of the elderly are looked after by the National Health Service (NHS). It is the job of the NHS to provide health care for all those who need it, regardless of whether they can pay for it.

There is also no doubt that the elderly make more use of the NHS than younger people.

For example, while only a small percentage of old people are in hospital at any one time, they occupy over half of the beds.

Some services which are provided by the NHS specifically for the elderly include:
- community nursing services;
- elderly assessment units;
- long-stay geriatric beds;
- rehabilitation units;
- special day care hospital units.

Many other physical and medical needs of the elderly are catered for by local government under the central government policy of **Care in the Community**.

Care in the Community

Since April 1993 certain needs of elderly people are catered for by Care in the Community.

The stated aim of this policy was to allow elderly people who had previously been cared for in **residential homes**, geriatric hospitals, or in some cases psychiatric hospitals, to leave these institutions and live their lives being cared for in the community.

The government claimed that this would enable elderly people to live a fuller life within the community.

Critics of the policy claim that it was introduced because the government was concerned about the ever-increasing costs of care for the elderly in residential homes and hospital wards.

During the 1980s there was a large rise in the numbers of Private Nursing Homes for the elderly. If an elderly person had savings of less than £3000 the Department of Social Security would pay up to £165 per week for them to be cared for in a home. The amount of savings a person can have has now been raised to £8000.

Paying for Care in the Community

Under Care in the Community, long-term residential care becomes the responsibility of the local authorities' social work department, not of the government.

Elderly people not in hospital or residential care are also the responsibility of local authorities' social work departments.

About 50% of the costs of Care in the Community are given to local authorities by central government. The rest comes from their own charges.

Since the Care in the Community Act, anyone who cannot pay the full cost of long-term residential care from their own resources is assessed by the social work department.

The Scottish Office makes a distinction between those who need long-term medical care, and those who need specialist medical and nursing supervision. The last of these is the job of the NHS and is free: those in need of non-specialist care must contribute to the cost.

In order to decide if individual elderly people can afford to contribute to these costs they are **means tested**. People with savings or capital of more than £8000 are expected to pay for their own care until their savings are reduced to £8000. They may then become eligible for income support towards the cost of their care.

This means that home owners have to sell their family home unless a relative continues to live there.

Since it is obvious that no one can live in their own home and in residential care, it seems a perfectly reasonable way to pay for care, until the money runs out.

It is a policy, however, that is at odds with Margaret Thatcher's vision of Britain as a 'property-owning democracy' and John Major's notion of 'wealth cascading down the generations'.

The government points to the fact that fewer than 10% of people pay the full charge.

A survey carried out by Age Concern found that the maximum charge which individuals had to pay varied depending on where they lived. In the Western Isles the maximum charge is £173.80, while in the Central Region this rises to £442.

Assessing needs

Local authorities assess the needs of individual elderly people in their area, as well as their means. This is called a **needs assessment**.

Social work departments have to work out the cost of meeting each needs assessment and the total cost of meeting the needs of all the elderly in the area. They then have to work out how they are going to pay to meet the needs.

These needs can be met by local authorities, the private sector or voluntary agencies. Often these agencies compete to provide care in the community for the elderly and thus earn themselves revenue.

The aim of this competition is to cut the costs of Care in the Community.

However, problems arise when the cost of meeting the needs of the elderly do not match up with the amount of money the local authority has.

175

QUESTIONS

1 Why did the government introduce its policy of Care in the Community?
2 Explain how Care in the Community actually works.
3 What do critics claim is the main drawback to Care in the Community?
4 What does means testing mean in relation to the elderly?
5 'It is a policy, however, that is at odds with . . . wealth cascading down the generations.' Do you agree or disagree with this statement? Explain why.
6 Suggest solutions to the problem of not having enough money to meet the costs of each individual's needs assessment?

Step by Step Guide to Care in the Community

Government gives up to 50% of costs to local authority.

▼

The needs of individual elderly people assessed by social work departments.

▼

Elderly patients means tested.

▼

Needs met by, or by a mixture of, local authorities, private sector, voluntary agencies who compete to provide services at the lowest cost.

▼

Local authorities	Private sector	Voluntary agencies
▼	▼	▼
Sheltered housing	Residential homes	Age Concern
Health visitors	Nursing home	Meals on Wheels
Nursing home	Residential home	Help the Aged
Home helps	Sheltered housing	Alzheimers
Social workers		Lunch clubs
Occupational therapy		Support group
Health services such as chiropody		Respite care

Figure 6.12

QUESTIONS

1 Look at Figure 6.12 and the two views on Care in the Community in Figures 6.13 and 6.14.

Write a report listing the positive and negative features of Care in the Community.

Different views on Care in the Community

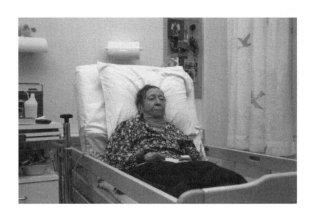

Half the specialists in Scotland caring for the old and the mentally ill think that services have become worse since the introduction of Care in the Community, according to a survey of doctors published in July 1995.

Doctors at the British Medical Association's annual conference in Harrogate said that they were particularly concerned by the distress caused to old people by the transfer of their long-term care to means-tested local authority services.

A survey of geriatrician and psychiatrists showed that only 31.6% thought that there had been an improvement, compared to 50% who thought there had been a deterioration.

Before the Care in the Community policy had been introduced elderly people who needed care received it free of charge from the NHS. Now their long-term care is provided by social services and it is means-tested.

Dr Arnold Elliott, chairman of the BMA Community Care Committee, said: 'Old ladies are having to sell their houses to pay for long-term care'.

GP Dr Nigel Rowell said old people who fell ill were praying for an early death, for fear of losing their savings. 'Fear of long illness and the financial repercussions of long illness are causing enormous grief among the elderly. Savings built up over a lifetime they see disappearing to fund a private nursing home place. No wonder they hang on for as long as they can at home and, if they do fall ill, they pray for a quick death.'

Figure 6.13   *Source: Herald, 6 July 1995*

It means 400 volunteers providing a bedding-down service in private homes, administering late-night medication, hairdressing, doing the shopping, collecting pensions, and just popping in occasionally for a chat.

Asked to sum up the experience, a 77-year-old volunteer worker says, 'I would say here is a community that has built up a nucleus of caring support for its elderly, which poses the question: what is happening in other areas that don't have it? How much loneliness and unhappiness is out there?'

Figure 6.14   *Source:* Herald, *19 September 1995*

Meeting the Elderly's Financial Needs

In Britain the **state retirement pension** is still the main form of financial help for the elderly. Women receive it when they are 60 years and men when they are 65.

From April 1996 this was £61.15 for a single person and £97.75 for a couple.

Most pensioners claim that the state retirement pension is not enough money to live on.

Elderly people who only have this state pension are also entitled to apply for income support.

This is means-tested and is calculated the same way as for other people whose income is too low to survive on.

Personal Allowance

Single person		£47.90
Couple		£75.20
Premiums		*add on*
aged 60–74	single	£19.15
	couple	£28.90
aged 75–79	single	£21.30
	couple	£31.90
aged 80	single	£25.90
or over	couple	£37.05

Figure 6.15   The elderly and income support from April 1996

Source: Labour Research, *April 1996*

The government also provides other financial help for people on low incomes. This includes other means-tested housing benefit and council tax rebates. This ensures that people who need it get help with their rent and council tax.

However, very often this is still not enough and many old people are faced with the problem of having to decide between paying for heating, buying warmer clothes for winter or buying enough food to keep them healthy.

Pensioners are also given a non-means-tested fixed sum £10 bonus at Christmas and a cold weather payment of £8.60 per week when the weather is very bad.

Pensioners groups say this is still not enough and point out the following.

In 1980, the present government decided to stop the practice of increasing pensions at the same rate as prices or wages, whichever was the highest.

Since 1980, pensions have only risen at the **rate of inflation**. The present-day pension would be £19.60 higher for a single person and £31.35 higher for a couple if it had continued to be upgraded by whichever was the higher of earnings or prices.

Similarly, if the Christmas bonus had increased in line with the higher of wages or prices it would now be worth £101.90.

One other major problem is that many people do not claim the benefits to which they are entitled, either because they do not know about them or because they are too proud to take what they consider as charity.

177

The Department of Social Security estimates that more than 25% of pensioners who are entitled to income support do not claim it. These pensioners are losing an average £13.45 per week.

Housing benefit is another area where pensioners miss out. 10% of pensioners fail to claim this. These people are losing an average of £13.90 per week.

Figure 6.16 *Source:* Benefits Agency Central Support Unit

QUESTIONS

1 What is the main form of financial help for the elderly?
2 What is the main means-tested benefit the elderly can get?
3 What other means-tested benefits can the elderly get?
4 What non-means-tested benefits can the elderly get?
5 What criticisms are made about the level of pensions and non-means-tested benefits?
6 Why do many elderly people not get the means-tested benefits they are entitled to?

Look at the worked example in Figure 6.17 and answer the questions which follow.

George is single, aged 66.

	£
His applicable amount is	
Single person	47.90
aged 60–74 single person's premium	19.15
Total	67.05
George needs	67.05
George's pension	61.15
George still needs	5.90
Income support entitlement	**5.90**

Figure 6.17   A worked example

QUESTIONS

1 Work out the applicable amounts and income support entitlements for:
  a Jim, aged 72 and Helen, aged 70, who are partners.

continued . . .

  b Jean, single, aged 78.
  c Anne, aged 84 and Robin, aged 86, who are partners.

Figure 6.18   This letter from Help the Aged highlights just one problem facing the elderly

Case Study

Heating or Eating

Some pensioners can't afford to do both during the winter. Marjorie is 75 and lives alone. This is what her living expenses are each week:

	£
Housing costs, e.g. maintenance, water	10.86
Fuel/light/power	10.13
Household goods and services, e.g. cleaning, phone*, insurance	11.02
Personal items, e.g. toiletries, dental and optical care	4.42
Clothing	3.26
Travel	2.28
Other, e.g. television* or newspaper	7.09
Total outgoings	68.54
But Marjorie only has a weekly income of	66.45

As you can see, to live properly Marjorie needs to spend more than her income allows.

Like thousands of other pensioners she simply cannot afford to do that. Like many pensioners Marjorie may be forced to cut down on food or heating.

*Telephones and TVs aren't luxury items. For many isolated elderly people, life without them can be dangerous or impossibly lonely.

Source: Help the Aged

QUESTIONS

1 What financial problems does Marjorie face?
2 What is hypothermia and why might Marjorie be in danger from it?
3 'Elderly people in this position either turn off the heating or cut down on food. Being constantly cold or hungry makes them more susceptible to illness. The more often they are ill, the weaker they get, and the less able to cope with cold and hunger. It's a vicious circle.' *Help the Aged Spokesperson.*

'There are a wide range of benefits available to pensioners in need. The government continues to do the utmost to ensure that no elderly person goes hungry or suffers from the effects of a cold climate.' *Government Minister.*

Which of the two statements do you agree with the most?

Give reasons for your decision and say why you reject the other statement.

Equality and Inequality

The main government proposal for increasing equality between men and women in retirement, and to deal with the extra costs of state pensions imposed by an ageing population, is to raise the retirement age for women to 65 years.

This is justified on the grounds of equality and by the fact that women live longer than men, but critics point out that the government wants older people to stay working for longer when many young people have to struggle to find jobs.

Many people would think that, given this, it would be more logical for men to retire earlier, but cost is a barrier to this idea. It is estimated that the total cost of lowering the retirement age for men could be as high as £5000 million.

Raising women's retirement age will be phased in over 20 years, beginning in the year 2000.

All women currently under 40 will not qualify for state pension until they reach 65.

Because of career breaks to raise a family or look after elderly relatives, women are more dependent on the state pension than men.

Fewer than half of all male pensioners receive an occupational pension, whilst for women the figure is 21%.

As a result of this there are over 1 million women of pensionable age claiming income support as opposed to one quarter of a million men.

Look at Figure 6.20 and answer the questions which follow.

Plans to equalise the pensionable age by raising it to 65 will drive them further into a poverty trap, according to the Economic and Social Research Council.

The average weekly income for older women was £61 and for men £106. This difference is caused mainly by the effects of occupational pension income, which is linked to occupation and lifetime earnings.

Older women were less likely than men to receive any income from an occupational pension, and the amounts were also less, because of the effects of child care and being a housewife on women's employment history.

Having children was the major factor influencing whether women had an occupational pension.

Professor Sara Arber, from Surrey University, said, 'For many women, who pay into occupational pension plans on the assumption that they are providing for their old age, the reality will be that they are no better off.

The small amounts of pension they accumulate will just take them above the benefits threshold.

It is a pension trap. Current government policies will result in large numbers of older women in poverty and dependent on state benefits.'

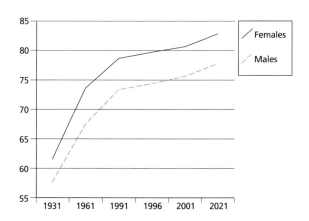

Figure 6.19 Expectation of life: by gender
Source: Social Trends 1995

Figure 6.20   *Source:* Herald, 12 September 1995

QUESTIONS

1 How does the government plan to deal with the extra costs of pensions due to the increasing number of elderly people?

2 What does Figure 6.19 tell you about the life expectations of men and women?

3 Why would the government not wish to lower the retirement age for men to 60 years?

4 'Older women were less likely than men to receive any income from an occupational pension.'

What reasons were given to explain this situation?

5 Using the figures in Figure 6.15, explain how an additional small occupational pension of £8 per week might affect a 66-year-old woman's entitlement to income support?

6 What effect might this have on her entitlement to other benefits?

7 'For many women, who pay into occupational pension plans on the assumption that they are providing for their old age, the reality will be that they are no better off.'

Write a paragraph explaining why this might be the case.

Inequality in retirement

It is wrong to assume that all old people are in the same financial situation. Not all pensioners are short of money.

Some may have savings of their own, an occupational pension, investments or even do a part-time job, as well as collecting their state pension.

This group of people has more money and a better lifestyle than people with only their state pension to rely on each week.

The most popular way of preparing for retirement is to contribute to the **occupational pension** or **superannuation scheme**.

Employees pay money into their company pension or superannuation scheme each week and when they retire they get money back each week in addition to their state pension. This means that they should be able to buy necessities, pay bills and still have money left over for things that other pensioners would consider luxuries.

Figure 6.21 shows the income received by the elderly as a whole.

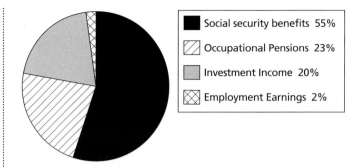

■ Social security benefits	55%
▨ Occupational Pensions	23%
▦ Investment Income	20%
⊠ Employment Earnings	2%

Figure 6.21   Source of origin Income of Pensioners (average) 1992

Source: Department of Social Security

The average income of UK pensioners in January 1996 was £150 per week.

Membership of employers' pension schemes varies depending on the type of jobs that people do.

Around 75% of professional and non-manual workers were members of their employers' pension schemes in 1993, compared with around 40% of semi-skilled and unskilled manual workers (see Figure 6.22).

Part of the reason for this is the availability of pension schemes to employees in different jobs.

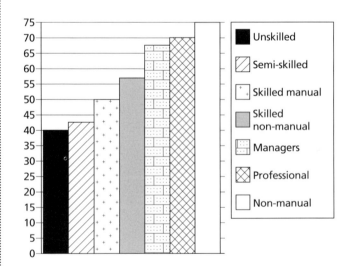

■	Unskilled
▨	Semi-skilled
⊹	Skilled manual
▨	Skilled non-manual
⊞	Managers
⊠	Professional
□	Non-manual

Figure 6.22   Membership of current employers' pension scheme: by socio-economic group, 1991–1993 figures as percentage

Source: Social Trends 1995

The value of the pension also varies depending on how much is paid in by the employee and how much is paid by the employer.

The more that is paid in, the higher the value of the pension on retirement.

Figure 6.23   Whoopies

This group of better-off pensioners go under the nickname of **whoopies** and **glams**.

Whoopies stands for well-off older people and glams stands for greying, leisured, affluent and married.

Many firms actively pursue these whoopies and glams for there are a growing number in these groups and they have money to spend.

Recent figures show that the over-55s have over 40% of the net wealth of the country. Building firms and holiday companies are especially interested in these groups and there is now a large market for private retirement property and off-peak holidays for older people.

Housing

One very important factor which determines the quality of life for many pensioners is the type of housing they live in.

It is especially true of pensioners that suitable housing will greatly improve their quality of life.

Good sheltered housing allows elderly people to be independent within a secure environment.

High-rise flats, on the other hand, are totally unsuitable. The lifts may be out of order, forcing the elderly to struggle up and down flights of stairs or to become prisoners in their own homes.

Being up high, or feeling the wind swaying the building, may also increase the fear experienced by the elderly.

Housing has traditionally been provided for the community by local authorities, housing associations and some specialised housing agencies, such as Scottish Homes.

Recent years have seen the increasing involvement of voluntary groups and private property companies in providing housing for the elderly.

There is also an increasing variety of different types of housing for the elderly. These include retirement homes, residential homes, sheltered housing (see Figure 6.24), care housing and nursing homes.

181

Figure 6.24   Sheltered housing in Glasgow area

Figure 6.25   A selection of household aids for the elderly

A new housing development opened recently by Scottish Homes illustrates what many think is the way ahead for elderly housing. The development provides 49 new homes including 24 sheltered homes for the elderly, 10 amenity flats, a warden's house, two for the disabled and 12 high quality properties for sale.

The aim of the development is to create a mixed community, providing housing for households ranging from young families to elderly people, some of whom will need support.

> **Q UESTIONS**
>
> **1** In what ways do the items in Figure 6.25 contribute to meeting the elderly's housing needs?
> **2** List them in order of importance saying which you think are the most important and why.

Catering for Other Needs

Day care centres

Day care centres meet the needs of elderly people who cannot completely cope alone. They provide a daily meal, at a small charge, and provide transport to and from the centre.

Individuals can take part in activities to meet their needs and interests.

These could include hobbies such as gardening, games such as bingo or dominoes, outside excursions, visits to the library and home cooking.

The idea of these centres is to cater for the emotional needs, such as loneliness, as well as the physical needs of elderly people.

Case Study

Figure 6.26   Dixon Community Carers Centre

Nell Ross had fun yesterday, and she can look forward to another good day tomorrow.

Every day she walks with a home help to an elegant building on the South Side of Glasgow where she is greeted by dozens of friends.

The main recreation room on an upper floor of the building is a kind of home from home for Nell and hundreds of other elderly folk who gather for a cup of tea and a chat, a game of cards or bingo, and regular social evenings.

It is the nucleus of a remarkable community which is highly regarded in the voluntary sector as a model of sympathetic and effective care.

It caters for more than 1500 people with a range of services from home helps to street wardens and residential facilities.

The woman at the heart of the organisation is Sheila Halley. 'There is a lot of goodwill out there,' she says. 'All we have done is to tap into it and help to organise it.

'If you have a lot of elderly people living alone and craving friendship and support, it's just common sense to bring them together.'

But what has distinguished the Dixon Community is the extent to which it has galvanised the residents of a large area, previously blighted by inner-city decay, into caring for each other.

And all on a shoestring budget.

What that means in real terms is a day centre which provides meals, bingo sessions, arts and crafts classes, carpet bowls, bus excursions and Saturday night dances and sing-songs.

A day at the centre, with meals included, costs £1.20, and most of the activities are organised by the elderly themselves.

INVESTIGATION

1 Find out if there is a day care centre in your area. You will get information from the local social work department in your area. You will find the number in the phone book.

2 Your teacher may help you to contact the centre to arrange a visit for a class group. Decide on some questions and things to find out before you visit the centre.

QUESTIONS

1 In what ways do day care centres meet the needs of elderly people?

2 In what ways is the Dixon Community a good example of Care in the Community?

3 Why is this centre not typical of other care programmes? What evidence is there to support the answer you have given?

Elderly Pressure Groups

The growing elderly population has led to some political commentators talking about the rise of **grey power**, meaning pensioner power.

Those who talk about grey power say that, if pensioners united, in numbers, they could use their votes to force political parties to pay more attention to the elderly's needs.

The elderly in Britain have not gone as far as their counterparts in Holland to form a grey power political party, but there are nevertheless many ways they can attempt to put pressure on central and local government.

A wide range of pressure groups exists in order to highlight the hardships which many pensioners suffer, and to try to fight for better treatment of pensioners in need.

These range from pensioner self-help groups such as elderly forums, to full-time voluntary agencies such as Age Concern and Help the Aged.

Figure 6.27

183

Elderly forums

Some elderly people are very independent and have formed groups known as **elderly forums**. These forums are pressure groups for pensioners.

They arrange meetings where everyone has a say on issues which effect elderly people, especially things which affect them in their own local community.

The forums consider it important to put pressure on the government and local authorities to persuade them to listen to what they have to say about certain topics.

Recent national issues which have concerned elderly forums have been VAT on domestic fuel bills and Care in the Community.

Figure 6.28

SOAPA, The Scottish Old Age Pensioners Association, is purely a pressure group and not a charity. They try to improve OAPs' standard of living and publish a monthly newspaper called *Scottish Pensioner*.

Their main aims include putting pressure on the government to increase pensions.

Voluntary groups

Help the Aged is a voluntary group which raises money by means of campaigns that highlight problems which many elderly face, including poverty, hypothermia in winter, fear of crime and inadequate housing.

It provides day care centres and publishes a monthly newspaper for elderly people.

Age Concern Scotland is another voluntary group. There are over 200 local Age Concern groups in Scotland working with over 12500 volunteers to help meet the needs of OAPs. They provide advice, information, transport and cash help to pensioners.

QUESTIONS

1 Explain the work of elderly pressure groups.
2 Design a poster highlighting one or more of Help the Aged's campaign issues.

Ageing Europe

Britain is not the only European country to have an increasing number of elderly people. It is a matter which concerns many other European nations.

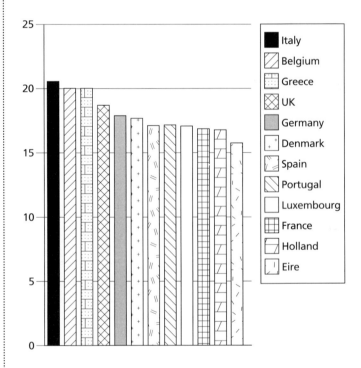

Figure 6.29   Per cent of elderly in the population by country

Source: Eurostat

Three other European Union (EU) countries have a higher proportion of people over 60 than the UK, and the number of people over 60 is projected to rise in *all* the countries of the EU.

So Britain is not alone in having an increasing number of elderly people, but are they all treated the same in the different European countries?

British pensioners do not think so.

They point to the fact that pensioners in other European countries receive more money in their state pensions and very often get other benefits that pensioners in Britain would like to have.

It is very difficult to compare pensions in the different countries of the EU as each country operates a different pension scheme, gives different benefits and has different **costs of living**.

Figure 6.30 shows the different rates of pensions for several EU countries.

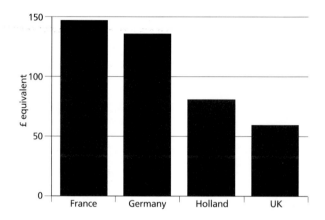

Figure 6.30 Weekly state pension

Source: Eurostat

Figure 6.30 shows that in purely financial terms British pensioners are the poor relations when it comes to European comparisons.

The government, however, would point to the fact that the cost of living is different in each of the EU countries. For example, the cost of living in Germany is 17% higher than it is in the UK, and prices in France are 9% higher than those in Britain.

Another way to examine pensions would be to look at how the amount that people get in their pensions compares with what they received when they were in work.

If we use this method we see that in Scotland a pensioner would get 46% of their former wage as their state pension, while in Germany a pensioner would get 82% of their former wage, and in France it would be 92% of their former wage.

QUESTIONS

1 What arguments might British pensioners put forward when complaining about British and European pension levels?

2 How might these arguments be countered?

Case study

Pensioners' benefits in EU countries
Belgium

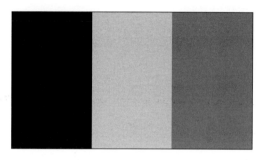

- no TV licence needed;
- half-price travel nationwide;
- half-price telephone charges;
- extra pension for holidays;
- an extra month's pension per year.

Britain

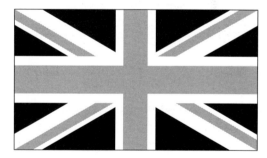

- Christmas bonus of £10;
- travel reductions dependent on region they live in;
- reduced TV licence if living in sheltered housing.

Denmark

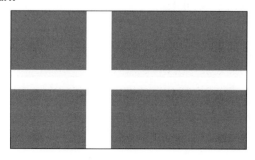

- half-price TV licence;
- half-price nationwide travel;
- no standing charges for telephone.

France

- telephones installed free;
- subsidised phone calls;
- free travel on Paris Metro;
- no TV licence needed;
- cheap nationwide travel;
- extra pension for big families.

Germany

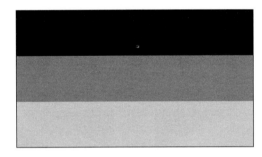

- cheap TV licence;
- cheap travel;
- cheap telephone calls, dependent on which part of the country they live.

Greece

- half-price nationwide travel;
- five free nationwide journeys per year.

Holland

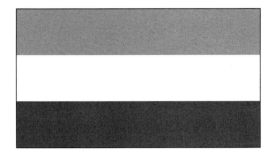

- an extra month's pension every year;
- extra pension for holiday allowance;
- a week's free travel every year;
- half-price travel nationwide;
- cheap TV licence.

Ireland

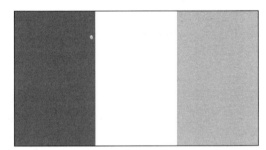

- free nationwide travel;
- free electricity;
- free telephone installation;
- extra pension for living alone;
- death grant of £100.

Source: Glaswegian

QUESTIONS

1 Put the countries in order of best for pensioner benefits to worst.
2 Are British pensioners as badly off as some claim? Give reasons for your answer.

Index

Figures in Roman refer to 'Foundation' chapters; figures in **Bold** refer to 'General/Credit' chapters